Published and forthcoming in KINO: The Russian Cinema Series

Series Editor: Richard Taylor

Cinema and Soviet Society: From the Revolution to the Death of Stalin
Peter Kenez

The Cinema of the New Russia
Birgit Beumers

Dziga Vertov: Defining Documentary Film
Jeremy Hicks

Film Propaganda: Soviet Russia and Nazi Germany (second, revised edition)
Richard Taylor

Forward Soviet!: History and Non-Fiction Film in the USSR
Graham Roberts

Real Images: Soviet Cinema and the Thaw
Josephine Woll

Russia on Reels: The Russian Idea in Post-Soviet Cinema
Edited by Birgit Beumers

Savage Junctures: Sergei Eisenstein and the Shape of Thinking
Anne Nesbet

The Stalinist Musical: Mass Entertainment and Soviet Cinema
Richard Taylor

Vsevolod Pudovkin: Classic Films of the Soviet Avant-Garde
Amy Sargeant

DZIGA VERTOV
Defining Documentary Film

JEREMY HICKS

I.B. TAURIS

LONDON · NEW YORK

1007

Published in 2007 by I.B.Tauris & Co Ltd
6 Salem Road, London W2 4BU
175 Fifth Avenue, New York NY 10010
www.ibtauris.com

In the United States and Canada distributed by Palgrave Macmillan,
a division of St. Martin's Press, 175 Fifth Avenue, New York NY 10010

ISBN: 978 1 84511 377 3 (paperback)
       978 1 84511 376 6 (hardback)

A full CIP record for this book is available from the British Library
A full CIP record for this book is available from the Library of Congress
Library of Congress catalog card: available

Typeset in Calisto by Dexter Haven Associates Ltd, London
Printed and bound in India by Replika Press Pvt. Ltd.

Contents

Acknowledgements   vii
List of Illustrations   ix
Preface   xi

Introduction: *Dziga Vertov – Defining Documentary Film*   1

1.   The Birth of Documentary from the Spirit of   5
      Journalism: *Cine-Pravda, Cine-Eye*

2.   Vertov and Documentary Theory: 'The Goal   22
      Was Truth, the Means Cine-Eye'

3.   'A Card Catalogue in the Gutter.' *Forward, Soviet!,*   39
      A Sixth Part of the World

4.   New Paths: *The Eleventh Year, Man with a*   55
      Movie Camera

5.   Sound and the Defence of Documentary: *Enthusiasm*   71

6.   Documentary or Hagiography? *Three Songs of Lenin*   90

7.   Years of Sound and Silence: *Lullaby*   106

8.   Forward Dziga! Foreign and Posthumous Reception   123

Notes   137
Select Bibliography   171
Filmography   179
Index   189

Acknowledgements

Thanks to the general editor of the Tauris KINO series, Richard Taylor, whose responses to queries were always prompt, pithy, and often amusing; to the School of Modern Languages at Queen Mary for giving me the sabbatical leave in 2004–2005 that enabled me to complete the book; to Zhenya Tsymbal for his inspiration; to Faya for her accommodation; and to Donald and Anna for the start in academic life. I am also grateful to Oksana Sarkisova and Valérie Pozner for letting me read their unpublished dissertations, and to the staff at a host of libraries and archives (especially SSEES and IWM) for their help. Most thanks to Inger and Nina for making all worthwhile.

List of Illustrations

1. Still from *Cine-Pravda* no. 1. Courtesy of   7
    BFI Stills
2. Still from *Cine-Pravda* no. 21 (*Leninist Cine-*   12
    Pravda). Courtesy of BFI Stills
3. Poster for *Cine-Eye* by Aleksandr Rodchenko.   22
    Author's Collection
4. Still from *Man with a Movie Camera*.   34
    Author's Collection
5. Still from *Forward, Soviet!* Author's Collection   44
6. Still from *A Sixth Part of the World*.   47
    Author's Collection
7. Still from *Man with a Movie Camera*.   55
    Author's Collection
8. Poster for *The Eleventh Year* by Stenberg   61
    Brothers. Author's Collection
9. Still from *Man with a Movie Camera*   66
    Author's Collection
10. Still from *Enthusiasm*. Author's Collection   75
11. Still from *Enthusiasm*. Courtesy of BFI Stills   78
12. Still from *Three Songs of Lenin*.   96
    Author's Collection
13. Still from *Lullaby*. Courtesy of Imperial War   111
    Museum, London
14. Still from *Lullaby*. Courtesy of Imperial War   113
    Museum, London
15. Still from *News of the Day* no. 3, January 1945.   121
    Courtesy of Imperial War Museum, London

Preface

I have chosen to translate *Kino-Eye, Kino-Pravda* and *kinok* as Cine-Eye. As a result readers will have to determine from context and italics whether I am referring to the film (*Cine-Eye*), the method, the movement (Cine-Eye) (all *kinoglaz*) or its members (Cine-Eyes) (*kinoki*). For reasons of consistency and so as not to confuse the reader I have correspondingly altered my quotations from Julian Graffy's and Kevin O'Brien's translations of these terms to *Cine-Eye* and *Cine-Pravda*.

In the text I have used familiar and more reader-friendly transliterations of Russian names and terms: Mayakovsky rather than Maiakovskii, Koltsov rather than Kol'tsov. In references to Russian terms, in the endnotes, and in the bibliography, I have consistently used the Library of Congress system for transliteration. All unattributed translations from Russian or French are my own.

In the endnotes I have given titles or descriptions, years and (where necessary) authors for materials quoted from anthologies and from Vertov's archive (RGALI Collection 2091) so as to retain a better sense of the evolution of Vertov's views and the critical climate. Similarly, I have supplied English translations, where they do not already exist, for the titles of Vertov's written works.

Introduction: *Dziga Vertov –*
Defining Documentary Film

This is the golden age of documentary. But what distinguishes it from other films? Is it devalued by bias or editorial manipulation? Can it capture the unperformed? What gives a film-maker the right to pry and show? These questions, still central for study of the form, lie at the heart of the thought and films of Dziga Vertov. Yet Vertov's reputation as director of a lone masterpiece, *Man with a Movie Camera*, does not reflect his deep commitment to exploring issues of structure, film activism, surveillance, the status of recording and performance. In fact, the true nature of his engagement with these concerns emerges only from a study of the whole body of his films and writings. That Vertov was the creator of a sizeable body of innovative and distinct films is a fact recognised by retrospectives at recent film festivals in Cambridge and Pordenone. However, as yet there exists no work in English covering his whole career. *Dziga Vertov – Defining Documentary Film* will fill this gap, enabling a broad swathe of readers to link the familiar and less familiar aspects of his film-making and thinking in a cohesive narrative.

At the same time this study challenges dominant views of Vertov solely as avant-garde artist and film poet,[1] showing instead how Soviet journalism inspired his creative transformation of newsreel into the new form of documentary film. While documentary has long been said to borrow from journalism,[2] this dimension of Vertov's work has never been adequately explored.[3] Yet the example of the Soviet press enabled him to turn newsreel from the illustration or recording of events into an overt attempt to persuade through images. Vertov nevertheless insisted upon intervening minimally in what he filmed, striving for a balance between recording and reworking. Claims that Vertov obviated performance in his films by exclusively employing hidden cameras are likewise an exaggeration. He, in fact, also used reconstruction but evolved methods to combat the tendency to pose.

Vertov's greatest works combine unstaged footage ingeniously so as to unleash a tremendous rhetorical force. They distil the sensibilities of newspaper column and Futurist poem into non-fiction feature films of incredible power and sophistication. In other words, they are classic

1

documentaries, as the book seeks to demonstrate. Yet the sheer novelty of documentary perplexed Vertov's contemporaries. Critics either would not accept their creative use of newsreel footage or denounced the apparently perverse rejection of acting. Vertov's struggle to make films, to describe and defend his film-making practice, was the struggle to define documentary as such.

The sense of documentary as a combination of recording and argument is a point that has to be made repeatedly when discussing documentary, even in the present. The assumption that a documentary must strive for balance and eschew political bias has led some of the most prominent historians of Soviet cinema to claim that there is a contradiction between documentary and the Communist world-view,[4] or to condemn Vertov's lack of 'objectivity': a false virtue he had neither claimed nor desired.[5] These same sorts of views still colour reception of contemporary documentaries, leading some to argue that the partisan approach of Michael Moore's *Fahrenheit 9/11* [USA 2004] meant it could not be a documentary.[6]

Vertov's achievements in documentary were soon under threat. Towards the end of the 1920s, and more markedly by the early 1930s, Soviet journalism and documentary began to subordinate news to commemoration and the cults of the hero and the leader. Soviet film criticism now began to attack the whole notion of a distinction between documentary and fiction film, insisting that the only point of a film was its ideological stance regardless of the means used to achieve it. Journalism and imaginative writing, documentary and fiction film became largely indistinguishable. After initially criticising these shifts in Soviet cinema and journalism, Vertov ultimately responded by making a cultic film that nevertheless strives to fulfil his own documentary agenda in *Three Songs of Lenin*. Yet this film earned him little or no recognition, because, despite its retrospective, folkloric and commemoratory character, it still espoused an original aesthetic and documentary authenticity alongside the articulation of a required message. Despite further attempts to accommodate, ultimately the only work Vertov could find was at the main newsreel film studio, editing compilations almost devoid of any recognisable individual style, as predictable and bland in their own way as the films he had reacted to when he began his career. With Vertov's defeat came the dissolution of documentary as a distinct film-making tradition in 1930s USSR, a situation changed only by the Nazi invasion of the Soviet Union in 1941.

Marginalised by the Soviet film-making community, Vertov looked abroad for sustenance in the early 1930s. However, where documentary film had developed in the West, it accepted reconstruction and staging to a far greater extent than Vertov. As a result, while his films served as important technical manuals for film-makers in the West, for many years he had few direct disciples here either. It was not until the 1960s that his more rigorous form of documentary led to him being rediscovered, both in his homeland and internationally. Curiously, though, the reflexive and overtly partisan qualities of *Man with a Movie Camera* have meant that Vertov is often seen as a gravedigger of documentary, rather than a pathfinder for it.[7] Only now is he beginning to be seen as a seminal figure of early documentary film, alongside Robert Flaherty and John Grierson.

This book is not a biography. Its focus is Vertov the film-maker, not the person. While a study of his life might shed light on the subject of Vertov's films, his single-minded devotion to cinema meant that he strove most fully to realise himself in his professional life. Analysing his films and writings broadly in chronological order enables us to re-examine Vertov's evolution and to challenge the typical view of his career as a steady progression away from journalism towards an ever more individual expressive form, peaking in *Man with a Movie Camera* before once more descending into the anonymity of Stalinist hagiography and newsreel.[8]

Jumbling up the messianic manifestos of Vertov's early career with films made later,[9] concentrating on a single film or a certain phase of Vertov's career, are approaches that facilitate the telling of this heroic story of Vertov, the modernist magician tragically tamed by the Stalinist behemoth. In fact, throughout his career, from the Civil War to World War II, Vertov adapts his art to the dominant forms of his time. There is always a compromise between a search for new and more striking visual – and, later, sound – solutions, on the one hand, and the need to articulate a message, on the other. Vertov never questioned this propagandist role of documentary and newsreel, seeing it as an inextricable part of the form: from the beginning his films exercised a right to see that, ultimately, derived from the state. Moreover, Vertov's later work still forms part of a coherent *oeuvre*, even if concessions to dominant stylistic and productional norms mean that the traces of his distinct approach became ever more rare. The later work is nevertheless a context aiding our understanding of the earlier films, showing how Vertov retains certain elements of style, such as his approach to the use of sound and the song almost until the end of his career.

While it would be foolish to deny the relevance of the avant-garde, Futurism, Constructivism, Productivism and the Left Art Front (LEF) to understanding Vertov's work, and much of it is clearly structured according to the norms of music, rhetoric and poetry, the atmosphere and generic conventions of journalism are no less germane. In revealing Dziga Vertov the documentary film-maker, rather than Vertov the

The first newsreel series in which Vertov was involved, *Cine Week* [Kinonedelia], initially displayed similar characteristics, including the same exclusive use of close-ups for portraits. Indeed, it has been argued that the concentration on personalities was a deliberate attempt literally to give the Soviet government a human face.[8] However, from October 1918 Vertov himself became increasingly involved in selection and compilation.[9] By December 1918 we begin to see editing employed to shape the material effectively, and a single theme being explored through a greater variety of shots. A good example of this is *Cine Week* no. 27 (10 December 1918), where the breakdown in communications during the civil war is shown by cutting together travelling shots from a boat, shots of sunken barges and of goods waiting on the harbour front. Similarly, the next issue (no. 28, 17 December 1918) edits together various shots of people having their papers checked by Reds so as to argue that the secret police are doing a good job.[10]

Soon, however, *Cine Week* too became a victim of war, and folded in July 1919. Over the next three years Vertov became involved with a range of documentary projects. He travelled to the front and for the first time supervised the filming of one of his projects, *The Battle for Tsaritsyn* (1919). He also participated in mobile filming and screening trips, such as on an 'agitprop' train. When unable to obtain fresh footage, Vertov re-edited earlier *Cine Week* newsreels into historical compilations, the most successful of which was *The History of the Civil War* (1921).[11] Here already images are manipulatively combined to articulate a marked point of view: an extended montage of the destruction perpetrated by the Whites is followed by shots of Trotsky speaking. In an intertitle he says: 'We will respond to White terror with Red terror.' Shots of battle follow. Already here Vertov is linking images to create a causality absent from the recorded material.[12] It is convincing because the images seem to relate to each other.

It was in 1919 that Vertov first met Elizaveta Svilova, a working-class Russian girl who worked as an editor at the Moscow Cinema Committee. The other newsreel editors refused to edit the short segments of film for *The Battle for Tsaritsyn* together with conventional longer shots in the innovative manner envisaged by Vertov, and simply discarded them as incomplete. Svilova took pity on the distraught Vertov and edited the film according to his instructions.[13] Henceforth she alone edited his films. Thus began an incredible life-long creative partnership.[14] It lay at the heart of the marriage that followed, in 1923, as it lay at the heart of every Vertov film. Joined the previous year by Vertov's brother Mikhail Kaufman, fresh from the Red Army, the three began to collaborate on a more ambitious newsreel series *Cine-Pravda*. It is with *Cine-Pravda* that Vertov truly begins to realise cinema's power to exhort in images.

Cine-Pravda no. 1 (June 1922) sets the tone for Vertov's newsreels in its sharply rhetorical style, downplaying the registering of events and instead editing together shots taken at different times and places so as to construct an argument.

Save the Starving Children

[Shots of emaciated children]

The removal of Church valuables

[Shots of icons being destroyed]

Every pearl saves a child

[Shots of children being fed]

These images may or may not be causally related. The children fed may not be the children starving, the confiscation of Church property may not have funded the soup kitchen. The camera does not record an already existing causal relation, it creates it. Through the meaning-creating power of cinema the three sequences describe a problem and propose a solution. Vertov's editing transforms non-fiction film from a means primarily of recording and informing into a powerful tool of persuasion and exhortation. Truly the genie of film 'propaganda' was out of the bottle. This transformation would have been unthinkable without Soviet journalism.

The Birth of Documentary from the Spirit of Journalism

This liberation of the 'expository'[15] potential of cinema was no chance discovery. Rather, it was the direct result of Vertov's explicitly partisan approach to newsreel. His brother and his cameraman from 1922 to the end of the 1920s, Mikhail Kaufman, recalls that Vertov aspired not to 'inform dispassionately' but, rather, to 'influence the mind in a certain direction'.[16] Yet this attitude was not the brilliant innovation of a genius. It was a commonplace of Soviet journalism. Vertov's most famous newsreels are called Cine *Pravda*, and borrow more from the leading Bolshevik daily than the title alone. Vertov's transformation of what was to become known as documentary cinema is inconceivable outside the context of the Bolshevik approach to journalism. Stylistically and in its approach to information, persuasion and communication, Vertov's film-making of the 1920s extends the model of the Bolshevik newspaper.

The Bolshevik Conception of the Newspaper

The focal point of their political activity, the Bolsheviks had long considered the newspaper the most important of all means of processing and distributing factual material.[17] For pre-Revolutionary Bolsheviks it had been a formative activity,[18] and it has been argued that their privileging of propaganda generally and the newspaper in particular enabled them to win the civil war, thereby maintaining power.[19] It is little surprise, then, that its example served to transform so many contemporary cultural forms: cinema, literature, photography, the poster, the wall newspaper and the acted or 'live' newspaper. All were either invented or revolutionised in this period, and the decisive influence was journalism. Yet, in order to understand the nature of this influence, we first need to grasp the specific nature of the Bolshevik newspaper.

The obvious place to start is with Bolshevism's founder: 'A newspaper is not only a collective propagandist and a collective agitator, it is also a collective organiser.'[20] Lenin's often quoted view of the newspaper stresses its importance less as a means for informing people but more as a means of influencing ('propagandist' and 'agitator'), and causing to act collectively ('organiser'). In stark contrast to the liberal conception of journalism prevalent in the West, the Bolsheviks never considered objectivity, independence or freedom of the press to be a primary consideration.[21] Consequently, despite the importance of persuasion in Soviet journalism, it is never in the context of free competition between different ideologies. This absence of free competition was crucial in determining the specific characteristics of the Soviet press.[22] Some have argued the resulting vacuum meant *Pravda* had no need of the techniques and methods of the popular press: certainly, it used few photographs, and its layout was dull. During the civil war, in particular, newspapers were distributed free, and readers had little choice. If they read anything, they still read *Pravda* and other Bolshevik papers despite their shortcomings in presentation. Moreover, readers were not able to access an account of events that contradicted that of the Bolshevik press: their statements as to the facts could not be contrasted with opposing views.

Yet the part played by compulsion in Soviet journalism can be overstated, particularly in the period of the New Economic Policy (NEP).[23] This approach fails to grasp that, for all the power of the Bolshevik state to ignore, censor and misrepresent oppositional opinion and inconvenient facts, there is still a considerable need to appeal to, attract and persuade the reading public, and, moreover, that misrepresenting the facts, even during the civil war, could potentially result in losing the trust of the reading public, since readily available eyewitness accounts of outside events, such as the approach of enemy armies, could prove them wrong. Bolshevik journalism took its distinctive form not solely from its lack of competition but, rather, from its goal of persuasion, and winning over with state support, in the absence of competition. Ultimately this enabled the Bolsheviks to refine the rhetorical side of their journalism, what has been called the interpretive sphere, even at the expense of information as document or reliable record.[24] This approach, a combination of the Bolshevik attitude to culture and the accident of their political power, enabled them to perceive and realise the immense power of film as means of persuasion. Similarly, this downgrading of information in favour of interpretation led to the reinvigoration of the established pre-Revolutionary Russian journalistic techniques of persuasion particularly through the genres of the essay-like *ocherk* and the feuilleton.

Soviet Journalism: A Tale of Two Genres

If Vertov transforms Soviet non-fiction film by subordinating the evidential power of newsreel to its discursive force, this shift is informed by the approach to information and persuasion of Soviet journalism. The character of this journalism is clearly illustrated in its dominant and most typical genres: the *ocherk* and the feuilleton. Both applied to journalism the methods of imaginative literature, engagingly reworking factual material in an attempt to reach out to as wide an audience as possible. These two genres represent two major tendencies in Soviet journalism: the tendency towards sharp juxtapositions, irony and a critical edge in the feuilleton, and the tendency towards description, praise and heroisation in the light of the ultimate goal of the *ocherk*. However, both tendencies can also be said to share a common attitude: they start from the fact, but elaborate on it so as to present it as powerfully and as engagingly as possible. Vertov too maintained a similar dual commitment, on the one hand to the capacity of cinema to record as a starting point, and on the other to exploring and unleashing its creative, persuasive, analytical potential. As we shall see, this duality is implicit in Vertov's key term '*zhizn' vrasplokh*', or life caught off-guard: it refers both to cinema's power to record and to reveal a deeper truth. Nevertheless, the innovation lay not in Vertov's commitment to recording but in his exploitation of cinema's discursive power.

'Newsreel is Life'[25]

At the very beginning of his career Vertov described the documentary cinema he would create as the recording of facts, which would then be organised into larger units such as the *ocherk*.[26] However, in the 1920s we frequently see his work resembling the feuilleton: the use of reverse motion (for example in *Cine-Eye*), or of superimposition in *Cine-Pravda* no. 22 'In the Heart of the Peasant, Lenin Lives' [V serdtse krest'ianina Lenin zhiv] is intended to force us to look at things in a different way and can rightly be considered feuilleton-like,[27] since a feuilleton similarly forces us to look at things anew by a startling juxtaposition or analogy. Such juxtapositions are something of a stock device for Vertov. Yet the influence of newspaper forms upon Vertov does not end there. Almost every issue of *Cine-Pravda* borrows something from journalism. *Cine-Pravda* no. 8 begins as a response to a newspaper report of the Right Socialist Revolutionary trial, in *Cine-Pravda* no. 7 the intertitles are all taken from a newspaper, and similarly, in *Cine-Pravda* no. 5, Vertov organises his material by showing someone turning the pages of a newspaper entitled *Cine-Pravda*. With each new page a separate episode appears. These examples are emblematic of Vertov's use of a journalistic approach to transform newsreel. However, with each issue of *Cine-Pravda*

Vertov increasingly sought to create an interlinked series of images rather than a simple recording of unrelated profilmic events.[28] Increasingly, he structured his films not solely according to their strict chronological order, but ultimately according to associations and logical, causal links between the various constituent elements. *Cine-Pravda* was conceived as a thematic newsreel in contrast to *Cine Week*, where the latest occurrence, the event, was all. It likewise stood in contrast to *State Cine Calendar* [Goskinokalendar´], the traditional-style newsreel Vertov turned out from 1923–1925 to buy himself time to experiment. *Cine-Pravda* was to be a revolutionary newsreel entailing a root and branch reassessment of the possibilities of film as a medium.

Similarly, the Soviet newspaper strove beyond the bounds of the classic newspaper organisation of stories based on events combined solely by virtue of their simultaneity towards the notion of a single theme underpinning a whole issue. Leading Soviet journalist Mikhail Koltsov's immensely popular weekly *Ogonek* had many such issues.[29] Initially, themed editions enabled the Soviet press to achieve greater power to make broader, more generalised points. Among the most successful of these were anniversary editions commemorating the revolution or the death of Lenin.[30]

The Thematic Issue: *Leninist Cine-Pravda*

Vertov's first themed issue of *Cine-Pravda* was *Cine-Pravda* no. 13, devoted to the fifth anniversary of the October Revolution in 1922. It combines related phenomena occurring at different times and places effectively. But his film made on the 1925 first anniversary of Lenin's death, *Leninist Cine-Pravda. A Film Poem of Lenin* (*Cine-Pravda* no. 21) [Leninskaia kinopravda], ranks among his most accomplished works.

In this film Vertov drew on 'The Final Journey' [Poslednii reis], a *Pravda* feuilleton written on the occasion of Lenin's funeral, by the man who had introduced him to cinema, Mikhail Koltsov.[31] In it Koltsov wrote:

> There he is! He hasn't changed a bit. How much he looks like himself! His face is calm, it almost smiles that unrepeatable, inexpressible, childishly arch smile, comprehensible only to those who saw it; his top lip with its stubbly beard is raised just as in life, provocatively. As if he himself can't believe what's happened: Lenin, but he does not move, does not gesticulate, does not rage, does not wave, does not hurry along at an angle with brief jaunty steps. Lenin, but he lies there, straight and hopeless, hands to attention, shoulders in his green army jacket.[32]

Vertov reuses Koltsov's central device of contrasting Lenin's familiar appearance with the fact that he is dead: 'Lenin, but he does not move.' Yet, whereas Koltsov evokes in words the familiarity of the sight of Lenin and contrasts that with his inanimacy, Vertov, through the medium of film, need only show Lenin lying in his coffin, because his photographic image is so immediately recognisable. It is iconic.[33] In particular, the expression on Lenin's face underlined in the feuilleton as 'comprehensible only to those who saw it' is presumably clear to the cinematic audience. All Vertov needs to do is name him: photography does all the describing he needs. He then underlines the contrast with Lenin's normal self through his use of intertitles.

Lenin

But he does not move

Lenin

But he is silent

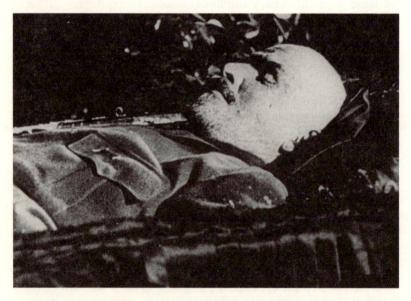

Although clearly inspired by Koltsov, Vertov is more ambitious. Whereas the point of the feuilleton is to evoke the funeral and a sense of loss, Vertov starts with the image of Lenin and a sense of loss, but then further employs these and other cinematic images of Lenin to insist that his cause lives on. Making an anniversary film, Vertov is keen to stress that, although Lenin himself may be dead, there is continuity in Soviet politics. He does this through an array of images of Lenin, flashbacks to important episodes in his life, interviews with people who met him, such as the worker who arrested his (alleged) would-be assassin Fanny Kaplan and shots of places he visited. The film also employs strange point-of-view shots tracking down streets and over crowds, accompanied by intertitles insisting 'Lenin's Force is with us' and hence implicitly visualising Lenin's presence among us. Similarly, a young woman's secret wishes are visualised as she seems to see Lenin appear above the mausoleum. All this is without mentioning the myriad things in the film named after or especially associated with Lenin. Vertov is emphasising Lenin's ongoing presence, and to do so he exploits to the maximum film's iconic power, its power to present and faultlessly reproduce a likeness so powerful as to enable us to recognise the person. It is this capacity inherent in film that Vertov is mobilising so as to stress that 'Lenin is dead, but Leninism lives on', one of the primary functions of the Lenin cult, of the lavish public funeral, and ultimately of the mausoleum.[34]

The argument that 'Leninism lives' is one Vertov makes not only through the image of Lenin. He also appropriates and extends the rhetorical structure of Koltsov's original piece.

The masses

[images of mourners filing past the coffin]

Move

The masses

[images of mourners standing silently]

Are silent

From the starting point of the single sentence in Koltsov's feuilleton – 'Lenin, but he does not move' – Vertov creates a structure of parallels by juxtaposing two sentences starting with 'Lenin' and two sentences starting with 'The masses'. Vertov is clearly underlining continuity by placing the words 'Lenin' and 'the masses' in the same place in these short sentences of identical structure. Unlike Lenin, the masses continue to move, in a visualisation of the unbroken tradition of Lenin's politics. Moreover, the first sentence about Lenin is negative, whereas the first sentence about the masses is an affirmative statement. Although, like Lenin, the masses are silent, their silence is not that of death, but of grief in reaction to his death. We see here clearly the structures of parallelism that might be adduced as examples of Vertov the poet, since poetry routinely employs such means of organisation. Indeed, this film is classified a 'film poem' by its subtitle. Yet its climactic moments take as their model not a poetic work but one of journalism. Here we have a very clear illustration of the intertwining of poetic and journalistic in Vertov. Like Koltsov, indeed, like so much of Soviet journalism of the 1920s, the resources of art and literature are trained upon the refashioning of factual material. As with the images themselves, intertitles too now play an expressive and not simply informational role in the film.[35] Yet the innovation is not limited to the intertitles' verbal substance but also relates to their visual texture. In particular, the intertitles for *Cine-Pravda* were carefully designed to maximise their impact. To this end they experiment with efficient, Constructivist fonts, and emphasise words by varying their size and number. The artist Alexander Rodchenko made some of them. The purpose here is to search for new forms not purely for the sake of novelty but to find the best way of getting a message across to as wide a group as possible, and influencing them as deeply as possible.[36]

This creative attitude to journalism, and factual, everyday genres, adopted by sectors of the artistic community must be borne in mind when considering Vertov's position within the avant-garde. In the years 1922 and 1923 Vertov published two of his most quoted writings, the manifesto 'We: Variant of a Manifesto' and the equally manifesto-like 'Cine-Eyes: A Revolution'. Published respectively in Alexei Gan's *Kinofot* and Vladimir Mayakovsky's *LEF*, iconic mouthpieces of Russian modernism, these sound many of the key themes of the avant-garde, particularly in their call for a renewed, mechanically perfected perception. However, it must be remembered that Vertov saw formal experiment as going hand in hand with the political task of creating a new kind of newsreel: 'Only the latest montage technique is capable of delivering an enormous quantity of instantaneous visual events within the narrow constraints of a cine-newspaper.'[37] It is only later, towards the end of the 1920s, that these goals of technical experiment and political persuasion come to seem incompatible.

In a film such as *Leninist Cine-Pravda*, the Bolshevik bias in journalism towards commentary and interpretation over the need to inform or record is very clear. It should, however, be equally clear that this bias was, at least initially, immensely productive for Vertov, enabling him to develop new kinds of proto-documentary newsreel cinema. Nevertheless, Vertov was also aware of the danger of filming only such politically stage-managed events, and in 1925, shortly after making *Leninist Cine-Pravda*, he tells his movement of Cine-Eyes to avoid filming such things:

Temporarily avoid photographing parades and funerals (we've had enough of them and they're boring) and recordings of meetings with an endless succession of orators (cannot be conveyed on the screen).[38]

Ironically, of course, Soviet documentary film of the 1930s came to be so dominated by films of such parades and congresses as to be virtually synonymous with them. With films such as *Leninist Cine-Pravda*, Vertov himself had made a considerable contribution to this development.[39] Films of events such as the annual 7 November Anniversary of the Revolution parade became part of an unchanging sequence of rituals as rigid as the Church calendar. Despite his complicity, Vertov's advice to his followers is informed by a certain suspicion of this growing marginalisation of journalism's duty to inform and to record. In the 1920s, both in Soviet journalism and in the work of Vertov, there was still a sense that there had to be a balance between artistic reworking and the fact, a residual commitment to factual reporting.

Cine-Eye and the Cine-Eye Movement

Vertov's films initially received a great deal of encouragement, especially from the pages of *Pravda*. This was aided, of course, by his friendships at the paper, especially Mikhail Koltsov.[40] The honeymoon had definitely ended by the time of the release of *Cine-Eye* (1924), which received mixed criticism in the USSR for what was seen as its excessive experimentation in film language.[41] Paradoxically, it is with this film that Vertov begins to be appreciated abroad, precisely for his innovative technique.[42] *Cine-Eye* is sometimes seen as marking Vertov's departure from journalistic cinema to a more poetic, experimental kind of film.[43] His first non-newsreel film aside from compilations, it is crucial to our understanding of this purported shift towards poetic cinema.

However, despite its undoubtedly opaque style, *Cine-Eye* can be seen as marking a higher stage in the evolution of Vertov as a cine-journalist.[44] *Cine-Eye* is an attempt to create a manifesto for a grassroots movement of cine-journalists whose purpose was to transform society, along with relations to creativity and technology. The attempt to found such a movement needs to be seen as a response to the practical, institutional difficulties he faced in his attempts to develop his own brand of Soviet cinema journalism. From his early days on *Cine Week* he had at times been forced to turn to commemorative and compilation work simply because the difficulties of filming meant it could not live up to its title's modest promise of regular weekly editions. Similarly, in an article entitled 'Cine-Pravda', which appeared in *Kinofot* in 1923,

Vertov elaborates on the obstacles facing any attempt to produce Soviet cinema journalism:

> *Cine-Pravda* needs and does not have: a permanent establishment of contributors, on-the-spot correspondents, and the means to maintain them and move them about, an adequate supply of film stock, and the opportunity for practical links with foreign countries. The absence of even one of these factors is enough to kill a cinema newspaper.[45]

Here we have something of an explanation as to why *Cine-Pravda* came out irregularly and ended up more of a journal than a regular newspaper: he found it impossible to make the kind of newsreel he really wanted due to insufficient institutional support.[46] Vertov's initial reaction is to attempt to change this situation, and he invests his energies in the Cine-Eye movement. In attempting to create this organisation, Vertov was following the model of Soviet journalism itself, which, during the Civil War, had appealed to its readers in an attempt to create its own network of correspondents virtually from scratch. For the Cine-Eyes, *Cine-Eye* was to be a programmatic film.

Vertov and Interactive Journalism: The Worker Correspondent Movement

On coming to power the Bolsheviks closed the old press, scared off most of the old journalists and set about replacing them, to create a new, expanded, Bolshevik press.[47] This meant creating a new network of correspondents, and finding language and formats appropriate to their new readers.[48] Since, initially, the population found their press difficult to understand, the Bolsheviks created new dailies aimed at peasants and semi-literate strata of the working class, which made much more of an effort to reach readers by writing accessibly.[49] The crucial ingredient of these mass newspapers' success was their encouraging of letter-writing. This served to encourage reader participation, and at the same time enabled the setting up of an amateur correspondents' network.[50]

Letters written to the papers served as source material for many articles and feuilletons, as such letters and those who regularly wrote them, worker correspondents or *rabkors* (short for *rabochii korrespondent*), tended to address local issues. This, of course, was their great merit as a source of information for staff journalists and the papers generally: they were a substitute network for the gathering of information over a wide area and the gauging of public opinion. Letter-writing and the activities of the worker and peasant correspondents were something like a space where independent critical sources found expression and independent opinion could survive.[51] At the same time they were increasingly institutionalised and controlled by the Party, and by the newspapers for which they wrote, in keeping with Lenin's notion that a newspaper should be an organiser. This interactive or participatory aspect of the Soviet press was its distinctive feature.[52]

Vertov was well aware of the worker correspondent phenomenon, as is clear from his writings. Moreover, his first wife's contacts included Lenin's sister, Maria Ulianova, the secretary of *Pravda* responsible for developing this movement.[53] She was in turn close to Nikolai Bukharin, the movement's most influential and enthusiastic advocate in this period, who in 1924 saw the worker correspondent as a vital independent conduit of information about the moods of the masses.[54] Vertov can be seen as extending the participatory principle to Soviet cinema in his conception of the Cine-Eye movement, modelled on the worker correspondents. Paralleling the abbreviated neologism *rabkor*, Vertov's invented Russian word for the Cine-Eyes 'kinok' itself unexpectedly combined 'kino', the word for 'cinema' (a Western loan word), with 'oko', the archaic and hallowed slavonicism for 'eye',[55] successfully fighting off a number of similar contending compound words, such as *kinkor*[56] and *kinorabkor*.[57] This neologism owed more to avant-garde poetry than to Bolshevik politics. Aside from its powerful incongruity, the term 'Cine-Eye' stresses the specifically visual and therefore cinematic aspect of his movement, intended as part of a revolution in the way we see and relate to technology. The Cine-Eyes are the individual instances of a collective political and cultural Cine-Eye.

The extent to which Vertov is modelling a movement on the worker correspondents is clear too from the way in which he conceives of the basic organisational unit as the circle or *kruzhok*, a term then closely associated with the worker correspondent movement, as its basic unit of organisation on the local scale. Moreover, the Cine-Eyes [Gruppa kinokov pri Goskino] were called upon by Vertov to contribute to their local wall newspapers,[58] just as worker correspondents too were to contribute in the first instance to their local wall newspaper.[59]

It is clear from his writing that Vertov thinks the participatory model of news-gathering extended to cinema would have effects far more radical than the worker correspondent movement. With the Cine-Eyes, Vertov is trying to

create an army of cine-observers and cine-correspondents with the aim of moving away from the authorship of a single person to mass authorship, with the aim of organising a montage vision – not an accidental but a necessary and sufficient overview of the world every few hours.[60]

Such a movement would transform newsreel and society, democratise technology and enact the slogans 'The world through the eyes of the millions' and 'The transfer of authorship to the people'.[61] This brainchild has been hyperbolised as a stunning vision prefiguring late twentieth-century TV news.[62] One could go even further. It is a collectively authored, interactive, 24-hour news channel perpetually delivering not just new stories but new perspectives on the world. Vertov's aspirations for the movement encompass the democratisation not just of technology but also of creativity, through a transcending of the distinction between art and work:

> All people – to a greater or lesser extent – are poets, artists, musicians etc. Or there are no poets, artists or musicians at all.

> A millionth of the inventiveness of every person in everyday work already contains within it an element of art, if we are to reckon with that label…there is no distinction between artistic and non-artistic labour.[63]

As symbols for this new cinema, part art, part newsreel but also examples of how it can be made, Vertov chooses children, the Pioneers of *Cine-Eye* (1924).

Cine-Eye and the Cine-Eye Movement

While originally intended as the first of a six-film series, *Cine-Eye* ends as a demonstration of the technique and method of Cine-Eye documentary, like the later *Man with a Movie Camera* (1929).[64] At the same time, *Cine-Eye* was projected as a concrete illustration of how to organise a documentary film movement analogous to the worker correspondents. As such it is a key film for understanding Vertov's relation to journalism. An uneven film, the most cohesive parts are the first few reels which focus on the Young Pioneers. The decision to use Pioneers (Soviet scouts) to show the possibilities for such a grassroots journalistic movement is crucial. Their very name 'pioneers' suggests innovation, and Vertov plays with the sense of them as pioneers not only of the new society but also, as we have seen, of a new approach to film that would make documentary cinema a tool for the transformation of art and life.[65]

In the first reel of the film, the Pioneers go through the market researching prices so as to show that meat is cheaper when bought from the Cooperative than from private traders. This kind of amateur journalistic research and observation was an important part of the work of Vertov's Cine-Eyes. The film also very clearly demonstrates the key techniques advocated by the group. Themes for initial observation can be split into roughly three categories:

1) *Observation of a place* (for example, a village reading room, a cooperative);

2) *Observation of a person or object in motion* (examples: your father, a Young Pioneer, a postman, a streetcar, etc.); and

3) *Observation of a theme irrespective of particular persons or places* (examples: water, bread, footwear, fathers and children, city and country, tears, laughter, etc.).[66]

In the film we see examples of observation of place and person in the market place, the bar and the Pioneer camp. Interestingly, the Pioneers are both what is being observed, especially in their camp, and the observers of market traders and bars. They are also shown actively agitating both for the Cooperative and against alcoholism. In this way the Pioneers become not just abstract symbols of the new world but also concrete illustrations of a new, socially interventionist grassroots journalism.

From the initial topical theme of the International Day of the Cooperative, the film strives to dig deeper into the analysis of a reality not immediately evident through its treatment of the themes of meat and bread, where reverse-motion is used to show the otherwise invisible processes of labour invested in the final product. This too belongs to the third category of the observation of a theme. In both cases the reverse-motion sequences are used to comment upon what has gone before. The bread sequence in particular begins with an intertitle from a Pioneer's diary, an activity also advocated by Vertov for the Cine-Eyes:[67]

From the diary of a Pioneer: … if the clock in our club went backwards the bread would return to the bakery
Cine-Eye continues the thought of the Pioneer.

In fact, the film shows the various processes of labour involved in bread-making not just to pursue the apparently unmotivated thoughts of the Pioneer. Rather, it is an attempt to mark a contrast with the illusionistic entertainment of the magician, the end result of which is 'to earn his daily bread', and is expressed 'in units of bread'. The film uses markedly filmic techniques to entertain, but not through the creation of illusion.[68] Instead, Cine-Eye reveals that everyday life, the normal appearance of bread, masks the labour invested in it. The Pioneer's diary indicates the beginnings of this analytical process, but Cine-Eye develops it into an illustration of the Marxist view of commodities and the labour theory of value. The Pioneers' activism, research and thinking are a starting point for the demonstration of the possibilities of film as an instrument of radical journalism.

Vertov and his group also encouraged the Pioneers to create a photonewspaper, a weekly newspaper engaging with issues in their daily lives. This achievement was proudly trumpeted, and was supposed to be mirrored by many such photo- and cine-newspapers around the country and, in the end, around the world.[69] Ultimately, the various circles of Cine-Eyes were to participate in the making of further issues of *Cine-Eye*:

> The Goskino Cine-Eye cell should also be regarded as an educational, model workshop through which Young Pioneer and Komsomol film groups will be drawn into production work.
> Specifically, all groups of cine-observers will be drawn into the productions of future Cine-Eye series. They will be the author-creators of all subsequent film-objects.[70]

Again, the decision to film the Pioneers seems significant: in being filmed, they are also learning about filming and are potentially the makers of subsequent issues of *Cine-Eye*.[71] Indeed, elsewhere Vertov even insists on an exclusive focus on teaching the next generation the methods of making cinema by concentrating on Pioneers and the Young Communist League (Komsomol). Needless to say, the lack of facilities, in particular cameras, and the expense of movie cameras were major factors hampering the development of this project.

Nevertheless, it is clear that Vertov in the film is attempting to illustrate with children what he in fact intends as a broad-based movement in cinema. Thus, when Ilya Kopalin, a young man of peasant stock wearing a soldier's greatcoat, appeared while they were filming, he was incorporated into the group and soon became an embodiment of the movement's ideals.[72] Making *Cine-Eye* transformed the likes of Kopalin into a film-maker. It turned Vertov's ideas into a method, enabling the perfection of a whole range of techniques as the basis for further films.[73]

The Fate of the Cine-Eyes

Even without considering Vertov's excessively optimistic assumptions about the possibilities for the development of the movement,[74] the Cine-Eyes faced ever greater difficulties. Journalism in Soviet society more generally was shifting away from the need to gather information or express opinions and towards the need to disseminate the views of the Party and the centre.

It is in this context that Vertov tries to deal with the problems of controlling the movement, while at the same time not stifling it or hampering its development. These were issues that the worker correspondents faced from the beginning, and they were the subject of heated political debate. The essential problem was that the Bolsheviks were unwilling to tolerate any independent movement: churches, cooperatives, trade unions, Pioneers all had to submit to Communist Party control, and so did the worker correspondents. Attempts were made to safeguard their independence, and to guarantee their freedom to criticise shortcomings in society, but by 1925 this was clearly impossible.

Given the expense of the technology involved, it was likewise almost impossible for Vertov to build a movement from the bottom up. His need for government funding meant that he was from the start keen to insist that his movement would be controlled centrally by the Party:

> In the area of vision: the facts culled by the Cine-Eye-observers or cinema worker-correspondents (please do not confuse them with cinema worker-correspondents assigned to reviewing) are organized by film editors according to party instructions, distributed in the maximum possible number of prints and shown everywhere.[75]

This need for control demanded a clearer sense of the movement's aims and a commonly agreed modus operandi. Vertov had to elaborate a programme and codify a method. This called for more sustained theoretical work than the provocative manifestos of 1922.

2

Vertov and Documentary Theory: 'The Goal Was Truth, the Means Cine-Eye'

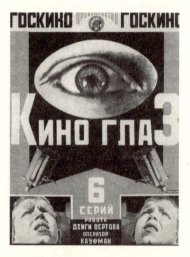

Vertov's theories are best known through cherry-picked terms treated as emblematic of his whole approach to film-making, the most famous of which is *cinéma-vérité*.[1] Similarly, analyses of Vertov's films refer to a 'life caught unawares' method of filming.[2] Typically this term is evoked, minimally glossed, in the hope of finding a partial explanation as to what the films attempt to achieve. But this theoretical construct is rarely subjected to extended scrutiny in its own right, and, equally, little thought is given to the extent to which the films embody and reveal the theories, rather than the other way around. Yet the potential rewards of such an investigation are rich. A sustained examination of key issues for documentary theory such as intervention, performance and ethics would enable us to relate Vertov to broader debates about and attempts to define documentary from the present day dating back to the 1920s. Such an enquiry is an indispensable precursor to any attempt to insert Vertov into his rightful position in the history of documentary film-making.

'Life Caught Unawares'?

As its title suggests, *Cine-Eye* is a crucial programmatic film in its demonstration of the Cine-Eye method for the eponymous movement. Its subtitle is no less significant: *zhizn' vrasplokh*, long translated as 'life caught unawares', is central in Vertov's theorisation of his documentary film practice. While Vertov's great innovation in newsreel was his mobilisation of film's persuasive power, he strove towards a balance between recording and the document on the one hand, and the 'interval', the interaction between shots, the need to reorder and make sense of them on the other. His insistence on capturing an unperformed reality stands at the heart of Vertov's claim to be following a practice of documentary distinguishable from fictional film-making and acted films. '*Zhizn' vrasplokh*' is the term Vertov uses to designate his capturing of the profilmic, his films' pretensions to 'ontological authenticity'.[3] Yet in order to understand the distinct nature of Vertov's brand of documentary we need to examine his use of this term very carefully.

Zhizn' vrasplokh in Dziga Vertov's Writings

Zhizn' vrasplokh has long been interpreted as referring to a hidden camera approach to filming. Probably the best examples of this comes in the index for the English translation of Vertov's works, where the reference for 'candid filming' reads: 'See filming unawares.'[4] Elsewhere in the same book *sniat' vrasplokh* becomes 'to film unobserved'.[5] Even the dominant English translation of the term as 'caught unawares' seems to suggest that Vertov's approach is to ensure subjects are unaware of the presence of the camera.[6]

On this reading, then, Vertov's great achievement is to have solved the problem of performance in documentary film definitively, something not achieved by anyone before or since: his hidden camera does not intervene in the actions filmed and therefore does not change them. In the view of Stella Bruzzi, this notion of a documentary truly capturing reality as it is, or as it was before the film-maker arrived, is 'a false utopian ideal'.[7] Rather, she contests, 'documentaries are inevitably the result of the intrusion of the film-maker onto the situation being filmed'.[8] As a result, 'the important truth any documentary captures is the performance in front of the camera'.[9]

Similarly, Brian Winston in the diagram reproduced below presents 'non-intervention' and 'total intervention' as opposite ends of a scale of reconstruction. By requiring no permission and employing no repetitions or reconstructions of any kind, Vertov supposedly occupies the implausible position of total non-intervention.

Figure 1[10]

Reconstruction Continuum
NON-INTERVENTION
PERMISSIONS
DELAYS and REPETITIONS
RE-ENACTMENT OF WITNESSED ACTION
RE-ENACTMENT OF HISTORY
RE-ENACTMENT OF THE TYPICAL
ENACTMENT OF THE POSSIBLE
ENACTMENT OF THE UNTYPICAL
ACTING WITNESSED HISTORY
ACTING
TOTAL INTERVENTION
WITNESS⋯⋯⋯IMAGINATION

Note: filming outside of the documentary tradition indicated by italic

However, a recent selection of Vertov's writings half-heartedly suggests an alternative translation: 'life off-guard'.[11] While at first sight there appears little difference between these variants, rereading Vertov's discussion of his methods through the prism of the new translation reveals that he does not in fact claim to employ hidden camera photography universally, but makes a clear distinction between filming people off-guard and filming them with a hidden camera.

In 'From the Cine-Eyes' Field Manual' (1924), Vertov's first instruction is: 'Filming unawares [s´´emka vrasplokh] – an old military rule: gauging, speed, attack.'[12] The need for a swift attack makes no sense in the context of the hidden camera, but it is of the essence for a cameraman intending to catch the subject off-guard.[13] Use of the hidden camera [skrytaia s´´emka] is advocated elsewhere in the third instruction, clearly illustrating that the two techniques were entirely different. Indeed, the 'manual' enumerates a number of ways in which the subjects can be photographed so as to minimise the role of performance. These are worth quoting in full:

From the Cine-Eyes' Field Manual

General instructions for all techniques: the invisible cameras.

1. Filming unawares [*vrasplokh*, i.e. off-guard] – an old military rule: gauging, speed, attack.
2. Filming from an open observation point set up by Cine-observers. Self-control, calm, and, at the right moment – lightning attack.
3. Filming from a hidden observation point. Patience and complete attention.
4. Filming when the attention of the subjects is diverted naturally.
5. Filming when the attention of the subjects is artificially diverted.
6. Filming at a distance.
7. Filming in motion.
8. Filming from above.[14]

Translating the term as 'unawares' feeds a widely held misapprehension that documentary is capable of successfully obviating performance. As Brian Winston puts it: 'Public reception of the documentary still turns on an unproblematised acceptance of cinematic mimesis.'[15]

As the above instructions make clear, Vertov's writings discuss a number of techniques to reduce the role of performance. 'Caught off-guard' is just one of these possibilities, as is hidden camera. Where the notion of 'off-guard' is used it suggests that catching people unprepared will reduce their tendency to perform and act, rather than entirely bypass it, as with the hidden camera. This more nuanced view of documentary also comes through in Vertov's 1927 diary, where he acknowledged the difficulties in overcoming performance:

With your camera you enter the whirlpool of life, and life goes on. The race does not stop. No one obeys you. You must adapt yourself so that your investigation will not interfere with others.

Your first failure. People stare at you, urchins surround you, your subjects peer into the camera. You gain experience. You use all sorts of techniques to remain unnoticed, to do your work without preventing others from doing theirs.

Every attempt to film people who are walking, dining, working invariably ends in failure. Girls begin to primp; men make 'Fairbanks' or 'Conrad Veidt' faces.

They all smile for the camera. Sometimes traffic stops.

Curiosity-seekers crowd around the camera and block the filming location.

It's even worse in the evening when the lights attract throngs of curious onlookers.[16]

While Vertov is here looking back at early difficulties, there is also more than a hint that these difficulties are ongoing. In fact the sorts of reactions discussed even remind us of the reactions to the camera we see in his later *Man with a Movie Camera*, where subjects frequently react to the camera.[17] Moreover, the text seems to face full-on the difficulty of overcoming the element of performance in documentary, the sense in which participants are aware of and react to the presence of the camera.

The ramifications of these insights into the irreducible component of performance in his documentaries need to be considered in the analysis of Vertov's films.

Staging and Performance in Vertov's Films (1918–1925)

There are many instances of what might be called 'staging' in Vertov's early films. In the very early *Cine Week* newsreel films this is particularly marked. Almost every single issue incorporates portraits in which the subjects pose: they are usually static and look directly at the camera. Sometimes they smile, or perform characteristic gestures, such as waving their sabres for the camera. In *Cine Week* no. 23 (5 November 1918), for example, we see a procession that is deliberately halted on the orders of the film-makers to make a better shot. Similarly, in *The Trial of Mironov* [Protsess Mironova 1919], witnesses seem to be testifying in front of a white sheet, probably put there by or for the benefit of the film crew, and one even appears to be repeating his speech outside the courtroom for the cameras. In these respective cases we have filming where the subjects are fully aware of the presence of the camera, but they pose, slightly alter what they are doing, and even repeat actions for the benefit of the cameras. Clearly, Vertov intervenes at least to the extent of obtaining the permission of the subjects filmed. In other instances, it seems likely that the subjects (for instance, Trotsky in *Cine Week* no. 22) were aware of the presence of the camera, but they deliberately do not look at it. In any case, Trotsky here would be giving a speech, or inspecting soldiers whether the camera was there or not. He continues what he is doing regardless. The latter makes the film visually more effective and more apparently natural, even though the subject has to overcome an equally natural desire to react to the camera. From the point of view of the spectator, this was clearly preferable, and widely practised in Vertov's films, even before the arrival of Mikhail Kaufman in 1922.

By the time of the *Cine-Pravda* series we see very few explicitly posed portraits, and far more footage of people involved in activities, and therefore less likely to stop to acknowledge the presence of the camera. Here we start to see examples of caught off-guard filming. This is clear already in *Cine-Pravda* no. 2, where the various participants arriving at the trial of the Right Socialist Revolutionaries are photographed while getting out of carriages, or having their papers checked, and they seldom acknowledge the camera directly. Or, if they do, such shots are discarded. In later issues of *Cine-Pravda*, this was developed into a system of representation in which workers are frequently photographed working, tending their machines, and consequently they have little time to acknowledge the presence of the film-maker. Feldman has even argued that not disturbing the activities of those filmed was one of the meanings of *zhizn' vrasplokh*.[18] The extreme version of this recording of work was the photographing of machines without the workers: in such cases there was no risk at all of performance.[19]

Nevertheless, even with the *Cine-Pravda* series, there are many instances where the presence of the camera has undoubtedly altered or even instigated some of the actions. Here we move further down Winston's scale towards the grey area of reconstruction, which is a consistent feature of documentary film throughout its history, beginning with *Nanook of the North* [USA 1922], one of the first examples of the form, where Nanook re-enacts long-abandoned hunting practices for the film. In 'About Love for the Living Person' (1958), a posthumously published article written towards the end of his career, Vertov attempts retrospectively to justify his view that the 'documentary-poetic unstaged film' can capture 'the living person'. To this end, he stresses that there are many 'unstaged' [neinstenirovannyi] episodes in *Cine-Eye* and his other, later films.[20] This is an interesting assertion, in that it implicitly accepts that there were many staged incidents in *Cine-Eye*, something that has long been clear to the most astute commentators, beginning with then film critic Vladimir Erofeev at the time of its release.[21]

Vertov's writings of the time go further than one might expect in confronting these issues, claiming of *Cine-Eye* that 'all the *dramatis personae* [deistvuiushchie litsa] continue to do what they usually do in life'.[22] The term '*dramatis personae*' suggests actors. Even if this is ironic, there is a tacit admission that the Pioneers' and others' activities have been repeated for the camera. At the same time, Vertov is photographing them doing the kinds of things that, as Pioneers, they would be doing anyway: setting up a camp or mending pots. While broadly this seems plausible, one might equally ask about the extent to which Vertov's team alter the actions of the Pioneers, the parades and flag-raising especially. While these are things the Pioneers would do, they are in a sense performing these typical actions for the camera. The proximity of the camera rules out any possibility of them being photographed without their knowledge: they are neither unaware nor off-guard. Instead, their actions are being choreographed or re-enacted for the camera.

Another similarly staged repetition of the subject's habitual actions in *Cine-Eye* is that of the Chinese conjuror, paid by Vertov to perform in a given yard, next to a road maintenance tent erected especially so as to film the magician and the children's reactions to him unnoticed.[23] This is the use of the hidden camera, but this effectively makes the magician a paid performer working for Vertov. The children are filmed unobserved, but the magician is consciously performing. In fact, the paying of participants is not by any means unknown in the Griersonian tradition: Flaherty paid the fishermen to go out in a gale in *Man of Aran* [UK 1934].[24] This notion of recording subjects repeating for the cameras what they would do anyway is important, in that this echoes very strongly the Griersonian tradition of realist documentary. In Vertov's own film-making this kind of practice was to dominate, notably, for example in *Man with a Movie Camera*, where all the actions of the cameraman, such as walking along with his camera, as well as collating the wall newspaper *The Filmmaker* [Filmar'], are clearly staged in the full knowledge that the camera is on him. Similarly, in *Three Songs of Lenin*, a (formerly) Moslem woman takes off her veil, an image already used by Vertov in *Cine-Pravda* no. 21 and *A Sixth Part of the World*. Once more, none of these incidents are acting in the sense of performing scripted actions one would not ordinarily do or has not already done, but they do involve performance for the camera.

Yet the film-maker's intervention can be seen as going beyond this kind of reconstructional practice (as Robert Flaherty and John Grierson did too): the researching of meat prices, the anti-alcohol campaigning in bars and the agitation for Cooperatives in general are things the Pioneers *should* be doing, but the presence of the camera ensures that they act in this model fashion. They give Vertov what he wants, or what they think he wants: they perform the role of perfect Pioneers. Just how much he wanted them to be exemplary is clear from the structure of the film, where the Pioneers represent the new in conflict with the old. Moreover, as we saw in the previous chapter, Vertov certainly intended the Pioneers in his film to represent not only a model for Soviet youth in general but also a model for a grassroots, cinematic news-gathering network. There are a number of similar episodes in the *Cine-Pravda* films, where people perform actions that have been instigated or choreographed by the film-makers, such as the episode in *Cine-Pravda* no. 15 where a man takes down an icon from his wall and replaces it with an anti-religious poster,[25] or that in *Cine-Pravda* no. 18 where a baby is symbolically baptised Vladimir before being passed to a Pioneer, to a Komsomol member, to a Communist and then to the mother. In each case, members of the public perform actions they might (or might not) have done anyway, but their behaviour is immaculately Communist. We may ask ourselves how typical this behaviour is for these subjects. It seems likely this was instigated by the presence of the camera. After all, what Soviet citizen would want to be recorded doing anything less than exemplary?

However, there are a number of incidents in which Vertov intervenes in what occurs to a far greater degree, staging action that is entirely conceived for the films. A minor example of this kind would be the person turning the pages of a specially mocked-up newspaper entitled *Cine-Pravda* in *Cine-Pravda* no. 5. This is obviously performed for the camera, and would not happen otherwise – indeed, it involves a prop. Yet probably the most egregious case of staging in these films comes in *Cine-Pravda* no. 8, which begins with Mikhail Kaufman and Ivan Beliakov discussing the trial of the Socialist Revolutionaries, arguing whether or not the defendants will be shot. The film then builds up suspense, showing the various participants in the trial, and culminating in the judges retiring to deliberate. The next day people crowd a news-stand to buy papers with the verdict. Again, members of the crew are visible acting out the roles of members of the public, as is Vertov himself, playing the role of a tram passenger buying a copy of the paper from a vendor, reading it and discussing it with the person next to him. The vendor also sells a copy to Kaufman and Beliakov, who are in a car. The verdict is guilty (this, of course, was never in doubt), and Kaufman asserts that the culprits will be shot; Beliakov disagrees, and they bet. Kaufman smiles as initially the headlines appear to bear out his point of view, but Beliakov smiles too as it transpires that the death sentence will be suspended for some of the accused.[26] They are both right: a happy ending.

What are we to make of this strange episode, entirely staged, possibly scripted, but differing from fiction in that the actors are not professional and the drama is that of the anticipation of the latest news story? Its purpose is quite clear: to impart an element of suspense to what might otherwise be considered something of a foregone conclusion – the accused will be found guilty and shot. It seems that the need to stage here is to give the impression of an anticipation and uncertainty that never really existed. In terms of Winston's classification, this is the re-enactment of the untypical, the greatest degree of intervention permissible within the documentary tradition. The purpose is deliberately to mislead the audience. This kind of staging, and the show trial it legitimates, are mendacious examples of the kind of staging that was to give Soviet documentary cinema – and, indeed, Soviet film in general – a bad name. It is dishonest, because it attempts not to reconstruct or repeat something typical or something already witnessed but to project a wished-for reality, conflicting with other evidence.

Frequently 'life caught off-guard' was not even an aim for Vertov. This is particularly evident in *Leninist Cine-Pravda*, where Vertov includes an interview with a worker who relates his role in arresting Fanny Kaplan after her attempt to assassinate Lenin. Often assumed to be an invention of 1960s documentary film, the interview is obviously neither off-guard filming nor hidden camera. Nevertheless, the fact that there are many instances of staging in Vertov's early work, and even in the *Cine-Pravda* period, does not of course mean that there was no use of hidden camera and that none of the subjects were caught off-guard or unprepared. On the contrary, Kaufman's camerawork is striking in its ability to photograph people in revealing ways. In particular, in *Cine-Eye* there are also sequences which apparently record black-market deals, with money changing hands. But the fact that anyone could ever have argued that Vertov exclusively filmed using hidden camera techniques is a tribute to the messianic power of his pronouncements, and to the success of his team, especially Mikhail Kaufman, in using their ingenuity to reduce the role of performance in documentary film.

Vertov's Brand of Documentary Reassessed

If Vertov does not universally employ hidden camera, nor even caught-off guard photography, but employs reconstruction, then to what extent does his brand of documentary represent a distinct variant of the form? Without question, one sense in which Vertov's approach is distinct is that reducing the role of performance in his films also meant avoiding detailed scripts. *Cine-Eye* can be seen as a bold attempt by the group to 'make sense of the phenomena of life around them'[27] to 'avoid getting tangled in life's chaos and to get [their] bearings in any surroundings

[they] happen[-] to come across'.[28] Apparently unconnected or random events are shown to be part of a pattern through the use of cinematography's analytical power. It is employed as an epistemological tool.[29] The episode of the elephant in *Cine-Eye* corroborates this interpretation, since it just happened to be on the same train as the Cine-Eyes and Young Pioneers as they returned to Moscow. In *Cine-Eye* it appears simply by virtue of this coincidence, an unmotivated occurrence that proves the film is a genuine attempt to make sense of random events. When reworked in *Cine-Pravda* no. 20, it has become part of a structured demonstration of the workings of the Pioneer troop: while one group of Pioneers goes to the countryside, the other group of Pioneers makes a trip to the zoo on the orders of their leader, for educational purposes. Yet, while this incident shows that Vertov was willing to film events that occurred spontaneously, the repeated hostility to the written scenario never meant the absence of any plans whatsoever. This is clear from his writings throughout the 1920s.

One unusual and characteristic feature of Vertov's approach to planning and conceiving a film was the stress upon the process of observation.[30] Moreover, the whole notion of 'life-off guard' needs to be tempered by the fact that Vertov believed in recording processes and underlying patterns, rather than just events. Hence the notion of 'Communist decoding' referred to repeatedly in his writings.[31] It seems that the Cine-Eye was supposed to select subjects to film, in such a way as to enable the editing process to make sense of the world. As a director this was usually Vertov's role, as is clear from some of the instructions he wrote to the other Cine-Eyes. Vertov would give commands as to the kind of footage he wanted his collaborators to take. Volchek, for instance, recalls how Vertov instructed him before setting off to the countryside at the height of the collectivisation campaign to ensure that every one of his shots of the fight against the kulaks 'was permeated with belief in the justice of the measures being taken against these criminal kulak elements...'.[32] Vertov even made precise suggestions as to how he could ensure the footage met these requirements. The film-maker was to be thoroughly prepared, and to shoot according to a precise, preconceived idea, albeit not a written script.

The eschewal of the detailed script, the emphasis placed on observation and on the filming of processes, are part of Vertov's conception of documentary as an analytical tool implicit in the very notion of Cine-Eye. Indeed, for Vertov, the cinema is presented as an optical tool analogous to the telescope or microscope, enabling him to reveal a new perspective on life: 'It is as if the eyes of children and adults, the literate and illiterate are opening for the first time.'[33] The need to get audiences to see afresh is absolutely crucial to Vertov's conception of the film *Cine-Eye*. Hence the choice of children as the 'weakest point'; both symbolic of and especially amenable to the new, they are ideal as the primary subject for this experimental and programmatic film. In this context, the avoidance of acting is not so much an end but a means to revealing something new about life:

> Not 'filming life unawares' for the sake of the 'unaware', but in order to show people without masks, without make-up, to catch them through the eye of the camera at a moment when they are not acting, to read their thoughts, laid bare by the camera.[34]

This sense of the general revelatory power of the cinema comes through strongly in Vertov's unpublished verse:

> There's sometimes a need
> to show a new plane of reality,
> free from banality.
> Upside down, juvenile.
> Human
> and Soviet-style.
>
> Cine-Eye is not the aim. Cine-Eye
> is a means.
> To show without masks.[35]

The total absence of performance was an ideal towards which Vertov strove, but which he was never quite able to attain. As Vertov's contemporary, Sergei Tretiakov, was to argue, the distinction between 'played' and 'unplayed' film is relative, since few documentaries succeed in employing solely 'off-guard', or what he calls 'flagrant', material.[36] As we have seen above, Winston takes a similar view. On such a reading, Vertov's peculiarity lies in the fact that he was actively hostile to performance and attempted to reduce its influence over his films, despite the fact that it features in each of them. He had at least freed documentary from the posed portraits and staging that dominated early newsreel.

His hostility is far deeper and his tolerance for staging more limited than the Griersonian tradition of documentary, even though he shares more in common with it than has been assumed. Grierson had assumed that making film an analytical tool involved far more directorial intervention.[37] Vertov's contemporary Grigori Boltiansky is also aware that films composed entirely of footage of people shot 'off-guard' are almost impossible to make, and similarly argues they are an 'ideal':

Ideally all footage for newsreel should be bits of 'life off-guard', the most persuasive, genuine, and unforced type of footage, but it cannot be obtained with an unwieldy camera that has to be set up, attracts attention, and creates unavoidable artificiality and tension.[38]

Here Boltiansky shows just how much there was an aspiration towards the ideal of fly-on-the-wall, observational cinema, to a great extent attained by 1960s film-makers. While the development of small, portable cameras facilitated direct cinema, in the 1920s, however, the very size of the cameras undermined the striving to record people and events without recourse to staging. Overcoming the problem of the subject's reaction to the camera was possible through various techniques, including the hidden camera for some shots, but this also meant the invoking of the model of intelligence work, of spying, to justify the observation and filming of people without their consent. Boltiansky stresses that the concept of a network of correspondent-photographers is the best way of ensuring that material really is 'caught off-guard'.[39] This prospect likewise recalls that of the network of correspondents, and once more raises the issues around surveillance suggested in the previous chapter: if Vertov was at all successful in attaining the ideal of hidden camera filming, or even the filming of people off-guard, then surely this raises certain ethical issues? Was Vertov the pioneer of surveillance photography?

Surveillance in Vertov's Concept of Documentary

In a 1936 diary entry Vertov commented upon something he saw in the paper:

A thief in the role of an auditor.
'Duty' – the bank auditor;
'Profession' – hardened thief.

(from an article about a thief in *Pravda* no. 262, 22 September 1936)

If Cine-Pravda is truth shown by Cine-Eye, then a shot of the auditor would be in accord with Cine-Eye only if his masks were to be discarded and if behind the mask of auditor could be seen the *thief.*

The only way to tear off the auditor's mask is to secretly observe him, through hidden filming, that is, an invisible camera, supersensitive film and lenses with a large aperture, film for night and evening observation; in addition, a noiseless camera (sight plus sound) in continual readiness, with instantaneous release, simultaneous with what's seen.[40]

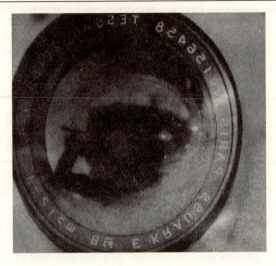

Hidden camera filming here is seen as a means of detecting crime, catching the culprit 'red-handed'. Here, once again, we have evidence of Vertov's prescience. To the twenty-first-century reader, what Vertov is describing appears to be the familiar techniques of the undercover investigative reporter or a system of closed-circuit television. While CCTV is widely held to help in the detection of crime or its deterrence, discussions about it also express unease about the loss of privacy, about the use to which unseen, unchecked agencies may put people's images and other data, and the use of surveillance, to enforce conformity. Although these anxieties about surveillance have been expressed most powerfully by Michel Foucault, Vertov's enthusiasm for surveillance is part of a strand of thinking stretching at least as far back as the Enlightenment and Jeremy Bentham's project for a panopticon-like prison, in which the visibility of the prisoners was to be the means to their reform.[41] The idea that observation could enforce behavioural norms was to influence school, factory and hospital design throughout the industrial world. While Vertov himself appears to use hidden cameras to record dubious or possibly criminal behaviour in *Cine-Eye* in the shots of the thieves and petty black-market traders exchanging money, the idea of film as a consistent means of penal or any other kind of reform is not one he pursues with any tenacity. His concern is, rather, to establish the fact that film can in theory be used in this manner.

Any failure by Vertov fully to exploit cinema's power as an instrument of surveillance was not due to any qualms about the individual's consent to be photographed or right to privacy. As he puts it, no member of the audience can be sure they will not appear in an issue of *Cine-Eye*.[42] On the contrary, Vertov's films are posited upon a sense of the camera's right to see whatever it wants: it is possible to argue that many of those who seem concerned to avoid being photographed, in *Man with a Movie Camera*, for example, are implicitly being criticised, whereas the workers are unconcerned by the presence of the camera.[43] Vertov is implying that all is public, there is no private sphere into which a camera has no right to intrude, and the camera therefore needs no consent on the part of individuals to film them. For Vertov, the personal is political.

What is Cine-Eye?

...Above all it is a striving to see better, a striving to explain the elusive visible world with the help of the film camera, the striving to penetrate so deep into life that the notion of the 'intimate' ceases to exist.[44]

The sequences showing mental patients illustrate this lack of concern for privacy or consent graphically. The patients are not in a position to grant it, and it is hard to imagine Vertov thinking very much about the possible effects of filming on the patients or their relatives. They are photographed primarily as an example of illness, as an analogy for unhealthy capitalist elements in Russian society. Unkempt, half-naked and with shaven heads, they react to and perform in front of the camera, whether it be by hiding their faces, denouncing the film-makers as tsarist policemen, or possibly alluding to the Kaufman brothers' Jewish identity: 'I demand that you stop the pogroms!' However, they are also made amusing through the choice of intertitles such as 'I myself haven't been born yet' or 'To hell with the icon! Bread is my God'. This seems to exploit these people for the delectation of others, and as such is still less ethical.

Vertov's Pioneer children in *Cine-Eye* are in a better position to consent, but they are not simply observed; they are themselves observers, as we saw in the last chapter. They serve as the model for a network of observers and do a great deal of surveillance themselves. There may be a play on words here: the scout movement became the Pioneers in Soviet Russia, translating a spatial metaphor of reconnaissance into the temporal one of being ahead in time. However, Russian uses the same word [razvedka] for both 'reconnaissance' and 'intelligence work'. Thus the person who does it is a 'razvedchik': both a scout doing reconnaissance and an intelligence officer spying. A Russian translation of the English concept of 'scout', the implicit model for the newly founded Soviet Pioneers, would yield a Russian word which also means intelligence officer or secret policeman. In this context, the choice of the Pioneers to illustrate the documentary movement he wants to create seems significant. Its significance is amplified when one realises that the words 'razvedka' and 'razvedchik' appear frequently in Vertov's writings about the film, but 'razvedchik' is normally translated as 'scout', just as 'razvedka', the subtitle of *Cine-Eye*, is usually translated as 'reconnaissance' – a choice that hides the unnerving reality of intelligence work and surveillance behind it.[45] Indeed, in discussing *Cine-Eye*, the film and the organisation, Vertov uses the term 'razvedchik' to refer to the activities of the Pioneers:

> The 'Cine-Eye' project for organising information work. Cine-scouts [Kinorazvedchiki]. Cine-observers. The first attempt to attract Young Pioneers to the investigation of the visible world.[46]

Similarly, Vertov refers to his other film which focuses on Pioneers, *Cine-Pravda* no. 20, as 'constructed on the basis of observations of young scouts [razvedchik]. It comprises three reports [donesenie] by Cine-observers.'[47] These 'reports' employ the word which typically refers to a spy's report to superiors.[48] Indeed, Vertov sees his network of observers or reporters as also constituting a network of informers and spies modelled on that of the GPU (the State Political Administration for Struggle against Espionage and Counter-Revolution) – firstly by using the term 'razvedchik', as we have seen, but, going further, by stressing that both the GPU and Cine-Eyes must '[from life's chaos] separate out and bring to light a particular issue, a particular affair'.[49]

Of course, it is true that, in evoking the model of the GPU, Vertov is attempting to find metaphors for the work of the cameraman, and the sense of reconnaissance and scouting ahead are significant to him as new metaphors for the commitment to experiment that lies at the heart of the similar notion of the avant-garde. Yet, at the same time, as we have seen, Vertov pays scant attention in his practice or his writings to the issues of his subjects' consent to being photographed and their rights over their own image. What greater principle does he invoke to justify this consistent disregard? The truth is that he never seems to confront this as an ethical problem. In passing he invokes the law and science. The liberal journalist's classic defence of the public's right to know is one he never seems to use. Art, too, would be a potential defence, and a more plausible one in the case of the mentally ill, since it requires no moral underpinning, but it seems unlikely Vertov would employ this, at least in the early 1920s. In the context of Soviet Russia, though, the more compelling argument is not the public's but the state's right to know: the classic justification of the secret police. The repeated references to the secret police and spying can be seen as filling the apparent void of consideration as to the ethical dimension of documentary film-making. Indeed, Vertov's efforts to obtain permission to film are directed primarily towards the state, and thereby bypass the need to obtain individual consent. Permits to film date as far back as one issued by the Revolutionary-Military Committee of the South-East Front in the civil war, and a mandate to film Lenin's funeral countersigned by Felix Dzerzhinsky, head of the GPU, are reproduced in the Russian edition of Vertov's works. Similarly, in planning *The Eleventh Year*, Vertov notes the need to ask the GPU for permission to shoot in various different instances.[50] In his notebook for 1934 he stresses that a pass enabling the film-maker to get in everywhere is indispensable for the documentary film-maker.[51] At the same time, this is one reason why Vertov's proposed grassroots movement failed: film-makers needed state permission.[52] Clearly, there can be no shooting without such permission, and Vertov is not in a position to grant it. Documents such as these, and not contracts or waivers with his subjects, give Vertov the right and the power to make films. His cinema eye was also exercising the state's right to see.

Yet this invocation of the state's right to see rather than the public's right to know is a sensible and very astute choice in the circumstances. Vertov's cinema grew, as we have seen, from Soviet journalism, in which the goal of informing was subordinate to interpretation, to editorialising. As a source of information the Soviet newspaper was inherently unreliable because it was too selective, too oriented towards good news, and became increasingly insular. As Sheila Fitzpatrick has argued, the government itself was aware of this and came instead to draw its information from secret police reports and citizens' letters, such as those sent by the worker correspondents.[53] Vertov, in modelling his Cine-Eye movement on the GPU, in its 'reporting function' and not its 'punitive function',[54] and on the worker correspondent movement was adapting for cinema the examples of the two most reliable channels of information available in his society. In fact, it is a sign of his acuity, and his ongoing commitment, for all his exploration of cinema's power of persuasion, to the informational goal of journalism and the documentary as record.

Nevertheless the right to see into any would-be private sphere is implicit in the notion of unmasking in the quotation from Vertov's diary. This was a metaphor frequently used by Soviet satirical journalism, and even more so by the secret police. Vertov, though, had a predilection for the metaphor not so much of unmasking but of unveiling: most notably in the image of a Bolshevised Moslem woman who casts off the veil, repeated in *Cine-Pravda* no. 21, *A Sixth Part of the World* and *Three Songs of Lenin*. When seen in this context, this image might be interpreted as signifying not only, or not so much, the woman's liberation to see the

3

'A Card Catalogue in the Gutter.' *Forward, Soviet!*
A Sixth Part of the World

In March 1925 Vertov released his last issue of *Cine-Pravda*. The following year he completed two seminal, feature-length documentary films that inspired or perplexed the film world. *Forward, Soviet!* and *A Sixth Part of the World* left no one indifferent. These two films in a year pulverised received notions of non-fiction film and newsreel. On the ruins Vertov constructed the mighty edifice of documentary, changing film for ever.

At the same time, this transition from newsreel was one Vertov had initiated with his *Cine-Pravda* series, and was largely inspired by journalistic models. *Forward, Soviet!* and *A Sixth Part of the World* use newsreel, found and unstaged footage, not simply to show, or record, but to construct an argument, to move and to persuade their audience. Their novelty lies in doing so in more extensive fashion and in more consistent manner than *Cine-Pravda*. Yet the reasons why Vertov moved to longer films owes much to the specific circumstances of Soviet newsreel in this period.

Decline of Newsreel in the 1920s

As we saw in Chapter 1, Vertov's evolution away from newsreel proper was in part because he was unable to secure sufficient resources to make the kind of newsreel he wanted. In the wake of his departure the new newsreel series, *Sovkino-journal* soon became a byword for ineffective and poor-quality factual film-making. A clear step backwards from *Cine-Pravda*.[1] Newsreel cinema in general fell out of favour in the NEP period, as distributors focused on profitability.[2] From its high point during the civil war, newsreel had fallen to a new low by 1926: the four years of

peace had yielded three times less newsreel than the four of civil war.[3]
Even archive footage was not preserved properly.

Yet Vertov was far from daunted by these straitened circumstances.
Having already left a distinctive imprint on the supposedly anonymous
genre of newsreel, he had plans to achieve something similar with
promotional film. His first practical experiments in this direction were
with the genre of animated shorts,[4] and in 1925 he published an article
called 'The Cinema Advert'.[5] In this article Vertov explores the advert as
a way for documentary film-makers in particular to make films. The
manuscript version of this article makes it clear that this is a compromise
engendered by the difficult circumstances for funding Vertov encountered
after the end of the civil war: 'The film advert can open the gates to work,
to production.'[6]

Showing characteristic skill in making a virtue of necessity, Vertov
and his team found new funding sources for even more ambitious films.
However, the changed economic climate meant expenditure was more
strictly audited, and he was not accorded the licence to experiment he
enjoyed with *Cine-Pravda*. Vertov's talent for finding a creative way of
fulfilling imposed tasks led to confrontations. Unable to succeed at this
new game, Vertov was fired from Sovkino at the end of 1926. However,
Vertov's failure to please his paymasters produced two remarkable feature-
length factual films, harbingers of the nascent form of documentary film.

Forward, Soviet!

Subtitled *The Moscow Soviet in the Present, Past and Future*, *Forward, Soviet!*
draws on Vertov's skill in using newsreel footage to show the country
transformed by Soviet rule and the Moscow Soviet. While, like the
Vertov group's first feature, *Cine-Eye*, much of the material was shot by
the Cine-Eyes themselves, *Forward, Soviet!* also employs the approach
evident in the earlier compilation films (such as *The History of the Civil
War*), where editing creates relations which may have no firm foundation
in fact. It would seem that Vertov was determined to escape charges
that the material was unstructured, the not entirely groundless criticism
levelled at *Cine-Eye*. The result is a highly coherent narrative which uses a
number of flashbacks from the normality of the present to the chaos of
the civil war, contrasted with which even a flushing toilet seems a
miraculous achievement. The film then depicts the contradictions of the
present before stressing those aspects that point towards the future
progress of the city and the country. In addition to the clear time
progression, the film finds inventive ways of introducing and structuring
factual material through rhetoric, rendering political speeches and

introducing lists in ways that were to be productive for the later documentary films of Vertov and others.

These narrative and rhetorical structuring devices are compounded by the film's treatment of space and time. The whole film treats Moscow not as a city apart from the rest of the country but as a microcosm or synecdoche for the country as a whole in the past eight years. The part represents the whole. In itself, this is not startlingly original. In novels this is the norm: the story of this or that character is the story of humanity, the class, etc. Moreover, Sergei Eisenstein had recently done something similar with *The Battleship 'Potemkin'* [Brononosets 'Potemkin', 1926]: the revolt that spreads from the battleship stands for the various events of the 1905 Russian Revolution, such as Bloody Sunday and the general strike. Indeed, ultimately it stands for world revolution. This use of synecdoche has been seen as typical of the documentary as a whole.[7] Yet not only does Vertov use the technique of part for whole in this broader treatment of the image of Moscow, he also uses it to construct individual sequences. Image and intertitle are linked so as to contrast representations of the civil war (before) with those of the country's achievements (after). One or two shots stand for the period.

One example is the repeated 'from … to' structure, in which ruined houses or factories are contrasted with newly built homes and full-tilt production. The intertitle implies that ruins are representative of the civil war whereas construction and industry sum up the present. The intertitle does not simply name the image or situate it in place and time, but also claims that it represents that place and time. The image becomes not solely an illustration but evidence in an argument:

Where previously it was impossible to drive …

[A horse-drawn cart skids pulling a broken-down car along a muddy track]

Now a there is a paved road

[A steamroller smoothes the tarmac on a road]

Rather than show us a recording of a muddy road at a certain time and place we are shown a muddy road as an image of the old Russia's backwardness, and a tarmac road as an image of the new Russia's progress. We are not being asked to dwell upon the relation of these images to the moments and places they capture except in the most general sense that they are of somewhere in Russia, at about the relevant time. Indeed, this vagueness is explicit in other images of destruction, such as those of famine and the dying horse introduced by the intertitle 'Somewhere...' [Gde-to]. The exact time and location is not important. What matters is how image relates to intertitle, making concrete the assertion that Russia has progressed in the last five years.

Nevertheless, if we do stop to consider the relation between these images and the moments, places and situations they capture, then we might realise that the impassable road and the tarmac road are probably not the same place. This high-handed approach to specific names, dates and places was to annoy the Formalist critic Victor Shklovsky, who wrote of the film:

> I think that newsreel material is in Dziga Vertov's treatment deprived of its soul – its documentary quality [dokumental'nost']... The whole sense of newsreels lies in the date, time and place. A newsreel without this is like a card catalogue in the gutter.[8]

For Shklovsky and his like, the sole purpose of newsreel is to record and name. There is no point in it attempting to do anything else. Vertov's film uses photography as evidence of the improvement not of specific roads, buildings or people but, rather, of the country as a whole, in a broader sense. The film asserts and argues rather than simply illustrating. This does not weaken *Forward, Soviet!* as a film. On the contrary, it demonstrates the incredible power of documentary film to persuade and exhort.

However, for the Moscow Soviet, which had commissioned the film, this was a catastrophe. There was no naming of specific achievements, politicians or figures, and they rejected the film as failing to fulfil its commission.[9] But both the Moscow Soviet and Shklovsky were ultimately in vain. Vertov had demonstrated the potential of the documentary form: newsreel footage can be combined to construct a powerful argument.

While the flashback-style narrative and part-for-whole conceit make up the general structure of the film, *Forward, Soviet!* is also highly effective in using rhetoric to present lists. One example of this is a variation on the part-for-whole pattern, where weapons of war are contrasted with tools of construction, with a single image used to represent the past but a list of images to stand for the present (and, implicitly, the future):

In place of bullets

[bullets being loaded into the breech of a rifle]

nails

[a nail is placed in a wooden block and drives itself in]

screws

[screws being screwed into wood]

bricks

Vertov displays here one of his great talents as a documentary film-maker: his ability not simply to create lists or catalogues of images but to link them up in an engaging way as a means of persuasion. This is a proclivity that we see throughout the rest of his films, to such an extent that his *Man with a Movie Camera* has been called the first 'database film'[10] for its brilliance in linking images on similar themes. In *Forward, Soviet!* the lists are made interesting through the judicious use of short intertitles such as the word 'Without', which is repeated at the beginning a number of times to link images of what people have now, but lacked during the civil war (such as bread and water). Here Vertov is drawing on the jingle and slogan devices elaborated in Mayakovsky's civil war posters, known as the ROSTA 'windows'. These were comic-book-style summaries of the news which employed an extremely laconic verse form in their captions. Conjunctions such as 'from', 'to', 'with' and 'without' dominate, and verbs are often replaced by a dash. Vertov's adoption of the latter device is illustrated in the sequence which can be read as 'The Soviet Helps the Sick and Victims of Industrial Accidents'. Exploiting a peculiar feature of the Russian language, the verb 'help' is replaced by a dash. It is implicit, and the spectator has to guess it.

As with *Leninist Cine-Pravda*, Vertov appropriates the devices of literature, here those of the Soviet Union's most prominent poet. However, the example followed is one in which poetic techniques had been innovatively applied to the treatment of factual material. Once again, the poetic and the journalistic prove intertwined.

A significant contrast between the poet and the film-maker is, as might be expected, that words dominate for the poet and images for the film-maker. Whereas Mayakovsky uses a single image per caption, Vertov tends to use a number of images per intertitle. Thus the question 'Where are you hurrying?' provokes a whole list of responses introducing diverse leisure activities. At the same time, this gives a sense of the bustle of the city and motion towards the future, and of the feverish activity of the present which is building it. Similarly, lists are introduced by fragmenting sentences. This creates a certain momentum almost bordering on suspense, as the viewer both anticipates the end of the phrase and strains to find out precisely what it is the Soviet is fighting for or taking care of. The answer is a list naming and showing the various items or activities.

This technique is used to represent political speeches, a sub-genre Vertov had refined over the course of the previous eight years in film. Initially in *Cine Week,* when we saw someone giving a speech, there were no intertitles explaining what it was about.[11] By 1919 Vertov shows the orator, and then gives the speech verbatim in an intertitle.[12] However, in *The History of the Civil War* Vertov had already shown a close-up of Trotsky before giving a few salient words in an intertitle followed by action sequences that were their consequence. Similarly in numerous issues of *Cine-Pravda* he had used images to illustrate and give a visual equivalent of a speech.[13] The final two speeches which conclude *Forward, Soviet!* are the acme of this technique. In the penultimate speech an orator in a workers' club celebrates the installation of light bulbs, 'Lenin's little bulbs'. We see the word 'Lenin' picked out in electric lights on the Soviet building. The orator exhorts people not to forget Lenin, and we see a shot of the dead leader at his funeral (anticipating a similar sequence in *Three Songs of Lenin*). The orator concludes his speech in four intertitles arguing 'each electric lamp/ each machine tool/ each machine/ continues the work of Lenin'. An image illustrating the speech follows each intertitle, but fragmenting the sentence lends the speech greater force.

Similarly, the final speech comprises only five intertitles: 'We are growing/ towards the construction of a new world/ Build, Soviet!/ Forward, Soviet!/ From NEP Russia will come Socialist Russia.' Instead of illustration, images of machines, buses, factories and speeded-up night-time traffic are intercut. The final shot is of Lenin by the Kremlin. Through intercutting the speech with images that echo his words, both words and images are made more dynamic: electricity is linked to Lenin and to the progress made by the Moscow Soviet, and night traffic becomes a metaphor for progress towards socialism. Neither words alone nor images alone could have achieved this.

Vertov was transforming narrow newsreel into something far more flexible. Yet *Forward, Soviet!* primarily builds on the achievements of his earlier work, developing the visualisation of political oratory from various issues of *Cine-Pravda*. Moreover, the basic structure of building a narrative of normalisation and progress by combining new and archive footage had been employed in *Cine-Pravda* no. 13, and even *Leninist Cine-Pravda* no. 21. Yet *Forward, Soviet!* does this in a more ambitious and extensive way. *Forward, Soviet!* exceeds the parameters of newsreel, but is still firmly rooted in it. Furthermore, its feuilleton-like contrasts and *ocherk*-like evocation unmistakably draw on Soviet journalism's licence in the reworking of factual material.

A Sixth Part of the World

If *Forward, Soviet!* treated Moscow as a microcosm for the USSR, Vertov's other promotional film of the same year, *A Sixth Part of the World,* took a diametrically opposite approach to the challenge of extended form: it attempts to squeeze the whole country into its similar 50-odd-minute span. Here Vertov did not draw on his skills in compiling a historical narrative but, instead, displayed his ability to draw together geographically contrasting phenomena, images encompassing the vast expanse of Soviet Russia. In so doing he revisited a sub-genre he had developed, of lightning travelogues or 'races' in issues 18 and 19 of *Cine-Pravda*.[14] The result was a remarkable synthesis of disparate images. This character, along with its description in the credits as a 'Film Poem', has meant that *A Sixth Part of the World* is often seen as marking the maturing of Vertov's poetic style.[15] Nevertheless, for all the film's poetic qualities it remains essentially a poetic take on journalism, and retains a strong imprint of the form from which it sprang.

Although some may doubt the value of drawing a parallel between poetry and film, this is a comparison prompted not only by Vertov's own classification of the film, but by critics as influential as Shklovsky.[16] But what does this elusive notion of poetic film mean, and what does it mean when applied to Vertov? It may be contended that *A Sixth Part of the World* resembles poetry in three main ways: subjectivity, reflexivity and structure. The subjective is sometimes seen as the poetic in cinema,[17] and the film's use of the first person form, such as the intertitle 'I see ...' in the first sequence, may be seen as making it subjective, imparting a personal sensibility to the material. But Vertov's use of the first person is not really lyrical or subjective, at least not in this film. In *Forward, Soviet!* and *A Sixth Part of the World,* if Vertov is striving to find a poetic voice, it is not that of the lyric poet offering a personal sensibility; it is poetry as oratory or rhetoric. In no sense was this Vertov's own intimate world: this is the 'I' as an instance of the collective 'we'.

Influential models for such personae in poetry are Vladimir Mayakovsky and Walt Whitman, whose works Vertov also knew well.[18] Whitman speaks with an 'I' that is spokesperson for and incarnation of the nation;[19] thus 'Song of Myself' is a song of America. Similarly, Vertov attempts to evoke the physical space of USSR, the composite nature of its identity. The film is poem as evocation and symbolic creation of nation through filmic enunciation.

This poetic persona of the intertitles of *A Sixth Part of the World* resembles that of Mayakovsky or Whitman, but it is also a further development of film as rhetoric. In fact, like *Forward, Soviet!* the film ends with a speech. It is a quotation from Stalin's Central Committee report at the Fourteenth Congress of the Communist Party in December 1925, in which he expounded the argument for building socialism in one country.[20] In Vertov's hands Stalin's lumbering speech becomes pithy and colourful. In reducing a 21,000-word speech to just 60 words, Vertov also changes the order of elements and employs liberal paraphrase. Nevertheless, the thrust is true to Stalin's message of socialism in one country. If this is poetic film, it is not by analogy with lyrical poetry.

A Sixth Part of the World not only uses the first person form but also addresses a number of groups, including the audience, as 'You': 'You that are sitting in this auditorium.' This too enhances our sense of the film as oratory, as a speech delivered to an immediate audience, again characteristic of Mayakovsky and Whitman.[21] At the same time, it draws attention to the film's palpability as film, and reminds the spectator that he or she is viewing a film. This kind of reflexivity, where art reminds us it is art, is also sometimes seen as being characteristic of poetry, particularly by the Russian Formalists.[22] There can be no question that Vertov in this film seeks to draw our attention on a number of occasions to the fact that we are watching a film. This ongoing theme in Vertov's work culminated in his film about film, *Man with a Movie Camera*, yet such reflexivity had been an element in Vertov's film-making practice for most of the *Cine-Pravda* period (issues 6 and 9 show film projection), and *Cine-Eye* intercuts shots of an eye with images of a mental patient. This reflexive character of Vertov's work serves as a model for what has been called metacinema, a cinema that questions its own processes of representation, as a model in turn for a society that questions and transforms itself.[23] However, this reflexivity is by no means unique to poetry.

Consequently, the claim that the film is poetic is made primarily on account of its structure, the way in which the shots are linked, and the effect this has upon the spectator. Typical of such claims is Shklovsky, who sees the poetic cinema as consisting in the repetition of images, in formal rather than semantic or narrative organisation.[24] In *A Sixth Part of the World* the dominant organisational principle is that of the list or catalogue. Sequences can be broken down into the various elements they seek to contrast. The second part of the film, for example, evokes a sense of the geographical and cultural contrasts of the USSR. It starts by comparing images of shepherds in different places, before listing far distant locations – 'Dagestan villages/ Siberian taiga' – and different peoples: 'Tartars, Buriats', etc. The film then juxtaposes the various ways they eat – 'You with your grapes/ you with your rice' – before almost seamlessly progressing to a comparison of young with old: 'You, who suckle at your mother's breast/ and you, hale 100-year-old.' The second part comes to a crescendo as various economic activities are counter-posed, and this whole catalogue of ethnic diversity is united by the assertion 'You are the owners of the Soviet land/ in your hands lies a sixth part of the world'.

While the list or catalogue is a significant device in documentary cinema, and as we saw Vertov was already employing it to great effect in *Forward, Soviet!*, it is no less significant in the poetry of Whitman. Simple repetitions such as 'I hear...', 'I see...', 'Where...' or 'And' introduce lists of images with no further grammatical structure. In 'Salut au Monde!' we find the same 'ethnological inventories'[25] as in *A Sixth Part of the World*. Indeed, analyses of Whitman's poems often consider their use of catalogue form.[26] So, does the use of the catalogue make Vertov's film poetic, or Whitman's poetry documentary? Lists and poems have much

in common: both weaken horizontal, narrative structures to invite comparison of their items as similar. It is not a great leap from a listing of items in a similar category to the poetic comparison of unexpectedly similar things. A given device cannot be exclusive to the style of documentary or of poetry. The difference lies in the purpose to which the device is put.[27]

Vertov's listing of the various nationalities in the second section of *A Sixth Part of the World* creates a powerful sense of the diversity of the USSR. At the same time these disparate elements are united as owners of their land. Whitman's catalogue of ethnicities in 'Salut au Monde!' similarly ends in an assertion, in this case of the equality and legitimacy of all nations.[28] The naming and description of the various peoples still contribute to the film's argument. The end result is not a dry listing or cataloguing, not simply an inventory of peoples, but, rather, the evocation of a seething panoply of ethnic difference united in common ideological aim. The argument is also strengthened by the sheer scope of the material with which it is illustrated. Catalogue and argument structure the film through dynamic tension, yet from the middle of the catalogue it may seem that we are being asked to see only analogical rather than logical connections, and thus that the film's sole purpose is poetic. The bigger picture, however, is one of logical argument and persuasion.

This single section of the film and its argument occupy a very definite place within a judiciously conceived, overarching expositional frame. A simplistic paraphrase of the underlying structure of *A Sixth Part of the World* clearly illustrates the methodical nature of the argument that it presents.

1) Capitalism is based on inequality and oppression. The rich amuse themselves, while workers and colonised people's labour is exploited, be it mechanised or manual.
2) By contrast, the diverse peoples of the USSR are rulers of their land.
3) They produce a great variety of goods from their land.
4) They export these goods by a range of means.
5) Even this traditional Saami produces furs that are exported to buy machines to build socialism.
6) There are many backward peoples in the USSR, but exports enable them to progress in cultural, economic and political terms. As Stalin argued, this will enable the USSR to produce machines that build machines, freeing the country from economic dependency on the West, and helping to free all the peoples of the world from capitalism.

Put like this, the film's highly structured argument becomes evident, but it seems less interesting. A major reason for this is that the incredible diversity of its catalogues of predominantly ethnographic images are what make *A Sixth Part of the World* visually striking. In making this expeditionary or ethnographic film, Vertov is deliberately engaging with an already marked tradition in documentary film-making. He does so in an incredibly knowing way, to the extent of incorporating footage from Robert Flaherty's pioneering ethnographic documentary *Nanook of the North*. As with Flaherty's film, Vertov photographed the material in expeditions, in his case a series of expeditions conducted by at least eight cameramen all over the Soviet Union. But, whereas the tendency in Flaherty, and more generally, is to seek out and record ethnographic difference for its intrinsic interest, Vertov is using these images to create an image of a nation.

Yet the contrast lies not only in the use made of the images recorded but also in the approach to the organising of expeditions. These are relatively short, targeted trips, where Vertov's primary role consists in dispatching his Cine-Eyes with clear written instructions as to the kinds of material he wanted. Whereas Flaherty, a professional explorer first and foremost, saw *Nanook of the North* as growing from the expeditions, from an immersion in the local culture,[29] Vertov sends his teams on short journeys of a month or so – just long enough to get enough footage to fill out the bigger picture. Concomitantly, he does not intend to achieve true and deep insight into the cultures of the various peoples of the Soviet Union, nor an image of ethnic difference that is arresting or challenging for more than a moment. This marks *A Sixth Part of the World* out from most of the Soviet exploration films that followed it, and especially from the work of the ethnographic film-maker Vladimir Erofeev, for whom ethnography was an end in itself facilitated by film. While it has been argued that Vertov emphasises the difference of these cultures from each other rather than their difference from developed Moscow,[30] they are ultimately made emblematic of a perceived backwardness, which the film suggests developed socialism will erase. Flaherty's Nanook bites the edge of a gramophone disc, but Vertov's Saami [Samoedy] listen to the sound of Lenin's voice on one. This may be seen as an implicit polemic with Flaherty's romantic elegy for traditional Inuit ways. While *A Sixth Part of the World*'s camerawork pays passing tribute to these peoples, they are ultimately to be civilised and Sovietised by the socialist society their pelts help develop.

The importance of fur exports in the film is curious, in that it is hardly a crucial economic imperative of the time. Yet this image serves to evoke the flaccid decadence of the West, symbolised by women wearing and adorning their houses with dead animals. At the same time, the film claims these items of fashion are obtained by trade with the Soviet Union.

As with jazz and the colonies, the bourgeoisie exploit ethnic difference to satisfy their appetite for amusement and luxury. The difference here is that this exploitation is aiding the development of the Soviet Union, a beacon of inspiration to such peoples the world over.

Unsurprisingly the film was little use in promoting trade and economic cooperation.[31] Part of the problem was that it set about trying to persuade a Soviet spectator that foreign trade was a good thing and could serve socialist ends, becoming too political, too closely tied to internal Soviet debates. Vertov had little idea how to appeal to the foreign capitalist and made little serious effort. This was a factor in his losing his job, but the debate provoked in the film press was even more significant as it suggested the inadequacy of existing film genres and categories for a description of the film.

In addition to being structured as an argument, *A Sixth Part of the World* possesses a journalistic topicality and focus on the burning issues of the day. While *Forward, Soviet!*, made as part of an election campaign, is obviously topical, it may not be immediately obvious to modern spectators that *A Sixth Part of the World* was no less topical. Yet the emergent theme of *Pravda* for 1927 is that of industrialisation. This, of course, is the main theme in *A Sixth Part of the World* and a major theme in *Forward, Soviet!*.[32] Even Vertov's most poetical films, *Man with a Movie Camera* and *The Eleventh Year*, treat this subject.

Throughout these films, his greatest and most innovative work, Vertov continues to follow an agenda determined by journalism, even if his approach to the subject may be original. Moreover, while *A Sixth Part of the World* was classified in the credits as a poem, Vertov's first feature-length documentary films, *Cine-Eye* and *Forward, Soviet!* were classified as 'newsreel'. Even his 1928 *The Eleventh Year* was so designated. Indeed, this classification of documentaries as newsreel, and the limited understanding of the emergent form, lay at the heart of 1920s responses to Vertov's films. Vertov was doing things with non-fiction film that no longer fitted the notion of newsreel. Rather than celebrate the new form, his opponents tried to draw attention to the un-'newsreel' aspect of his work as if it was a shortcoming, and refused to accept that it had gone beyond and transformed the genre as conventionally understood. It was judged not for what it attempted to do but for things it never aspired to do in the first place. Vertov put it vividly: 'When a critic denounces a horse for its inability to miaow, he is saying something about himself, and not the horse.'[33]

The Horse that Would Not Miaow

From as early as 1922 Dziga Vertov had been transforming newsreel, making films that so far superseded the category that it became increasingly misleading. When critics and industry figures eventually realised what was happening many of them condemned him for not making conventional newsreel. Part of the problem here was the Russian term for newsreel: 'khronika' applied to all films of record at this time. While it enjoyed widespread currency, its sense was restrictive and implied a jumble of events given sense by chronological sequence alone.[34] The weakness of 'khronika' as a term to describe the burgeoning sphere of documentary film was a major factor leading critics such as Shklovsky (as we have seen) to criticise *Forward, Soviet!* for the absence of dates and figures. Elsewhere, he repeats the view that a newsreel requires a strictly chronological sequence with unobtrusive editing and that Vertov has been taking unacceptable liberties.[35] The assumption that newsreel should strive simply to record implied a style of few set-ups, long takes, little editing and few if any close-ups. None of the means now at the disposal of the cinematographer were to be used either to present material engagingly or make directorial commentary.[36] Shklovsky, the champion of the feuilleton and innovative non-fictional literary forms, grants cinema no such licence. Vertov comments in his diary in response to Shklovsky's attack that every fact recorded by the camera remains a fact even if it is not numbered and indexed.[37] It is precisely this disregard for the protocols of naming and recording that enables Vertov to forge a new, more flexible and expressive non-fiction form, through techniques such as associative editing, flashback and reverse motion.[38] Documentary is founded on such freedom.

Yet Shklovsky was not alone: other critics too criticised *A Sixth Part of the World* as flawed newsreel. In such a view, the film's crime was this very same refusal to confine itself to the 'mundane illustration of life' expected of the genre, and to attempt to evoke the deeper meaning, the greater sense of the epoch.[39]

However, for critics willing to accept the creativity of Vertov's approach, it was his continued use of newsreel footage that was the problem. Such detractors criticised Vertov for the opposite failing: for recording too slavishly, for not imposing meaning on the material, for not being artistic [khudozhestvennyi] enough and not revealing the deeper connection between phenomena. The notion of 'khudozhestvennyi' is a problematic one for Russian documentary in that it means both 'artistic' and 'fictional'. Vertov opposes the latter, the notions of 'fiction', of made-up, imaginary plots and scenarios, but clearly is not opposed to 'artistic', in the sense of works made with artistry, with care and competency.[40] Similarly, the notion of a director, a term borrowed from the theatre, was one Vertov contested. While in his early less experimental works he briefly attempts to appropriate the term, during the crucial *Cine-Pravda* period he eschewed it.[41] Instead, Vertov's 1920s films credit him as 'supervisor' or 'Cine-Eye', although his role appears to be broadly that of a director.[42] In his writings of the 1920s he likewise associates the term 'director' with a theatricality he rejects. An unintended effect, however, of these panegyrics against fictional cinema and directors was to supply ammunition to those fostering the impression that Vertov was unwilling to structure his material.[43] It was in this spirit that a critic called Levidov argued that Vertov's 'caught off-guard' approach to material was something of a dereliction of duty for a director.[44] This was Eisenstein's critique of Vertov too. In Eisenstein's view the role of the director was to use editing to shape '*reality* and real phenomena', whereas Vertov simply recorded passively.[45]

As we shall see in Chapter 5, such condemnation of unstaged documentary as passive and contemplative was to become so intense in the early 1930s as to all but destroy the form and effectively erase the distinction between documentary and fiction film. It would, however, be some time before staging became ensconced as the norm for documentary film-making. In the meantime, from the early 1920s onwards, Vertov was willing to mount a vigorous defence of documentary film as record. For Vertov the need to register went hand in hand with the need to construct an argument, and he had to defend his view of this combination against both sides: those who felt his films should simply record and name on one side (Shklovsky), and those who felt he should neglect no means available in the promotion of a tendentious argument on the other (Eisenstein). In each case, Vertov's opponents assumed documentary, or newsreel, completely devoid of creativity.

'The Future is in the Hands of ...'

On the other hand, an enlightened minority realised that exceeding the confines of newsreel by not simply naming and showing is not necessarily a bad thing. A number of contemporary critics grasped the novelty of *Forward, Soviet!* and *A Sixth Part of the World* and attempted to understand, or even welcomed, this departure from generic convention. Indeed, many of the critics appeared relieved they had not had to suffer a tedious newsreel of the kind they had expected to see. V. Fefer also stresses this sense that *Forward, Soviet!* is infinitely more engaging than newsreel as audiences had known it hitherto:

> The Cine-Eyes refuted the usual approach to these kind of 'stock-taking' films of dry illustration with accounts in figures and diagrams. Over the seven reels of the film there is not a single figure, not a single dry-voiced intertitle, and that is precisely why the visual facts presented in condensed form on the screen persuade by their concreteness.[46]

As secretary of the editorial board of *Sovetskii ekran*, Izmail Urazov put it: 'Dry commissioned newsreel has grown into a heroic chronicle of the revolution.'[47] Yet is it really still newsreel, still chronicle? Rather than simply assert that this is newsreel of a new type, a number of the enthusiasts for these films grope towards new definitions. Vladimir Blium's celebration of *A Sixth Part of the World* was typical: 'Dziga Vertov has...given an undoubted model for the "non-fiction" artistic film (not "newsreel").'[48] G. Osipov similarly recognised the novelty of *Forward, Soviet!* and tried to define it as something between narrative and lecture:

> Here newsreel stops being newsreel – a plotless succession of pictures, like in a Sovkino-Journal – and turns into a narrative, into a film lecture, where every sequence proves something; it turns into a harmonious whole, with a beginning, an intensification of the action, and a denouement.
>
> The future is in the hands of *this kind of newsreel*.[49]

Fefer argues likewise that the film combines the virtues of fiction's capacity to hold an audience with newsreel's scope, whereas a conventional newsreel approach would have lasted five times as long and if the film had concentrated on particular individuals in the manner of fictional films, it would have lost breadth.[50] Like Fefer, fellow *LEF* film-maker Vitali Zhemchuzhny recognises *A Sixth Part of the World* cannot be called newsreel and suggests a journalistic analogy: 'This is not information but an editorial.'[51]

Despite the acclaim for these films and recognition of their merit, the Moscow Soviet's rejection of *Forward, Soviet!* meant it was not distributed or promoted properly and never given a chance to attract a mass audience.[52] By contrast, *A Sixth Part of the World* was shown quite widely, at least in Moscow, and did fairly well.[53] As Victor Pertsov commented at the *New LEF* round-table debates, Esfir Shub's *Fall of the Romanov Dynasty* [Padenie dinastii Romanovykh, 1927] was the first feature-length Soviet documentary to be publicised adequately. Certainly, it was the first to enjoy popular success.[54] However, it can be argued that Shub's film was aided by an atmosphere of curiosity and openness towards the possibilities of the new forms of newsreel, or documentary, created by

Vertov and *A Sixth Part of the World* in particular.[55] Indeed, *A Sixth Part of the World* was the first feature-length documentary to be shown at Moscow's premiere cinema, the Malaia Dmitrovka.[56] The success of Shub and subsequent documentary film-makers in the Soviet Union was in large part a measure of Vertov's success in creating documentary where previously there had been only newsreel. This was a product of his written and spoken advocacy, but it was above all due to his achievements in film.

A major factor in *A Sixth Part of the World*'s broader appeal was its use of the expeditionary form. These expeditions across the USSR had meant that Vertov's team shot a great deal of new material for this film, and as a consequence used relatively little archive footage. This in itself was a problem, because in 1926, the Soviet year of 'economy measures', Vertov shot a film which because it used non-actors demanded the team shoot a great deal of material that was not used. This is generally the case with documentaries, but even more so when employing Vertov's hidden camera and caught off-guard techniques.[57] This got him into trouble with the film authorities, who remained unsympathetic to this aspect of documentary film, as Shub was to complain.[58] From their point of view this was an argument in favour of staging, and the scenario, since they produced little wasted footage. Vertov's uneconomic approach was probably a reason for his sacking from Sovkino at the end of 1926. The formal pretext was his refusal to produce a preliminary written scenario for his next intended project, *Man with a Movie Camera*.

He had transformed newsreel, freeing it from the need slavishly to record and document. *Man with a Movie Camera* would release documentary from naming altogether, entirely dispensing with the intertitle and creating an unbroken visual idiom. However, Vertov first had to find a new film studio willing to employ him. An offer of work from Kiev's VUFKU studios provided the perfect opportunity.

4

New Paths: *The Eleventh Year, Man with a Movie Camera*

With Vertov's departure for Ukraine in May 1927 the Cine-Eye movement fragmented, the wider circle remaining in Moscow. Nevertheless, former Cine-Eyes continued to transform the persuasive power and visual appeal of Soviet newsreel and documentary film.[1] Ilya Kopalin was probably the most prominent, forging a highly successful career culminating in *Moscow Strikes Back* [Razgrom nemetskikh voisk pod Moskvoi, 1942], an Oscar-winning film of the Battle of Moscow.[2] Indeed, Vertov's films and polemics had imparted incredible impetus to Soviet film even beyond newsreel, to opponents as much as to allies: in their location shooting, rhetorically conceived construction and casting of social type, Eisenstein's acted films appropriated key features of the Cine-Eye documentary style. Vertov had unleashed a whole wave of documentary forms: his achievements in the compilation film were inspiring Esfir Shub, just as his commitment to recording was inspiring the former editor of *Kino-Gazeta*, Erofeev, to make a new kind of ethnographic film. When Mayakovsky's journal *LEF* was relaunched in 1927 as *New LEF*, it turned to documentary as a key strategy for the transformation of art and society. Yet this was a revolution occurring without its instigator, and over whose course Vertov had lost control. Instead, from his new post in Kiev, accompanied by Svilova and later joined by his brother Mikhail Kaufman, he was preparing a new coup: the ultimate purification of filmic expression, the swansong of silent cinema.

The Eleventh Year: The Minimal Number of Intertitles

Of all the comments made about his films, one in particular rankled: *A Sixth Part of the World* was condemned for subordinating the images to its intertitles.[3] For radical Russian film-makers it was an article of faith that film's development as a distinct medium required it to cast off the encumbrances of literature and drama. Vertov himself frequently denounced fictional films for the very same excessive influence of literature. Whether or not their purpose was to respond to such suggestions, Vertov's next two films nevertheless constituted a more than effective riposte: *The Eleventh Year* uses minimal intertitles, and *Man with a Movie Camera* uses none at all.[4] Vertov was now going one better, having himself introduced a range of widely adopted innovations in intertitles. With these films Vertov pushes his experiments with film as a discrete visual medium to the utmost. They appear as a kind of visual coda to silent film: conscious of its impending demise in the wake of the 1927 'invention' of sound, Vertov seems to demonstrate silent cinema's incredible versatility in the articulation of ideas.[5]

This new course towards films of even greater formal experiment seems incredibly bold, given that Vertov's previous two films were already innovative. Yet, by the late 1920s, avant-garde artists increasingly had a sense that their time had gone, that the revolution no longer had any place for them. As one of Vertov's associates, Alexei Gan, put it in 1925: 'The time of slogans for the present has passed.' The choices were either to return to hack work in the old, pre-Revolutionary way, or to abandon all practical work and produce theoretical work exclusively.[6] While Vertov would ultimately be forced to return to the plodding kind of newsreel he had once transformed, for the moment he took the second path, choosing something akin to theoretical work, only in film. Unable to reach wide audiences in the present, he produced arcane works aimed at future artists. This is certainly one way of understanding *The Eleventh Year*, and especially *Man with a Movie Camera*.

Such films are clearly envisaged by Vertov in an October 1926 article in which he describes five different types of film work he anticipates for the Cine-Eyes in the coming period. These include current newsreel weeklies, thematic newsreels covering several months, complex newsreels summarising a year, scientific or educational films and finally '[e]xperimental film studies, laboratory research, laying down new paths for all the Cine-Eye movement as a whole'.[7] While *Man with a Movie Camera* fits the category of experimental film work, an aid primarily to film-making, *The Eleventh Year* may be seen as something between newsreel and experiment.

Contemporaries were struck by the unusual style of the film. As Zhemchuzhny commented, *The Eleventh Year* was more of a laboratory experiment than something for broad usage.[8] This was especially evident in its intertitles, which Vertov claimed set a record low number for all Soviet films.[9] Similarly, Vertov stresses the film's visual style, anticipating his statements about *Man with a Movie Camera*: 'The 100 percent language of cinema... designed to be perceived visually, to be thought about visually.'[10] Certainly, for large parts of *The Eleventh Year* themes of construction are rendered by dynamic lines of workers marching, together with trucks and tractors moving in the same direction, and then by myriad shots of exploding and hammering rock all punctuated by barely a single intertitle. The intertitles are reduced to a minimum so that the pictures speak for themselves.

Nevertheless, there are sequences in which the film also uses intertitles with greater frequency. The film begins travelogue-style, identifying geographical features, and towards the end of the film the repetition of 'We are constructing' and the triad of 'On the earth, under the earth and above the earth', intercut with images of trains, mining and aeroplanes, is very much in the style of *A Sixth Part of the World*. Moreover, *The Eleventh Year* is classified by its own titles as newsreel, and correspondingly the film begins by setting out a clearly defined space in the construction of the Dniepr hydroelectric dam. In fact, it almost seems ploddingly well situated in time and space when compared with Vertov's previous films. This initial geographical integrity is clear from the fact that, while planning the film, Vertov drew a map showing the location of the various elements in the film in relation to each other, showing the Nenasytets or 'insatiable' rapids upstream from the dam.[11] This is almost certainly the only Vertov film for which it is possible to draw such a map relating the main elements in it. Nevertheless, the film then moves on from the single place and theme to take in greater thematic and geographical sweep, incorporating material from Kharkov, Sipov and the Volkhov hydroelectric dam.[12] Vertov recognised the tension between the manner in which it sets out a clear sense of space before progressing to a more metaphorical, fluid style:

> The first part is obviously at a level at which it is easier for the viewer to take it in; the fourth and fifth parts are constructed in a more complex way. They contain far more montage inventiveness than the first two parts; they are looking more to the future of cinema than the second and third parts. I have to say that the fourth and fifth reels have the same relation to the first reel as a higher education does to a secondary school. It is natural that more complex montage forces the viewer to experience more tension and demands greater attention in order to be taken in.[13]

Aware that his films would not necessarily find willing spectators in the present, Vertov is in part appealing to future generations of film-makers. This hedging of bets was wise given the at best mixed reception of his other full-length films. Yet, even with regard to posterity, *The Eleventh Year* has not fared terribly well and is seldom seen as many times as it requires, by contrast with *Man with a Movie Camera*. On detailed scrutiny, however, *The Eleventh Year* emerges as one of Vertov's most accomplished works.

Despite its orientation towards the future spectator, this is a film set in the present time to a greater extent than any Vertov had made since *Cine-Pravda*. Throughout the time-frame is clearly of the present day: we see none of the ability to use archive footage to construct a narrative. It appears that he no longer has at his disposal a whole library of film footage dating back to the revolution.[14] In the new context of Ukraine, Vertov has little choice but to shoot new footage, and from this material forge his narrative. Consequently, rather than use the before-and-after flashback structure of *Forward, Soviet!*, where images of ruin are contrasted with those of construction, Vertov extends the approach adopted in *A Sixth Part of the World*, where images of traditional and modern life are juxtaposed to articulate the same narrative of socialist transformation. In *The Eleventh Year* Vertov tells the same story by drawing on images taken exclusively from the construction of the Dniepr hydroelectric dam. The dam is contrasted with the image of the archaeological remains of an ancient Scythian uncovered during the excavations. Here we have spatial continuity but with sharply discontinuous temporal associations.[15] The First Five Year Plan is a turning point in history, an epochal moment setting history free from the bonds of the past.

In order to articulate this narrative Vertov draws deeper than ever on the resources of metaphoric association, structuring the opening of the

film upon the contrasts of sky and land, water and rock. After the opening aerial view, the film then shows a whole number of rock structures with names associated with the past: 'Catherine's Chair' 'Warrior [bogatyr']
Cliff', 'Love Cliff'. These are followed by a shot of the Scythian photographed against the earth, and contrasted with shots of water. Shots of rock and of the earth are associated with the passive, dead-weight burden of a history that is to be overcome through the intensity of labour building the dam. To this end workers are framed against the sky, in low-angle shots that make them appear as silhouettes, hammering and breaking down the resistant earth. Superimpositions show apparently giant workers hammering flat huge rocky outcroppings. The incredible energy of the Bolsheviks transforms the physical properties of earth, so that by the end of the film it is not static but seething with activity above and below ground. The land is blown sky-high and flooded (in superimposition), it is transformed by labour and by water, so that the separation between earth and water no longer holds. After the key event of the dam's construction the film's earth too becomes socialist, and, from barren rock, becomes rich soil churning under the mechanically drawn plough. As such it is now to be defended by the stern ranks of the Red Army, marching confidently towards the camera.

The dynamic flow of water is made emblematic of the Bolsheviks' own unceasing application, and symbolic of the magical, transformative power of electricity itself, of Lenin its patron and of revolution. This points to the importance of water imagery in Vertov's work as a whole. As early as *Cine-Eye* he had shown Pioneers marching over a dam, allowing the camera to linger on the water rushing under it, and likewise showing them washing. Similarly, in *Man with a Movie Camera* washing serves as a crucial metaphor for renewal and transformation.[16] The building of a hydroelectric dam represents an economic trans-formation enabling electricity, the energy of Lenin, to revolutionise the Soviet Union, but it is also a symbol of a deeper, elemental renewal.

With no archive, the photography has to create fresh footage capable of supporting this incredible metaphoric weight. Mikhail Kaufman endows the images with the symbolism of nature he was to perfect in his own film *In Spring* [Vesnoi, 1929]. As a result, *The Eleventh Year* marks a higher stage in the creative partnership between the two brothers: Kaufman's own sensibility is more evident than ever before, which leads to heightened tension. Clearly, this is what leads Osip Brik to criticise *The Eleventh Year* for its lack of journalistic edge: the shots may appear to be determined purely by their visual interest, with no attempt to report.[17] They may even seem static.[18] Unquestionably, much of the film's allure lies in its photography: its beautiful shots of water, of scenery and of sky.

However, the visual style of *The Eleventh Year* is not defined by breathtaking photography alone. The editing plays an equal role in creating the layers of metaphors dynamising apparently simple themes. Superimpositions within shots are more significant than in previous films, and create richly palimpsestic imbrications of images in the superimposition of rippling water upon shots of traditional village life, in the double exposure of the dam itself combined with a detail of its construction, or the multiple exposure of six images of pumping pistons. This dynamic aspect of the film, its thematisation of movement and energy as such, was heralded by no less a figure than the artist Kazimir Malevich.[19]

Yet, for all their visual appeal, these images are are all part of a system of associations which is highly political and ultimately topical. It is not true that the photography impresses solely as aesthetic spectacle devoid of any striving towards reportage or journalism. While this criticism clearly picked up on the more subtle poetic mood of much of the film, the claim that it lacked any journalistic characteristics is belied by the theme. Industrialisation, the building of dams, hostility to the past are all themes with a highly topical resonance. Even the incredible superimpositions and process shots do not serve aesthetic ends alone but enhance the sense of movement, of feverish but purposive activity, towards a socialist future. They convey the sense of electricity as the magic ingredient transforming all spheres of society, changing history, as a growing and unstoppable force ultimately underpinned by military might. *The Eleventh Year*'s evocative dynamism and energy are a reflection on the major issue of the day: industrialisation. As we have seen, this was already emerging as the leading theme in the press of the time in 1926. The rapid industrialisation of the First Five-Year Plan, accompanied by the collectivisation of agriculture, dominated news in the Soviet Union. Vertov's first Ukrainian film was his response to this agenda.

Reception of *The Eleventh Year*

The Eleventh Year was released in Kiev in April 1928 and the following month in Moscow. It apparently did well for a documentary, particularly in Kiev, and was even shown in smaller cities such as Rostov-on-Don.[20] Broadly, though, the critical reception displayed the usual prejudice against 'newsreel'. As one critic intoned: 'An artistic synthetic image is beyond the capabilities of a non-fiction newsreel film.'[21] Such voices again outweighed those ready to recognise Vertov's success in reinventing the form. Zhemchuzhny was again insightful, hailing the film as a further departure from previous conceptions of newsreel:

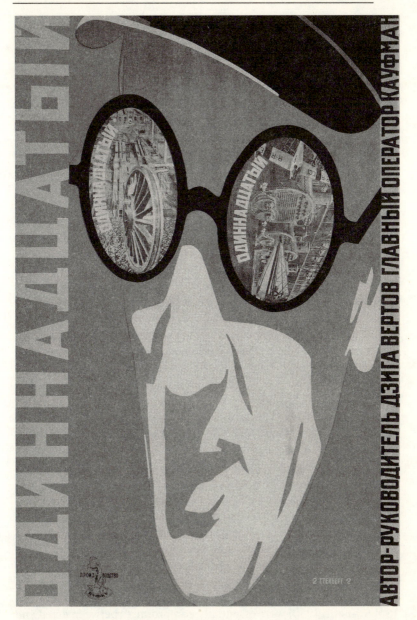

We are shown on screen not a specific factory or machine, but some
generalized abstracted factory – 'a factory in general'. This
generalized material is not arranged through…spatial or temporal
sequence, but is gathered into thematic parts: electrification, 'people
of coal', 'the Red Army', and so on.[22]

While it was encouraging that such critical responses recognised the need to take films of fact beyond the confines of newsreel, there was still no consensus as to what such films might be called. One candidate was the German term 'Kulturfilm'. Initially associated with the popular genre of the expeditionary film,[23] it soon became synonymous with the notion of popular, accessible films with an educational purpose and correct political content.[24] Was *Kulturfilm* the answer to the long-held aspiration of making popular political films? It was this promise that enthused the March 1928 Party Conference on Cinema Affairs, which met in Moscow, while Vertov was editing *The Eleventh Year* in Ukraine. The conference is seen as moving away from debates about newsreel or documentary film.[25] Embracing the notion of *Kulturfilm* was a way of doing so.

Yet the conference was also a clear sign that the government was taking cinema more seriously than ever before.[26] This meant money would be invested in the production of film, especially *Kulturfilm*, on an unprecedented scale, and there would be taxation and distribution concessions too.[27] However, the term's emphasis on political purpose meant that it made no distinction between approaches to production, including both acted and unacted films.[28] Consequently, documentary film-makers themselves resisted it tooth and nail, hostile to its potential undermining of documentary as a distinct form. In 1929 Shub condemned 'the so-called "kulturfilm"' as the invention of those 'unable or unwilling to define the new form of cinema...the unplayed film'.[29]

Needless to say, Vertov was equally vocal in his opposition. As early as 1926 he derided *Kulturfilm* as representing a dangerous blurring of distinctions between documentary and fiction, undermining 'unplayed' films by subtly eliding them with acted films under this general category. As such, it was to theory what Eisenstein's brand of film-making was to practice.[30] The real distinction had to be drawn, he insisted, between films that recorded life and those that recorded acting.

As a description of their practice, *Kulturfilm* was successfully resisted by documentary film-makers, and failed to survive far beyond 1929.[31] Nevertheless, this did not mean the defeat of its proposed elision of acted and non-acted films in practice. Acclaimed by contemporary reviews, Viktor Turin's *Turksib* [1929] and Mikhail Kalatozov's *Salt for Svanetia* [Sol Svanetii, 1930] were essentially compromises between acted and strict documentary.[32]

Despite his opposition to *Kulturfilm* in both theory and practice, Vertov described *Man with a Movie Camera* to the censors as a 'so-called "kulturfilm" on the subject of film-making',[33] albeit consisting purely of newsreel (i.e. non-staged) footage.[34] This was a tactical manoeuvre indicative of Vertov's willingness to bend current terminology to his own ends to ensure further funding for his films. Yet this kind of critical sleight of hand could not last. In return for making greater resources available, the Party now demanded a more uniform and accessible film style, embodied in the conference's key slogan: 'Intelligible to the millions'.[35] Critics were quick to seize on this, interpreting it to mean clearly recognisable central figures in documentary as well as fiction film. Consequently, *The Eleventh Year* was seen as sidelining the human being by featuring no particular worker, miner, peasant or sailor.[36]

Man with a Movie Camera is in part a tongue-in-cheek response to such calls to foreground the human being. Here we have not actors but genuine film-makers photographed doing their job: filming. Vertov's conception of documentary, in which acting is obviated, is foregrounded as never before in a parody of the acted instructional *Kulturfilm*.

In its very form *Man with a Movie Camera* is a defence of documentary. For Vertov, however, the defence of documentary was inextricable from the defence of the integrity of cinema itself, since documentary was its purest, least theatrical form.[37] Prompted by Brik's accusation that the film's intertitles functioned as a poor substitute for a script,[38] Vertov defended the visual purity of *The Eleventh Year*.

> The film was constructed visually; it was 'written' directly in sequences and shots, and only when the edited film was completed were a few cheerful slogan-intertitles inserted.[39]

If any doubt as to his commitment to the pure language of cinema remained, Vertov made sure Brik could not possibly repeat this comment of the even more machine-oriented, even more unstaged and unscripted *Man with a Movie Camera*. If *The Eleventh Year* combined laboratory experiment with commission, then in *Man with a Movie Camera* the experiment dominated. This was a film truly made for and appreciated by posterity, to show the future possibilities of film. Aware that time was running out for experimentation, indeed for documentary, Vertov made a film that flew directly in the face of the emerging orthodoxy in Soviet film.

Man with a Movie Camera: An Isolated Masterpiece?

Since at least the 1960s *Man with a Movie Camera* has been widely regarded as Vertov's masterpiece (see Chapter 8). In contrast to the rest of his work, it is readily available, and has already generated two books in English and a host of articles. Even the philosopher Gilles Deleuze makes the film emblematic of an influential treatise.[40] It has been approached from a myriad of angles, as epistemological experiment,[41] political tract,[42] database[43] and cyborg film,[44] as both contesting[45] and as confirming[46] the objectification of woman, as Cubo-futurist,[47] Formalist,[48] Constructivist[49] and Productivist.[50] Despite the breadth and wealth of these interpretations, they share a common tendency to stress the film's exceptionality. The film's acclaim has misled us into seeing it in isolation, and therefore treating it as unprecedented either in film history or in Vertov's own filmography.[51] Sometimes, despite their best efforts, books devoted to single films tend to emphasise the film's structure as a self-contained unity, and give less prominence to its place in a larger *oeuvre*. While recognising that *Man with a Movie Camera* stands out as the salient moment in Vertov's career, deserving of the attention it receives, it also draws together a number of tendencies in Vertov's films and thinking, contributes to ongoing themes and concerns in his work and initiates approaches more marked in his subsequent films. Seeing the relations between *Man with a Movie Camera* and Vertov's other films uncovers facets of it that would otherwise be ignored or remain obscure.[52] The film emerges less a manifesto than a reformulation of the documentary principles and method Vertov had been employing throughout the 1920s. An embattled 'statement of commitment to the documentary approach',[53] it was a defence of documentary in the increasingly hostile circumstances of attempts to dissolve documentary, a desperate counter-attack against the core shift in Soviet non-fiction film towards scripting and staging. This context grants us further insight into the film, but should not detract from its power and relevance, still growing three-quarters of a century since its release.

Ongoing Themes in *Man with a Movie Camera*

While *Man with a Movie Camera* represents the culmination of a whole process in Vertov's early career, it also prefigures the greater prominence of women in Vertov's subsequent work. The film displays a profound fascination with 'women at machines, women in machines, and woman as machine'.[54] Where there are men we see fewer portraits. Recent criticism has accented the way in which the motif of the female body brings together the film's central themes of modernity, the machine and experimentation.[55] Indeed, the translated title's use of 'man' as a generic term is misleading, and the less attractive *Person with a Movie Camera* is actually more accurate.[56] Despite the fact that the cameraman is clearly male, the film is about every stage of film-making, not just shooting, and the no less crucial cinematic process of editing is practised by a woman, suggesting an equalising feminine gaze of the editor in contrast to the cameraman's male gaze. Indeed, it is Svilova's pale blue iris that dominates the film's finale.[57] The eye associated with the shutters is female, the train wakes up this same woman, and the central image of liberated vision is the ironic subversion of the film poster for *The Awakening of a Woman*, counterposing its salacious promise of sexual awakening with a deeper filmic coming to consciousness.[58] This is a deliberately staged episode, intended to parody the very conventions of fiction cinema contested by the film; as Tsivian calls it, a 'mousetrap' at odds with Vertov's film-making practice as a whole.[59] This scene is intended to show sleep, followed by waking up into true vision. Thus woman is associated with cinema itself, and is rescued from the slumber of the unreal to be resituated in the productive realm of editing, sewing and weaving. This image of the redemption of woman as redemption of vision is a key element in two of Vertov's later films, *Three Songs of Lenin* and *Lullaby*, where it is articulated through the image of a Moslem woman's unveiling. Moreover, *Man with a Movie Camera*, Vertov's most radical film, in fact anticipates these less acclaimed and less ambitious works in the way in which this pivotal moment is the most highly scripted and staged point in the film.

Largely, however, the film expands and builds upon techniques and themes recognisable from Vertov's earlier documentaries. In particular, the motifs of cleansing, of sleep and awakening, as well as the images of children, magic and water, are all familiar from *Cine-Eye*. Similarly, in its splicing together of a range of shots, of 'a' market, of 'a' bar and of 'a' group of drunken peasant women, the earlier film also created the kinds of composite image typically associated with *Man with a Movie Camera*.[60] This is a coincidence in more than theme alone. As a number of commentators have mentioned, Vertov is building upon the experience of *Cine-Eye*.[61]

As we saw in Chapter 2, *Cine-Eye* was partly an instructional film, illustrating key methods for Vertov's Cine-Eye movement. Similarly, *Man with a Movie Camera* shows us how to make film, as well as how to think about it. Vertov is attempting to leave some kind of manual, if not now for an already existing movement but then possibly for a movement yet to come, a blueprint for a future 'cinematic democracy'.[62] The film's openness towards film-making and its future is a large part of its enduring appeal.

In another sense, too, *Man with a Movie Camera* develops and expands the project initiated in *Cine-Eye* exploring film's capacity as an instrument of cognition, a means of understanding the world. Yuri Tsivian comments on the sequence where we see a chimney, followed by shots of coal mining, that this is a lesson in Marxist economics, showing us the origin of energy in the miner's labour. The sequence also shows us the various machines set in motion by this power, as in *The Eleventh Year*. Yet *Cine-Eye* pioneered this approach too, revealing the various forms of labour that magically produce the conjuror's apparently prosaic bread. However, *Man with a Movie Camera*'s greatest achievement was to pursue this process to its logical conclusion, unveiling not just the mysteries of bread-making or electricity, but revealing the process of revelation itself, the secrets of film-making. An investigation of the way we make sense of the visible world, this is a film about film, and an apologia for documentary.

Man with a Movie Camera as Documentary Credo

In references to *Man with a Movie Camera*, Vertov evokes a number of generic models, including 'an experiment', 'a feuilleton', an 'excerpt from the diary of a cameraman', a 'production film' and a 'symphony'.[63] Ultimately, though, these are all vehicles for the same central concept of a film about film-making:

> We felt that we had an obligation not just to make films for wide consumption but, from time to time, films that beget films as well. Films of this sort do not pass without leaving a trace, for one's self, or for others. They are essential as a pledge of future victories.[64]

However, while Vertov argues that *Man with a Movie Camera* was a film for film-makers, enabling further films to be made, he remains hostile to sharp distinctions between spectator and film-maker. These aspirations are embodied in the image of the *Filmmaker* [Filmar'] wall newspaper as a model for a deprofessionalised and accessible approach to film-making in which all can contribute. Throughout its length the film stimulates all to reflect upon the path and purpose of cinema, demanding a new, invigorated, active spectatorship.[65] The result is a film that is doubly about cinema: it scrutinises cinema's role and place in society, as an example of industrial process, and at the same time it stimulates thinking about the devices of cinema, and attempts, through what Vertov called the 'decoding of mystification',[66] 'to familiarise a wider audience with the mysterious world of cinema that was hitherto unknown to it, and at the same time to display the devices of cinematic production'.[67]

This is done by showing spectators how the film is made. Numerous sequences show the cameraman cranking, the camera focusing, the editing process, the cameraman getting into and out of position to take high- and low-angle shots. At one point we see him being told to get out of the way. Certain critics were highly sympathetic to this approach, arguing that a major difference between fiction film and documentary was that knowing how a film was made disenchants the audience of a fiction film but increases the interest of a documentary.[68] Revealing the nature of cinema is, for Vertov, inseparable from denouncing fiction film and proving the power of his documentary method.

For this reason *Man with a Movie Camera* goes out of its way to insist upon the filmic nature of film, right down to showing people's reactions to being filmed and reminding us of its projection. In drawing attention to itself as a film, *Man with a Movie Camera* is not only fighting the illusion of realism, which for documentaries usually meant greater staging, but also stressing that it is made with techniques specific to film: 'A film about cinema must be expressed in the authentic language of cinema.'[69]

The sense that a film about cinema must eschew intertitles is very much bound up with a strong imperative in early film theory to define what was and was not specific to film as an art. In a number of Soviet theories, such as that of Kuleshov, this notion was editing. Vertov was no less keen to establish film as a distinct medium, rejecting acting, staging, script and plot since for him these were all alien to pure film, most perfectly expressed in documentary. This pure, wordless, cinematic nature ensured cinema's international reach as 'a film on film-language, the first film without words, which does not require translation into another language, an international film'.[70]

With Vertov's *Man with a Movie Camera* silent cinema's aspiration to a visual language unhampered by national borders comes closest to fulfilment. It has, equally, overcome the barriers of time, since, while hard to decipher, it requires little knowledge of historical context, of the importance of the events or figures depicted.

Vertov's brother and cameraman, Mikhail Kaufman, was beginning to develop a distinct perspective on documentary of his own and was no less committed to the ideal of the film with no intertitles, but for different reasons. Regarding *Man with a Movie Camera* as a failure, it seems his objection to the film was that the intention had been to show a cameraman making sense from the chaos of life, but the end result was still chaos rather than any clearly expressed ideas.[71] It was too obscure, too experimental, whereas Kaufman was keen to make films that were easy to understand. He was less concerned with the rhetorical, persuasive or analytical side of the cinematic art that can be seen in Vertov's films. The disagreement over the film brought to a head simmering tensions over creative control, already evident in Vertov's demand that Kaufman repudiate Brik's independent praise for the photography in *The Eleventh Year*.[72] This time, rather than loyally backing Vertov's authority, Kaufman asserted his own, and parted company with Vertov acrimoniously and definitively. Starting with *In Spring*, he began to direct his own films in a distinct but more accessible style: 'Speaking in pure film language, without recourse to the help of literary explanations (intertitles), [*In Spring*] turned out to be comprehensible to a broad audience.'[73]

Upholding its pure filmic nature, *Man with a Movie Camera* must also eschew the use of actors, from Vertov's point of view a theatrical intrusion. However, Vertov is accused of employing a great deal of staging, or even actors, in this film.[74] Clearly, Kaufman as cameraman, Svilova as editor, the projectionist, the orchestra and the woman sleeping at the beginning are all posed for the camera. In fact, as we saw, the woman waking up stands as a sequence apart in the film, whereby she performs everyday actions such as sleeping, getting dressed and washing, but very much for the sake of the camera. While this is, admittedly, a level of performance greater than he had employed previously, it is a performance intended to end performance comparable with a film released the previous year, *Glass Eye* [Stekliannyi glaz, Lili Brik and Vitali Zhemchuzhny, 1928], which demonstrates the inferiority of acted films to documentary through an extended comic parody with real actors. Vertov does not venture anywhere near that far from the parameters of documentary, if at all, since reconstructing habitual action is so much part of the documentary tradition: in *Man with a Movie Camera* the woman's performance is of her habitual actions. The other episodes are even more legitimate examples of reconstruction, since Kaufman is photographed doing what he usually does: being a cameraman. Likewise, Svilova is editing, the projectionist is projecting and the orchestra is playing. The element of performance is minimal. In contrast to the mannequins, these are real people, and, like the workers, they are doing their normal jobs.

However, some of the film's most striking footage comes in the examples of caught off-guard photography, the pinnacle of this technique. Shub lavishes praise on Kaufman's photography in the film:

[H]is ability to capture characteristic moments of someone's behaviour whether it is by hidden camera or by an unexpected assault on a human subject enabled Kaufman to capture such convincing sequences as the girl with the bow in her hair next to the magician, the people in the bar, the homeless boy waking up, the young woman getting up from the bench on the boulevard, the crying woman at the graveyard, the birth.[75]

Similarly, the film contains a lot of perfectly actorless, 'caught off-guard' machines. Clearly visible as a category in the archive of Svilova's editing suite, the theme is central. Partly this was because machines do not act and do not react to the presence of a camera. Consequently, Vertov and Kaufman refined the photography of machines to a peak in *Man with a Movie Camera* with the striking shots of spinning bobbins, whirring pistons, wheels, cogs and cams. It has become customary, however, to treat this prominence of machines solely in the context of the avant-garde, and of modernism:

Vertov's film was, like the speeding cars, the intersecting trolleys and spinning gears depicted in it, a high-speed machine meant to shock the viewer into empathy with the industrial age. It was a high point in early modernism's desire to wed art and the machine.[76]

While recently the film has been celebrated for its supposed merging of humanity with machine, as a cyborg film,[77] in the 1930s the perception that Vertov was unable to create characters was a factor in his marginalisation.[78]

As well as rejecting acting, the film famously eschewed the fixed, written scenario prior to shooting. For Vertov, this was so important that he refused to give his Sovkino bosses a written scenario before filming even though it was made clear that failure to do so would result in his dismissal.[79] Opposition to the preliminary written scenario is part of an ongoing commitment to a sense of film as process and as record. In this respect too, *Man with a Movie Camera* is a defence of Vertov's conception of documentary. As some contemporary critics suggested, it is refusing the script which opens up an extremely rich vein of material.[80]

Vertov's view of documentary likewise emphasised shooting in public spaces, remaining hostile to the private sphere. However, the opening scenes of the film, unusually for Vertov's work, treat the theme of private space and take place in the room of an unidentified woman, granting us an apparently intimate look into someone's private life. Once more, this was not for its own sake but, rather, an attempt to upstage the private and domestic with the drama and dynamism of the public and social. The interior scenes of the woman sleeping give way to the outdoor scenes of increasing activity. This opposition, implicit throughout Vertov's films, is explicitly thematised in the allegory of awakening.

Although this sequence has been seen as 'an exercise in voyeurism',[81] rather it is intended as a denunciation of cinema voyeurism as well as an assertion of the right of the camera to see anything and be anywhere.[82] *Man with a Movie Camera* can justifiably be called 'a film about total surveillance'.[83] If there is no such thing as the private sphere the only permission the documentary film-maker need ever seek is that of the state. Like the secret police, the Cine-Eye has the right to be everywhere.

Following lively debates at screenings in the Ukrainian cities of Kiev and Kharkov,[84] and a press campaign, *Man with a Movie Camera* ran for a week at prominent cinemas in Moscow. Despite well-attended screenings, it was replaced with a Harold Lloyd film. The authorities were no less hostile to Vertov than when he left for Ukraine. Behind this opposition lay a strengthening conviction that Vertov represented a dangerous and unacceptable challenge to the Party's imperatives for cinema.

While there were some sympathetic reviews, the film's formal complexity meant it was open to accusations of aestheticism and formalism.[85] In the Soviet Union it would long be criticised as the way not to make a film, because it is so reflexive, because the continuity of time and space are so fractured in it and because it privileges recording over dramatic structure.[86] However, it was to outlast just about every Soviet film of its era, as it eventually found its true addressee: the spectator of the future.

5

Sound and the Defence of Documentary:
Enthusiasm

The Coming of Sound in Soviet Documentary

Jazz Singer [USA, 1927] decisively announced the shift to recorded sound films. American studios and cinemas were virtually all refitted by 1929.[1] Soon American audiences found silent film worthy only of derision.[2] In the Soviet Union the first completed sound films were made in 1930. Only in the 1940s did they stop making silent versions of newsreels.[3] This delay meant that sound's arrival was all the more anxiously awaited, and its potential uses debated. In their as yet still silent films, Soviet montage directors became increasingly skilled in rhythmic editing and the use of visual images to evoke aural associations. The rhythmic editing of the Odessa steps sequence in Eisenstein's *The Battleship 'Potemkin'* is legendary.

Vertov was no exception, using aural images in the 'gathering of buses' in *Forward, Soviet!*.[4] He claimed of *A Sixth Part of the World* that he had created not intertitles but a 'contrapuntal construction of a word-radio-theme'.[5] The intertitles, rather than naming and identifying the images, are part of a constant stream of imagery built from word and picture alike. The film dispenses with the old hierarchy whereby intertitles created a meaning confirmed by the images. Vertov went even further in his final silent films. *The Eleventh Year* creates a sense of sound in its images of a bugler, a bell, a loud-hailer, rushing water, hammers and explosions. The implicit noise of the hammers and explosions comes at climactic points in its structure, and is intended to make it 'a film-object of sight and sound, edited to be heard as well as seen'.[6] Similarly, *Man with a Movie Camera* contains sequences that have a powerful sound concomitant. The orchestra heard on the radio in the workers' club would be a good example. Vertov's 'Musical scenario' for the film requires the

71

freeze-frames near the end to be accompanied by sudden silence, before being contrasted with the pendulum swinging, itself illustrated with a muffled ticking clock. *Enthusiasm* uses recorded sound to create such images.

Yet, while others also created images of sound in their films, Vertov unambiguously welcomed sound itself. His anticipations of sound enabled him to respond to the end of the silent era better than fiction film-makers.[7] Certainly, Vertov was one of the first Soviet directors to write about sound, and his experiments with it predate his film debut.[8] As early as 1923, four years before the first sound film, Vertov envisaged the extension of Cine-Eye to the realm of sound in an article entitled 'Cine-Eyes: A Revolution'.[9] Nowhere in Vertov do we detect a trace of the guarded attitude to the 'double-edged invention' of Eisenstein, Pudovkin and Alexandrov in their famous 1928 'Statement on Sound'.[10]

Vertov's openness to this new dimension of film not only differed from the attitudes of other radical directors but also contrasted with wider expectations that sound would put an end to documentary, since all sounds would have to be reconstructed in the studio.[11] Abram Room assured him that location recording of sound was impossible,[12] and Ippolit Sokolov claimed it would yield little more than 'caterwauling'.[13] Nevertheless, Vertov insisted upon the importance of location sound recording as the only way of 'preserving the advantages of location shooting in the production of sound documentary film'.[14] Certainly, there were incredible difficulties in recording and producing synchronised sequences in any unfamiliar place, especially in factories, where electrical currents often interfered with the recording apparatus.[15] Yet, having experimented by taking the apparatus further and further from the studio in Leningrad, Vertov and his team eventually made their first location sound recordings. He sent a euphoric telegram declaring a 'victory in the field of documentary recording...for the first time we have recorded the sounds of factory machines, a locomotive, and other documentary material for our film'.[16] Recordings were then made on location in the Donets Basin (Donbas) 'in conditions of clanking and crashing, in workshops shuddering with sound'.[17] The result was *Enthusiasm*, which Vertov proclaimed the first full-length sound documentary film,[18] 'the first train of sound to have burst through the velvet studio walls on to the open expanses of audible life'. It had disproved the doubters, 'definitively exploded the shell of the sound studio and...resolved the vexed question of sound documentary recording'.[19]

Enthusiasm demonstrated the applicability to sound of Vertov's established methods of hidden and off-guard recording.[20] With its completion in November 1930 and release on 1 April 1931, Vertov had further defied the film-making establishment's hopes that sound would precipitate a more pragmatic approach to documentary.[21] Vertov was once more setting the pace: 1930 and 1931, the Soviet Union's first years of sound, were dominated by documentary sound films which similarly extended the location recording approach.[22]

Making Sense of *Enthusiasm*

Despite the influence of its example, initial responses to *Enthusiasm* at Moscow and Kiev previews were hostile, possibly influenced by poor-quality sound projection facilities.[23] While there may have been any number of underlying reasons for these reactions, many spectators appear simply to have been confused by the film: the film's form and challenging use of sound are an obstacle to understanding for contemporary and present-day spectators alike. Yet the film is far from the disorganised wall of sound described by its detractors.

i) Structure and Themes

Even though the themes are readily identifiable and the essential message of the film rather straightforward, the film does have a narrative that emerges only after repeated viewings.[24] One reason is that, like Vertov's previous film, *Man with a Movie Camera,* it attempts to present the spectator with a perceptual process, a gradual emergence into sense.[25] The opening section of the film uses the assault upon religion to illustrate the process of overcoming false consciousness,[26] with the woman wearing earphones, who appears only in this section, drawing our attention to the act of listening itself.[27]

This section stands apart from the rest of the film as a representation of the past and its revolutionary transformation. Images of the old dominate, and the new is introduced by the efforts of Communists and Pioneers, turning a church into a workers' club. This is both a literal and an allegorical transformation, the switch in the building's function standing for a change in society, since this key event enables society's successful response to the coal shortage later in the film.

This acts as the first part in a characteristic Vertov narrative strategy of comparing and contrasting the pre-Revolutionary past with a revolutionary present, in turn containing the seeds of an imminent socialist future. As with the previous two Ukrainian films, though, the past is evoked not through archive footage but images of the present with associations to the old. Marking a transition between the two sections of the film, the passage of time is implied through the speeded-up image of clouds passing. In the second part the theme that dominates is work, and the need for the whole Donbas, the whole of society, to work harder than ever to make good the shortfall in coal and build socialism – a stark change from the stasis and inebriation of the old.

If the film's first part resembles *Man with a Movie Camera* in its contrasts of old and new as well as in its reflexivity, the rest of the film resembles *The Eleventh Year*, particularly in its dynamic images of workers filing purposively past the camera. Coincidences in the visual textures of the film are not coincidental, since the cameraman here, Boris Tseitlin, had been Kaufman's understudy on that film.[28] However, despite its being based in and dedicated to a clearly named place, 'the Donbas', this film does not even show *The Eleventh Year*'s initial spatial integrity: shots relate more through association than geographical continuity.[29] Alongside *The Eleventh Year* and *Man with a Movie Camera*, *Enthusiasm* forms part of a Ukrainian triptych in which a sense of Ukraine as a place is insistently erased in favour of a universal, international, Communist space.

Enthusiasm skilfully uses opposing formal features to underline its juxtaposition of past and present. This is evident in its sharply contrasting low- and high-angle shots.[30] In the opening sequence we see a large number of low-angle shots of churches. There are high-angle shots of a statue of Jesus on a church, but this serves to contrast the immense sculptured form with tiny, barely visible human beings below. People throughout this sequence, whether worshippers or drunks, are photographed either from a high angle, as they prostrate themselves, or straight on. Sometimes their faces, and especially their eyes, are partially obscured. Moreover, they are predominantly static, or, like the final drunk's feet, shot with a wobbly hand-held camera, barely able to walk. With the exception of the radio-telegraph woman and the conductor, who seem to stand outside the world represented, the portraiture captures age, decrepitude, vacant, alcohol-addled expressions and bearded pomposity. Notably absent are youth, beauty and energy.

All this changes when the church becomes a workers' club, after which we see a huge array of low-angle shots of workers framed against a light sky. Frequently they are looking upwards. Typically they are hard at work, or in motion, filing past the camera before a red flag. As with *The Eleventh Year*, Vertov marshals his considerable resources as a film-maker to evoke a sense of the energy and enthusiasm expended in work. These workers' faces radiate joy, health and vitality.

Vertov has deployed the array of expressive devices from his previous film, but to articulate a clearer narrative: whereas previously God was all-powerful and humanity stagnant and reviled, now humanity has power and is everywhere active in building a new, vigorous society. Yet the contrast between stasis and motion is developed not only through this structure of contrasts but also through the verbal structuring of the voice-over and orators. One orator argues that the shortfall in Donbas

coal production must be made good by the whole of society's efforts. Soon we are told that Komsomol members went to the Donbas. They are followed by shock workers and then enthusiasts. In each case a form of the same verb 'to go' (*idti*) is used: *shli komsomol'tsy; idut udarniki, entuziasty idut*. The motion of these three groups matches three results described with the same verb: coal is flowing (*ugol' idet*), metal is flowing (*metall idet*) and the Donbas goes onto the attack (*Donbass idet na vstuplenie*). One of the final voice-over interventions of the film announces 'The construction of socialism is going ahead at full steam' over the image of a train. Once again, the same verb is used. In each case motion, already a key metaphor in the images, is underlined by repetition of the same verb of purposive onward movement.

However, in bending his visual idiom to the ever more narrow remit of the Five-Year Plan period, Vertov restricted his use of certain techniques. Highly expressive subjective camera, reminiscent of *Man with a Movie Camera,* is used a few times in the first section to ape the movement of a bell, the bowing of a penitent and the staggering of a drunk, but is absent from the Five-Year Plan section. This suggests a deliberate strategy to associate such devices with negative phenomena in order to legitimise their use. It is also indicative of Vertov's sensibility to the criticisms of *Man with a Movie Camera* for over-concentration on machines and lack of portraiture: Vertov compensates with a myriad of portraits. Unfortunately, this still fell short of creating a character, the sort of named, individuated image increasingly required of documentary and fiction film alike. One reason was Vertov's approach to sound.

ii) Use of Sound and Music: Sound–Image Interaction

The film's complex use of sound, famously condemned as a 'cacophony',[31] can be seen as an attempt to reveal its constructed nature.[32] Vertov's purpose, on this reading, is to disrupt naturalistic expectations of sound, manipulating or detaching it from source to remind the spectator that this is a film.[33]

However, Vertov is not attempting solely to 'break the aural cinematic illusion'.[34] There are naturalistic uses of sound too, especially speeches. Frequently the film shows a person making a speech. Moreover, there are marching bands recorded in synchronous sound, as well as numerous industrial machines including hooters, pit-head lifts, coal trucks, drills, trains, whistles and hammers, all recorded on location and combined synchronously with the image. The synchronised sound appears almost exclusively in the Five-Year Plan part of the film. Indeed, in the first part of the film the bell-ringing alone is matched to an image of its source.

The film's pioneering use of synchronised speeches predates Soviet film's first interviews. It seems that technical difficulties meant further material had to be excluded.[35] Nevertheless, despite the paucity of synchronised speeches and the general tendency towards sloganising, *Enthusiasm*'s use of synchronised sound is worth noting because it was to become more pronounced in Vertov's later work. Moreover, the speeches are used in such a way as to dispense almost entirely with intertitles (there are a handful of superimposed titles), and they simultaneously introduce voices identifiable as those of various individuals: they are far from the impersonal, unquestionable authority of the 'voice of God' commentary that was soon to dominate sound documentary. In fact, speeches given by embodied individuals in synchronised recordings function in the same way as disembodied off-screen voices by making statements and exhortations to which the film's subjects respond. The hierarchy of authoritative commentary and less dependable recorded voices that was to dominate sound film is here fascinatingly contested, and very much prefigures Vertov's later exploration of the interview.[36]

Yet by far the most interesting use of sound in this film is in the repetition and the detachment of industrial sound from its source and its use as a motif. Good examples of this are the uses of a chugging, locomotive-like sound and the use of a steam hooter or whistle.

Normally announcing the start and end of the working day, the hooter seems associated with new beginnings.[37] In the film, the hooter first appears in the religion sequence immediately after the staggering drunk's feet. It is immediately followed by the film's first marching band, a troop of drumming Pioneers. We then see the hooter again whistling and letting off steam. This causes the radio telegraph operator to put on her earphones. The next time we hear the hooter sound, but do not see it. The noise accompanies a striking, low-angle *contre-jour* shot of a metal plant. This is the first such shot. Until now low-angle shots of buildings had been of churches or the church transformed into a workers' club. Now this image, accompanied by the sound of a hooter, introduces the theme of industry, the film's main theme. The sound of the hooter continues, accompanying images of workers going to work and delegates assembling at a congress, intercut with a voice warning of the shortfall in coal. Having now established its meaning, the image and sound of the hooter also underline other moments in the film, such as the hammering sequence used to proclaim Stalin's slogan that work is 'A matter of honour, a matter of glory, a matter of valour and heroism'. Similarly, it signals the beginning and end of the sequence depicting the competition or 'socialist emulation' of the steel plant's furnace and rolling machine. Overall, the sound serves to punctuate the film, proclaiming the coming of the new and introducing themes.

More impressive still is the use of a chugging sound resembling a steam locomotive. This sound is first heard in the mining sequences following the orator's call for 'the whole mass of the public to liquidate the shortfall'. This chugging sound unifies an extended sequence in which shots of mining and pit ponies pulling trucks are intercut with shots of miners on the surface, rhythmically practising walking in a mine and using picks. The chugging here seems to emphasise the coordinated and collective aspect of mining. Its next use comes in the hammer sequence, the culminating point in a number of shots of steel-working. In none of these cases does the sound appear to be created by any of the images we see. Consequently, we come to see it as associating these three kinds of labour, suggesting they share a common purpose. This is ultimately an image of the country's furious pace of development, a rhythm to be contrasted with the ticking and the bell-ringing of the now transformed old world.

Vertov's approach to sound differed from the other leading Soviet documentarists, Erofeev and Shub, who were wary of incorporating location recorded sound into montage-style constructions. Vertov described his three ways of recording synchronised sound sequences: if sound and film are recorded on different strips of film at different times then the image is superior to the sound; if on different strips of film at the same time then the sound is better than the image; and if they are recorded on the same strip of film at the same time then both image and sound are satisfactory. This is compounded by the fact that ease of synchronisation makes for difficulty of recording and vice versa.[38]

Vertov claims Erofeev only accepts the recording of sound and image on the same piece of film – i.e. the third of these methods.[39] Certainly, his early sound films, such as *The Olympics of the Arts* [Olimpiada iskusstv,

1930], strive above all to record, and do so at great – indeed, excessive – length. Shub too followed this path. In her *Komsomol: Patron of Electrification* [Komsomol – shef elektrifikatsii, 1932] there is genuine location sound.[40] Rather than sound working as a separate, independent element, often contrasting with the image, as in Vertov's film, Shub respects the integrity of each sound, its real length and relation to the event, and consequently synchronises far more.

Despite recording most of the sounds synchronously, on the same piece of film, Vertov sees sound and image interacting. Arguing that either coincidence or non-coincidence of image with sound are possible, Vertov is distancing himself from both the synchrony position of fellow documentarists and the commitment to a consistently non-synchronous, 'contrapuntal method' championed by the 'Statement on Sound':[41]

> [T]he question of audio-visual montage is resolved not according to the simplest coincidence of sound with image, and not according to the simplest opposition of sound with image, but according to the complex interaction of sound with image.[42]

Characteristically, Vertov maintained a commitment to recording equalling that of the other documentarists, but not to the detriment of film's expressive power. Recording was never an absolute for Vertov. This approach, and his outspoken defence of it, continued to antagonise exponents of documentary and fiction film alike, and continues to perplex those seeking to appropriate Vertov either as documentarian or reflexive cine-poet.

Yet, for all Vertov's keenness to defend the integrity of documentary, *Enthusiasm* employs music, effectively accommodating art. It is, however, worth remembering that music had typically accompanied silent showings of film: since silent film had been accompanied by music, then so should sound film.[43] Indeed, Vertov himself gave indications as to the music to be used to accompany a number of his earlier films, including both *The Eleventh Year* and *Man with a Movie Camera*, so his use of it here was not unprecedented. Moreover, Vertov's theorisation of film was informed by music, most notably in the theory of intervals. Film was already a rhythmic art, one which structured time, and needed to find its specific rhythm.[44] Music was in this sense too already part of film, or, rather, film was already musical: even if Vertov's rejections of alien influences upon cinema do mention music, they do so far less than theatre. The greatest danger of sound film was seen as the talkie, of the re-theatricalisation of cinema through synchronised dialogue so typical of much early sound film in America. This was seen as a continuation of the intertitle, and was therefore, like it, an offence against movement, the essence of cinema.[45]

In this hostility to dialogue at least, Vertov and Eisenstein could agree. By the end of the decade both would be embracing music in film, but extremely stylised, non-naturalistic music.

His subsequent use of it notwithstanding, Vertov introduces music into *Enthusiasm* tentatively, as part of the old, aesthetic world ultimately superseded by the found sounds of the new socialist society. A radio announcer's voice announces the music as '"The Final Sunday March", from the film *Symphony of the Donbas*'. Identifying the music enables the viewer to fit it into the film's thematic tension between old and new. Moreover, this framing device indicates that the woman with earphones is listening to recorded music on the radio, the same music we hear. It is not inserted from without, non-diegetically. This is possibly why the credits refer to 'musical documents', suggesting that the music is something recorded and reproduced on film, like the other elements. The image of the radio-telegraph woman, and a sound that resembles a radio tuning in, function as something of an aural equivalent of Vertov's iconic image of the Cine-Eye, encouraging us to see or listen reflexively.

Yet we first hear the music before the radio announcer introduces it. Vertov is up to the kind of metapoetic trick he played in *Man with a Movie Camera*: the unwary think they are getting conventional soundtrack music, before Vertov shows us the conductor of the music. Indeed, Vertov initially intended to intercut shots of the cameraman and editing as work in general starts. While this in fact ended up in *Man with a Movie Camera*, the final version of *Enthusiasm* gives us a reflection on the documentary perspective on sound rather than on film itself. Like *Man with a Movie Camera*, this film is Vertov's defence of documentary, but only extended to sound. The self-referential nature of his work is not the result of formalism as such but a need to defend his conception of documentary film.

Like *Man with a Movie Camera*, *Enthusiasm* is also intended to challenge our concepts of work and entertainment, workdays and celebrations. The notion of the final Sunday, or final sabbath, means the end of a distinction between rest and labour. This is a theme close to Vertov's heart. In keeping with the spirit of the First Five-Year Plan, henceforth all will be work, and celebration will be part of work. Vertov's personal life is itself an illustration of this attitude in his marriage to Svilova, a fellow film-maker, and in their all-consuming shared devotion to this work. It is probably no accident that this dedication becomes so much more pronounced to the extent of being explicitly thematised in this, the first film made by the couple after the departure of Mikhail Kaufman, whose attitude to life had tended to be more easygoing, and who had a family life distinct from work.

To illustrate this synthesis of work and leisure, the intermingling of sounds and images of industrial work with those of Mayday and other demonstrations, such as in the sequence where the rolling machine and furnace compete, is intended to suggest that there is no longer any distinction: '[A]ll work on the liquidation of the shortage in the Donbas turns into a gigantic "subbotnik".'[46] Similarly, the film projects a sense of the musicality of machines: 'Is this the rattle of machines or music?'[47] Just as work comes to resemble celebration, so machines come to sound musical. The composed symphony on the radio gives way to the direct presentation of sounds of the living Donbas:

> The march dedicated to the Donbas (art) and authentic sounds of the Donbas (reality), the past (Tsarist) and the present (Soviet), theory and practice, plan and real situation, the concept of 'holiday' and the concept of 'labour', cine-language (the visible) and radio-language (the audible) in the film are in a state of uninterrupted interpenetration and interaction.
>
> *Enthusiasm*, written by the voices of machines, the voices of shock-workers and radio-telegraph reports, ends in an audio-visual symphony, where industrial sounds take root in holiday demonstrations, where the sounds of holidays take root in the Donbas working day.[48]

The implicit question is: which is the true symphony of the Donbas – the music or the factory sounds? Yet this was a reflexive vision of the documentary film, whereby music gives way to industrial sound, that Vertov could not even maintain throughout the whole course of the film, using a distorted Tsarist national anthem to accompany images of drinking. For Vertov this kind of stylisation, without the parodic element, was indicative of the way he would use music in his remaining films.

Enthusiasm as Documentary

For Vertov, extending documentary film-making to sound meant a commitment to the location recording of sound, but also to editing together sounds and images from different times and places. Similarly, in the visual sphere *Enthusiasm* applies caught off-guard and hidden camera photography: drunkards waving the camera away, workers hard at work (and therefore distracted from the camera) and shots of industrial processes. As with *Cine-Eye*, Vertov's first 'off-guard' film, and *Man with a Movie Camera*, the most striking use of hidden camera comes in photography of the socially deviant. Here it is the drunks, some of whom clearly do not want to be photographed.[49]

There is far more performance in the positive scenes. As with *The Eleventh Year*, there are numerous shots of workers filing past the camera, often with symbolic backdrops such as red flags or Communist banners. Yet this is the kind of reconstruction using real workers photographed at their workplace Vertov had been doing since *Cine-Eye*. Vertov was right to insist that this was a successful adaptation of documentary principles to sound, and that any shortcomings be seen in the context of the incredible obstacles overcome in making it.[50] Nevertheless, the film's hostile reception is an indication of the difficulty spectators had in understanding it. *Enthusiasm* was an overt challenge to the slogan 'intelligible to the millions'.

While scope for experimentation was narrowing, there were also greater resources for Soviet cinema, especially non-fiction film. The founding of Soiuzkinokhronika in 1932 as a separate organisation for Soviet 'newsreel' was indicative of its greater weight. However, the stress was upon newsreels proper and documentary shorts, not feature-length documentaries: in 1932 Soiuzkinokhronika produced only two, alongside 45 shorts and over 100 editions of various newsreel series.[51] The emphasis was on the regularity and immediacy of journalism, the very goals Vertov had concluded to be impossible with the available resources when abandoning newsreel proper in 1925.[52] Now resources were available and newsreels came out punctually, but they were bland in form. Better funding entailed greater control,[53] a goal aided by the nature of sound film, which literally spoke the same language as politicians.[54]

Meanwhile, *Enthusiasm* had shown the Soviet film industry what a consistently documentary approach to sound might be like. Moreover, in discussing *Enthusiasm*, Vertov consistently uses the term 'documentary' as in 'documentary film' [dokumental'naia fil'ma], and employs it increasingly from this point onwards.[55] A recent import, Vertov may have acquired the term from his younger brother Boris, in France, where it had long designated non-fiction films.[56] In Russia, in the early 1930s 'documentary' was generally kept in inverted commas, or carefully glossed, signalling the novelty of the word and a writer's distance from it.[57] Whatever its precise path into the Russian language, it still felt new and foreign at a time when Russia was turning in on itself and away from outside influence.

Vertov's sway over young film-makers is evident from debates among Leningrad newsreel makers, where one group argued that preliminary scenarios destroyed newsreel.[58] Former Cine-Eye Ilya Kopalin made *One of Many* [Odin iz mnogikh, 1930], a film that eschewed voice-over and used location-recorded sound as widely as Vertov had. Even in his absence from Moscow, Vertov's mere reputation was exerting influence upon emergent Soviet sound film. The time had come to destroy it. The term 'documentary' was seized as a weapon in a virulent campaign to annihilate documentary as a distinct film form, and Vertov's influence over it.

The Struggle Against Vertov is against Documentary as Such[59]

While the choice of term owes much to political expediency, there was a deeper motivation: the concept of documentary makes a claim for evidentiary power, stressing the importance of film material as evidence and record. Despite juxtaposing disparate phenomena to construct an argument, Vertov was still committed to a residual concept of documentary film as record. The form's integrity was now an obstacle to the emphasis upon regular newsreels, heroic portraiture, written scenarios and a willingness to stage. The minimally staged documentary Vertov championed left too much to chance and had to be crushed. The 1931 rebranding of leading cinema journal *Kino i zhizn'* (Cinema and Life) as *Proletarskoe kino* (Proletarian Cinema) signalled an intensification of polemics. Its first task was to attack 'documentalism': documentary as a distinct tradition promising privileged access to the real.[60]

According to one critic, Borisov, the problem with Vertov's *Enthusiasm* and Kopalin's *One of Many* was their 'fetishisation of fact'. By limiting themselves to recordable 'facts' they had made films that missed unrecordable but crucial factors, such as 'underground counter-revolutionary work'.

> In this way the fetishisation of fact inescapably leads to the artist, for all his striving to show reality in a deeper way, being limited to those phenomena that can be easily recorded, and the deeper and more complex processes without which it is impossible to understand reality will fall from his field of vision.[61]

Documentalists give no sense of the bigger picture, a significant failing for Bolshevik cultural criticism, which stressed the Hegelian notion of 'totality', the artist's task of making sense of the world. Yet this bigger picture contained things such as kulak conspiracies, which simply did not take place and could therefore not be recorded. The only way cinema could solve this problem was through 'the creative relation to reality': either a new kind of documentary involving extensive staging, or acted films. Never willing to do this in the manner required, Vertov's scope for film-making was rapidly curtailed.

Vertov's response to the attack is to take 'documentalism' as referring to a hybrid form of acted films borrowing the style of *Cine-Eye* or *Cine-Pravda*: 'acted films with a newsreel form',[62] such as Eisenstein's 'acted newsreel', and use of an actor to play Lenin.[63]

Vertov had always opposed such 'attempts to efface the boundaries between newsreel and "typage" films'.[64] This is not just a blind attack or a rant on Vertov's behalf,[65] but an attempt to preserve the film form he had spent his whole adult life defining and developing. In 'Documentary Film and Documentalism' (1931) he distinguishes the various competing terms:

> Question: What is the difference between newsreel, Cine-Eye, documentary and unplayed film?
> Answer: There is no difference. These are different definitions of one and the same branch of cinema production: it is 'newsreel', which points to its continuous link with the accumulation of the current material of newsreel; it is Cine-Eye, which points to the recording of this newsreel material with the eye armed with the cine camera, the Cine-Eye; it is documentary, which points to its being genuine, to the authenticity of the accumulated material; it is unplayed, which points to actors being unnecessary, to acting being unnecessary in the production of this kind of film.[66]

In reply, Vertov's opponents make it clear that 'documentalists' refers to 'those working in newsreel, instructional-newsreel, scientific, unplayed or documentary film'.[67] Soon they call for '*implacable struggle* against documentalism' with the aim of 'destroying it completely'.[68] Terms are hurled as abuse as 'documentalism' is dubbed formalist and Trotskyist:

> [T]he very basic premise of documentalism – the division of films according to the way they 'glean their material' into 'played' and 'unplayed' ignoring the quality of their content, is a formalist premise.[69]

Curiously, this discussion covers the same ground as more recent discussions as to whether a meaningful distinction can be made between fiction and non-fiction film, since both depend on similar methods of construction.[70] As with the work of contemporary Structuralist-inspired criticism, there is a dismissal of the notion that cinema's indexicality, its capacity to record, makes it in any sense a privileged tool for grasping reality. However, whereas Structuralists downplay relations of reference between films and reality, Proletarian critics argue that art reflects reality no less than document does.[71] 'There can be and are "documents" that interpret reality falsely. There can be and are fabrications that reflect reality correctly and to a large extent completely.'[72] Documentary cannot provide any extra information unavailable to acted films, because the important thing is the ideological position of the film-maker, not the method.

This was the key point: if documentary afforded the viewer no privileged knowledge of the world, it could be judged like any other film on whether it succeeded in attracting, entertaining and persuading audiences. Newsreel was now said to be an art, and its maker an artist. The First All-Union Conference of Newsreel Workers opened with an assertion that documentary and fictional (artistic) cinema cannot be opposed, since a skilful newsreel film-maker must be an artist too.[73] In an uncanny echo of Eisenstein's criticisms of *Cine-Eye*, rejection of the terminology of art and the artistic was now taken to mean denial of the documentary's need to organise recorded material and persuade:

[P]eople completely forgot that the task of newsreel is not only the creative cognition of the social reality that surrounds us, but also the active transformation of this reality through the influence of art.[74]

Nikolai Lebedev pointedly quoted Marx: 'The philosophers have merely interpreted the world; the point, however, is to change it.' Newsreel's capacity to record was now condemned as 'dispassionate objectivism',[75] as an obstacle to the propagation of the Party line. Since recorded events are important only to the extent that they advance the cause, facts must be selected and combined so as to show their connection with the bigger picture (as determined by the Party), 'as a drop of water reflects the sun'.[76] To include any fact simply because it is a fact (i.e. simply because it is true) is not acceptable, it is to be a 'fetishist of the fact'.[77]

The campaign against 'documentalism' routed Vertov and marked a watershed in the reorientation of Soviet non-fiction film towards the scripted, staged documentaries and abusively inaccurate historical films with which it became synonymous for the next 20 years.[78] This becomes clear if we examine exactly what kind of newsreel and documentary films were now to be made in Soviet Russia.

The Change in Style

From approximately 1933 onwards newsreel and documentary film differed radically in its use of sound, its tendency to stage and its use of a detailed written scenario.

i) Sound

Bulky sound cameras hindered location and hidden filming, often leading to poor results. In Erofeev's *Olympics of the Arts*, an orator has to pause as noisy machinery briefly drowns out his speech. Fear of unpredictable quality was probably a factor leading to the ever less frequent use of location sound recording in Soviet newsreel and documentary. This is why a 1932 issue of the *Soiuzkinozhurnal* newsreel recorded Leonid Utesov's jazz band in a sound studio rather than at a concert venue. In consequence, as Erofeev observed, while documentaries had pioneered Soviet sound film in 1930 and 1931, it was now fiction film that was more innovative in using sound.[79] Only the most important moments were shot with synchronised film, the rest on silent stock with sound added in the studio.[80]

Roman Karmen epitomised this approach, using voice-over effectively in *Moscow–Kara-Kum–Moscow* [Moskva–Kara-Kum–Moskva, 1933]. This film struck the correct note with its telegram from Stalin and sense of triumph over nature: as the crews work hard to get their cars through the desert, the voice-over proclaims: 'The desert begins to understand what a shock worker is.' Here sound is predominantly a strident voice-over, with a synchronously recorded official speech at the end which sums up the narrative and restates the race's importance in carrying out goals set by the Party and the government. Karmen's film uses its sound to echo a message of maximum political orthodoxy.

Significantly, in the resolutions of the Second All-Union Conference of Newsreel Workers, *Moscow–Kara-Kum–Moscow* is singled out for particular praise as an example of the sharp increase in the quality of newsreel film by Ioselevich, the head of the Soviet newsreel organisation, Soiuzkinokhronika.[81] Throughout these discussions quality is synonymous with unambiguous and accessible form. It is almost another way of saying 'intelligible to the millions'.[82]

By 1933 the format of voice-over commentary plus music already dominates US newsreel. In the Soviet Union this pattern is slower to dominate, but it dominates documentaries well before World War II despite Vertov's alternative example. However, in Russia at the beginning of the 1930s, film-makers held greater sway and saw the voice-over as a way of disguising a weak film, since it is particularly important when a film is shot badly.[83] It was attractive to the film industry and political authorities for precisely this capacity to turn base metals into political gold.

ii) Staging

N. Karmazinsky, at the 1932 Conference of Newsreel Workers, poses the choice of methods as '"staging" [instsenirovka] or "life off-guard"'.[84] Defeating Vertov, the incarnation of an alternative, would clear the way for staging. This was a practice particularly attractive as a means of meeting tight deadlines and making films efficiently. A film such as Alexander Lemberg's *The White Sea–Baltic Canal* [Belomor–baltiiskii vodnyi put´, 1933] was criticised for its lack of close-ups, biographies and portraits, and not released. That this was the result of a reluctance to stage was no defence.[85] If staging was the only way to achieve the desired results, then the film-maker had to re-enact the whole thing in the studio.[86] An early example was a 1932 edition of *Soiuzkinozhurnal*, where a meeting, including the speeches, was re-enacted in the studio. As Lebedev put it: 'We are not against moments of staging. Just because we shoot this or that real shock-worker in more convenient circumstances for recording, the essence of the shock-worker will not change.'[87] This approach led to the widespread use of studio reconstruction.

While studio reconstruction was staging at its most egregious, there were many subtler types of intervention by the film-makers. These included provoking an action, such as getting someone to dance[88] and rearranging a banner to suit filming.[89] More flagrant examples involved getting participants to perform uncharacteristic actions, or even using professional actors.[90] The distinction between reconstruction and staging becomes somewhat tenuous: Mikhail Slutsky's *People* [Liudi, 1934] was seen as reconstruction at the time but more recently has been treated as epitomising staging.[91]

Just how endemic staging had become is evident from the universally hostile reaction to Erofeev when he denounces such practices at the 1932 Conference of Newsreel Workers:

> I start from the position that newsreel should be the recording of authentic reality, since to create phenomena here in the studio is to falsify those phenomena.
>
> If we are to stage in the studio, then there is no reason for newsreel's existence anymore.[92]

Erofeev is interrupted repeatedly, universally derided, and denounced in the resolutions.[93] Once again this position is condemned as documentalism, and 'simple recording'.[94] Medvedkin's response catches the conference's mood:

> Comrade Erofeev's formulation of recording the facts of reality does not suit us at all. Our approach is to make film the mouthpiece of the politically active public.[95]

This was a position embraced by Medvedkin's cine-train comrades, such as N. Safronov. This overt advocate of staging argued that directing a film involved 'educational Party work with the masses' to ensure the film shows the right outcome.[96] The cine-train's integration of film-making with activism entailed a fundamental shift towards both acting and staging in the treatment of contemporary non-fictional material. For those on the cine-train, observational and caught off-guard approaches were luxuries they could ill afford, as is clear from Karmazinsky's detailed discussion of how to reconstruct events and activities: political persuasion is too important to be potentially sacrificed to the niceties of recording unprovoked events.[97] This politically pragmatic approach found exponents throughout the country:

> As for staging. Where we live in Siberia this question is often asked, and whether good or bad, we stage. If we take a single shift at an enterprise and film not only its actual achievements, but make this shift show a way of organising a number of things characteristic of other shifts, collecting this experience together, then this enables the experience to be transferred to related sectors. Can you really pose the question here: is this a document?[98]

Such approaches testify to the essential danger in all such staging and reconstruction: it becomes easier for the film-makers to show what should be occurring than what actually is occurring. However, staging to represent the typical rather than the factual could also be motivated for formal reasons, to make the work more dramatically engaging. One 'visiting editorial board' film-maker proudly proclaimed his successes in staging:

> In this film there is not a single shot that has not been staged. Everything, right down to the most distant long shot is staged yet at numerous screenings no one noticed...
>   Since we organised the facts ourselves, we were able to impart a certain dynamism, we could choose what to include, and so the work acquired a dramatic spine.[99]

As well as being more economically and politically efficient, staging enabled stronger narrative development. As such, it went along with the scenario.

iii) Scenario

At the 1932 Conference of Newsreel Workers, Erofeev outspokenly linked the scenario with staging:

> A scenario presupposes staging, it issues a directive to the cameraman to get such and such a shot even in the event that this shot does not actually occur. Newsreel should reject this kind of scenario.[100]

Erofeev's proposals were immediately rejected as too time-consuming.[101] Instead, the method endorsed involves both drawing up detailed literary scenarios and reconstruction. The greater the element of staging involved, the more detailed the scenario had to be, involving a shooting plan even specifying dress.[102] In this context, Vertov's reluctance to present more detailed scenarios makes sense as part of his hostility to staging, and championing of optimal authenticity.

A major imperative to use the scenario is the desire to economise on film stock. Participants in the first conference of newsreel workers proudly announced that using a scenario had enabled them to achieve ratios of footage in the final film to stock used of 1:2.[103] This might be compared with Vertov's *A Sixth Part of the World*, where the ratio was said to be 1:20.[104] As Shub commented, working with real people and not actors required more film stock.[105]

This approach meant an upsurge in films of predictable occasions such as expeditions, sporting events and parades. The genius of Karmen's *Moscow–Kara-Kum–Moscow* is that it is both race and expedition, combining newsreel and popular documentary genres. Moreover, besides having intrinsic narrative structure, the camera can easily capture the important moments: the setting out, the arrival in this or that place, the obstacle overcome, the homecoming. There is no particular need to stage with such a film: it is like a football match – spontaneous, but regulated within clear spatial and temporal boundaries. Similarly, Arkady Shafran recalls how, from the outset, he and Troianovsky had plotted three possible conclusions for their film *Cheliuskin* [1934].[106] As they were shooting they noted extra episodes that might need to be shot depending on how the film ended. In fact, none of the proposed endings foresaw the ship sinking, which made the film more engaging than they envisaged.

The emphasis upon planning individual films was likewise mirrored by an overall plan for the industry, in which officials claim they can predict the news sensations of the coming year 1934. These include the opening of the Moscow Metro.[107] Ironically, it was not opened until May 1935, a year late! Nevertheless, this astonishing arrogance revealed the underlying aspiration behind Soviet newsreel of the 1930s: the suppression of the event and recording in favour of entirely staged and scripted ritual pseudo-events. Documentary had changed utterly.

6

Documentary or Hagiography? *Three Songs of Lenin*

After the domestic hostility to *Enthusiasm* and 'documentalism' Vertov left the Ukrainian film industry, obtaining a job at Mezhrabpomfilm. As the Moscow production arm of Workers' International Relief, Vertov's new employers might have hoped the next film would build on the international acclaim of *Enthusiasm*. It was certainly designed to. Since his 1925 *Leninist Cine-Pravda* Vertov had been planning *Lenin* (*Proletarians of all Countries Unite*) [Proletarii vsekh stran soediniaetes´], a feature film in which the image of Lenin was linked to internationalism.[1] The finished product, *Three Songs of Lenin*, expressed this idea through the peoples of the Soviet Far East.

Three Songs of Lenin has been seen as falling short of the standards of Vertov's earlier films,[2] and as a renunciation of everything Vertov previously stood for: it deploys the tools of cinema not to demystify but to sanctify Lenin.[3] The fact that the film became the most acceptable example of Vertov's work in the Soviet Union after his death was retrospectively adduced as proof of its conformist approach.[4] It was 'an example of the heavy hand of Socialist Realism methodically crushing Futurist and Formalist experimentation',[5] the diametrical opposite of *Man with a Movie Camera*.[6]

Others assert that it is Vertov's 'greatest film',[7] or that it subverts socialist realism.[8] Taken in the context of the style that dominated the early 1930s, *Three Songs of Lenin* stands out as 'almost non-conformist'[9] and 'a development of the experimental tradition',[10] transposing documentary to sound in an approach analogous to the earlier reflexivity. Vertov demonstrates anew the mastery of archive footage that characterised his work of the early 1920s. Since these arguments are anchored in accounts of the film's reception, it is worth considering the fate of *Three Songs of Lenin* with the Soviet public and critics before analysing the film proper.

Reception

Recently arrived in Moscow, American Communist Jay Leyda claimed *Three Songs of Lenin* rendered 'all other documentary films of the period a little ordinary by comparison' and was 'outstanding for now and a long time after'.[11] Nevertheless, it was not immediately influential in the Soviet Union itself, where it encountered a series of obstacles delaying its distribution and was not screened at the Bolshoi Theatre on the 24 January tenth anniversary of Lenin's death, despite being ready.[12] Vertov's efforts to get the film shown 'ended in splendid victory'.[13]

On 1 November it opened at 11 of the largest cinemas in the land,[14] and was supposedly discussed at 200 public screenings.[15] Yet it lasted only a few days. Vertov claims that this was despite substantial receptive audiences and implausibly blames minor bureaucrats for keeping the film from the public despite its good press.[16]

Certainly, where reviewed, the film's hallowed theme meant criticism was, at worst, guarded. A good example is a *Sovetskoe kino* review of various films released near the fifteenth anniversary of Soviet cinema, which praises *Three Songs of Lenin* as evidence that Vertov has reformed: '[T]he logic of events comes first, the meaning of these events and not the frequent succession of Formalist visuals, of brief montage shots, as in Vertov's previous works.'[17]

If this compliment seems backhanded, the rest of the review directly criticises *Three Songs of Lenin* for concentrating on the non-Slavic ethnic groups of the Soviet Union, and not portraying industrialisation in the centre of the country. This hostility towards the film's Eastern theme came directly from Stalin himself. Boris Shumiatsky recalled that prior to showing Leningrad Party boss Kirov his favourite film, *Chapaev* [1934], Stalin commented on *Three Songs of Lenin*:

> [F]undamentally it was incorrect: Lenin is shown purely using Central Asian material. This places completely unwarranted emphasis on Lenin the leader and standard bearer solely of the East, solely as 'the leader of the Asiatic peoples' which is profoundly mistaken.[18]

The true problem could not be voiced. Vertov had placed undue emphasis on Lenin: he alone inspired emancipation. The cult of Stalin was eclipsing that of Lenin, and Vertov had failed to make Stalin and his achievements sufficiently prominent. On the tenth anniversary of Lenin's death Stalin occupied over half the front page of *Pravda*, whereas Lenin was part of the background.[19]

Stalin preferred *Chapaev*, also released for the October celebrations. Critics competed to praise its combination of historical truth with artistic licence.[20] This free adaptation of a famous civil war diary in fact sacrificed all accuracy to dramatic effect. If acted and fictionalised films of recent history were treated as trustworthy, then documentary was threatened still further. Although *Three Songs of Lenin* helped win Vertov the Order of the Red Star at the celebrations of the fifteenth anniversary of Soviet film in January 1935, it was *Chapaev*, and not *Three Songs of Lenin*, that dominated the inaugural Moscow Film Festival later that year.

The East

Given that it was the ostensible reason the film failed to impress, why did Vertov choose the peoples of the East to illustrate his Lenin theme? Vertov's own answer is that the women of Soviet Far East were 'triply emancipated',[21] and therefore, as Drobashenko explains, the progress of the revolution was most dramatic and evident there.[22] Official appeals to Soviet Central Asian women as the 'surrogate proletariat' of the East, called upon to liberate their societies under the aegis of the Soviet state, were commonplace.[23]

In keeping with this vivid account of sexual, cultural and class liberation, the structure of the film traces a narrative from the opening song's deliberately slow rhythm depicting the oppression and stagnation of traditional Asiatic society, symbolised by women wearing the veil. The revolution overturns this and the final sequences of the third song employ Vertov's familiar fast editing style.[24] The final quotation confirms the film's progression from the liberation of individuals and peoples of the East to that of the whole country, and humanity: 'Centuries will pass, and people will forget the names of the countries in which their ancestors lived but they will never forget the name Lenin, Vladimir Ilich Lenin.'[25] The third song mirrors the first, so that 'my collective farm' becomes 'our collective farm', indicating the same movement from specific to general emancipation.[26]

While this shift may be seen as a forgetting of the East in favour of the implicit hegemony of European Russia,[27] it is also bound up with the film's central theme of memory. The quotation at the end of the film echoes the quote from the second song: '[A]nd neither we nor our grandchildren's grandchildren will ever forget him.'[28] Lenin's memory enables all emancipation. The inspirational act of remembering Lenin is represented through the intercutting of Far Eastern women with the scenes of Lenin's funeral, and by placing this episode at the film's centre. The women's actual distance from Moscow is paralleled by their actual distance in time from the funeral and Lenin's life. Yet not only does the editing suggest that they are looking upon Lenin's body laid out in state, but even the way in which they all sit down at the end suggests a link with the preceding shot of Lenin's bench at Gorki. The film collapses the distance between the Far East and Moscow, just as it splices present and past. It is a celluloid mausoleum trip.

This interpretation suggests that Vertov is expressing an implicitly Eurocentric universalism (although not enough to please Stalin). In fact, he is using the East as a cinematic image of distance from Lenin's life and Moscow, be that in terms of space, time or ideology. The East has become a cipher of distance overcome by memory, standing for the act of remembering. Nonetheless, the film draws not only upon the East but upon images of women: there are nearly three times as many close-ups of women as men.[29] In so doing, Vertov produces the first of his female-centred films.[30] This is more than simply an image of political liberation.

The unveiling of a Moslem woman can be interpreted as a typical gesture of 'orientalism', whereby the exotic beauty of the East is uncovered to the Western male gaze and opened to sexual or economic production. Public unveilings were encouraged in the Soviet Far East from the mid-1920s.[31] Yet the image of the veil and of unveiling is, like the film's structure, part of a reflexive cinematic and not purely a political conceptualisation. It is a consistent motif in Vertov's work from *Leninist Cine-Pravda* to *A Sixth Part of the World*, representing more than just a typical Western attitude to Islam. Using the veil as an image of blindness, Vertov implies that Moslem women can now see, whereas previously they could not. This is, of course, nonsense, in that the veil blinds or restricts the vision not of the woman wearing it but of the person looking at her. It presents a way of seeing resistant to the camera's gaze, its panopticon.[32] Yet, as a public assertion of privacy and the individual's right not to be seen, this is a very particular affront to Vertov's arrogation of the camera's right to see all, proclaimed from the early 1920s onwards. For Vertov, the image of unveiling represents not only the political trope of casting off the shackles of religion, opening onto light as knowledge, but also filmic awakening. Unveiling becomes a metaphor of liberated vision, embedded within a political metaphor. It is another image like the eye superimposed on the camera lens, standing for the renewed and enhanced vision granted by cinema alone.

There are almost certainly other cinematic reasons for choosing to shoot *Three Songs of Lenin* in Soviet Central Asia. These may relate to the practical: the greater hours of bright sunlight made it easier to plan filming and facilitated the film's exploration of the theme of light, itself a central metaphor. The remote location almost certainly also aids Vertov's desire to get away from audiences – and indeed, subjects – spoilt by fictional cinema's harmful effects. Vertov claims that peasants reacted better to factual cinema than fiction:

> This sharp divide between the reception of film-drama and newsreel was evident everywhere a film show was being given for the first, second or third time, everywhere the poison had not yet penetrated deeply.[33]

While this refers to the spectators' attitudes rather than those of the filmed subjects, those who have not seen films will presumably also have no idea how to perform in front of the camera. As with the pioneers in *Cine-Eye*, Vertov is looking for subjects unaware of conventional notions of how to pose for the camera. This was the experience of fellow Soviet cameraman Boris Nebylitsky in Kolyma in the early 1930s:

> The life that opened up before us was so interesting, so colourful and at the same time simple and thrilling, that there was never any occasion to reconstruct it artificially for the camera.[34]

Vertov is making a film with more staged elements than before, but the subjects are non-actors unspoilt by cinematic culture who therefore do not perform in the way that adult metropolitan Russians would. Yet the peoples of the East influence the film in a deeper sense: their folklore furnishes the film with a generic structure and poetic idiom.

Folklore as Documentary

The film grew from the idea of a contemporary woman's tribute to Lenin, originally an article in a wall newspaper by Olga, a Russian shock worker.[35] The whole concept changed after hearing a folk song about Lenin.[36] Clearly, Vertov decided these songs could perform the same function of grassroots tribute, claiming he had found a new kind of authentic material for his film: 'song-documents'[37] or 'documents of popular creation'.[38] These were early examples of the widespread and officially encouraged pseudo-folkloric genre.[39] Nevertheless, these songs existed prior to the expedition and the making of the film, and Vertov records them like a folklorist. However, like all documentarists and folklorists, he is selective and records only those songs and variants that suit his vision. What is more, he retells, recontextualises and stylises them: 'Some songs are on the sound track, some are expressed in the images, still others are reflected in the intertitles.'[40]

This approach effectively places the images within speech marks; it is a frame narrative. Whereas the intertitles of Vertov's silent films usually function as a kind of authorial voice, albeit poetic and visually striking, here the whole film is told in the words, and from the perspective, of women of the Soviet Far East: '[T]he entire film passes before the viewer-listeners in the light of folk images, from Turkish, Turkmen, and Uzbek folk songs.'[41] In *Enthusiasm* too there had been an attempt to avoid impersonal voice-over by using a variety of voices and in the use of synchronised speech. *Three Songs of Lenin* adds the folk song as a further means of avoiding 'voice of God' commentary. Alongside synchronised speech, the folk songs function as a reformulation of documentary for new times, a coherent adaptation of Vertov's poetics and vision to the increasingly narrow parameters of Soviet sound film.

The folkloric form also gave Vertov a new justification for his startling juxtapositions of images. He could be poetical since he was showing the world through the eyes of a folk poet rather than a Futurist. This latitude was all the more important as the language of Soviet documentary became increasingly flat and inexpressive. Thus Vertov is free to associate dandelions and flowers budding with Lenin so as to suggest 'Lenin is springtime'. Lenin becomes a flexible image for the new society, freedom and all that is good. This is clear from a 1933 diary entry: 'Lenin is when the melancholy songs of slavery grow gay and lively.'[42]

For all its poetic qualities, the song genre provided an accessible form enabling Vertov to describe it using the canonical slogan 'intelligible to the millions'.[43] Vertov's shift anticipated Maxim Gorky's famous endorsement of folklore at the 1934 First Congress of Soviet Writers.[44] While Vertov took this as a vindication, Vertov's approach to folklore is, in fact, not at all typical of Soviet Russia of the period. Gorky was calling for a hyperbolic, heroic folklore. It went hand in hand with a collapse of the fiction/non-fiction distinction. *Chapaev* epitomised the new heroic myth that displaced sober history.

This tendency went beyond historical films. Documentaries too were required to illustrate the heroic nature of Soviet life.[45] Expedition films such as *Cheliuskin* were particularly suited: shots of it appear in *Three Songs of Lenin*. Aviators too were represented in epic tones.

This was an extremely narrow view of folklore. The heroes were not one of many but exceptional, and the use of folklore was intended to elevate them.[46] Similarly, this was a folklore increasingly stripped of its comic element: soon even *Pravda*'s veteran satirist Demian Bedny found himself marginalised and his works censored.[47] While some have elided Vertov with this heroic folklore by interpreting *Three Songs of Lenin* as collapsing real time and space,[48] Vertov's film in fact stands out in its reflection on memory and the past–present relation. The editing together of 1924 and 1934, as well as of the Far East and Moscow, is not an attempt to create an atemporal, mythical realm but an explicit thematisation of the present–past relation. Moreover, the use of folklore in *Three Songs of Lenin* conveys a strong sense of anonymous collective power, rather than individual heroism. It is a symbol of Communism's international dimension. Soviet folklore was *Chapaev*, with its heroic and national vision of both folklore and Communism.

The Genre of the Film-Song

As we have seen, one attraction of the film-song genre for Vertov was that the song could act as a document. Yet, for all the importance of the songs as quasi-folklore, the film-song genre also presented an attractive resolution of the problem of sound.

In discussing *Three Songs of Lenin*, Vertov made it clear that he understood he could no longer employ the sort of overt reflexivity characteristic of his earlier films, most notably *Man with a Movie Camera*, where 'the construction of [shooting] methods was open and visible'.[49]

All the same, there are diegetic sound sequences that refer to the film's own aural form. In the first song, there is an episode in which people in the East listen to a Red Square parade on the radio. Earlier, we see a male musician in the workers' club playing a stringed instrument, followed by an image of a woman playing a similar instrument. Although we are being shown the woman's cultural development, at the same time this is an image of a Far Eastern folk musician that appears to portray the playing of the song we can hear. Similarly, the film-song genre enabled Vertov to recall the reflexivity of his earlier films, by making the music a theme of the film, so that its role here was explicit. Here Vertov seems to be accepting art, in the guise of music, provided it is in some sense thematised in the course of the film. Compared with *Enthusiasm*, where there was a displacing of music by found sound, this is a further step back from the rigorous sense of documentary as a form renouncing mediation.

While the folk songs still smacked of documentary, the film has other music too. Indeed, it can be argued that it has a musical hierarchy in which the Western orchestral forms of Shaporin's music ultimately prevail, while the folk songs simply 'add local colour and credibility'.[50] In his diaries, Vertov frequently complains of the limitations of his sound equipment. It may be that these obstacles prevented him recording as much location sound and as many folk songs as he wished.[51] Moreover, while the film ends with Shaporin's strident martial band music, this is something of an automatic conclusion. The role played by the songs is pivotal as the central image and motif, the source of the imagery, and even as the model for the film's structure. The idea of the sung tribute to Lenin enables the combination of archive and present-day footage as an image of Lenin's enduring legacy.

However, the deeper problem that seems to hinder Vertov's use of Central Asian folk songs is that their messages are not explicit enough, or at least not to Vertov's anticipated Russian and Western audience. Here cultural difference is a barrier, so that, rather than representing something, the songs risk standing for the unvariegated category of Central Asian folk music. This is presumably why Vertov inserts a number of Western musical themes with unmistakable associations for his audience, employing them almost as he employs stock archive shots of famine or ruin. Chopin's funeral march signifies death and mourning, Tchaikovsky's *Swan Lake* evokes water and elegance, the trumpet and drum suggest revolutionary awakening, and the *Internationale* stands for the universal appeal of Communism.

These limitations are clear in the first song, where the folk song accompanying shots of veiled women and men praying is interrupted by an image of a woman reading next to a window and a bugle call. The intertitle then announces the arrival of Lenin, 'the light of truth', and we see marching Pioneers blowing bugles. As the woman leaves the house to go to the women's club, the music returns to folklore. The bugle as an image of revolutionary awakening is, of course, familiar in Vertov's work from *Enthusiasm*, but here the director inserts Western music with a clear meaning, rather than an appropriate Central Asian folksong.

Similarly, in the third song, folk music announces that a visit to the mausoleum will cause grief to drain away like water. This notion, established by folk song, is illustrated through shots of a Red Square gymnastics display, shots of irrigation, a woman with a small child, abundant ripe vegetables and a dandelion. These are all linked up by Tchaikovsky's *Swan Lake*. The music suggests elegance and water, and the theme of water is expanded by shots of the Dniepr hydroelectric dam. It is also evoked by the snow of Lenin's funeral, on the bench in Gorki, and by the ice of the *Cheliuskin* expedition, which is shown turning to water as the explorers arrive in Moscow. Water, from a theme of grief, becomes an image of a dynamic new society. The theme of electricity as the generation of light through water neatly synthesises the film's imagery. Lenin is repeatedly associated with light, but his death is associated with water. The water of mourning becomes the water of the dam producing the light of electricity.

In each case the song sets the tone, but Vertov requires Western music to enhance the film's imagery. The search for a form accessible to the predominantly Russian-speaking audiences led to the folk song, but also limited its use. Similarly, the film's most extensive use of synchronised sound comes in the final song, in which Russians speak.

The Interview

In adapting his method to sound film, Vertov once more innovated by introducing a journalistic form: the interview.[52] In part the interview was a response to criticism that *Enthusiasm* gave more space to machines than to human beings.[53] Nevertheless, this was a consistent extension of Vertov's conception of documentary. While it would, of course, be impossible to interview someone without him or her being aware of it, Vertov did nevertheless strive to catch the subject off-guard during an interview, to see beyond the performed veneer to the 'moment of nonacting'.[54] Clearly, this would be a challenge, since synchronised sound in the Soviet Union already tended to mean the performance of a previously memorised speech. Vertov, however, claimed to have revealed the unrehearsed 'synchrony of word and thought' in his interview with the concrete worker Maria Belik in *Three Songs of Lenin*,[55] and counted it among his greatest achievements.[56] While he claimed that Belik's interview even moves foreigners ignorant of Russian,[57] it has been commentators sensitive to the nuances of the language who most persuasively praise the natural and vivid feel of this interview.[58]

There is debate as to whether or not this is the first sound interview, but it is certainly among the earliest, and among the best of the earliest.[59] It is the way in which Maria Belik tells us about herself rather than what she tells us that grants insight into her feelings. She uses dialect, has verbal ticks, forgets words and imparts a human dimension to the cliché of the Lenin Medal-winning worker. The result approximates the modern interview.

Quite how significant Vertov's achievement was in having sound interviews recorded on location is implicitly acknowledged by the (London) Film Society's inclusion of the verbatim text of the speech in the programme for their showing of *Three Songs of Lenin* in 1935. Aptly it was screened alongside Arthur Elton's *Housing Problems* [UK, 1935], likewise innovative in its location recording of talking heads.[60] However, not only does it predate *Housing Problems* but its interviews are less stilted. Nevertheless, both films make significant strides towards what was for the 1930s 'the impossible ideal of using sound to make subjects come alive on location'.[61] The Maria Belik interview indicated the way Vertov would develop documentary in the sound era: towards synchronised recordings and the interview, even when this became a highly marginal practice in the late 1930s and the 1940s, as the so-called 'voice of God' voice-over came to dominate. Moreover, Vertov's use of the interview pointed ahead, beyond the norms of his era, to the 1960s revolution in documentary film-making.

For Vertov, this hostility to the voice-over is a resistance to the domination of film by words informed by his commitment to the purity of filmic expression. He continues to resist demands for a preliminary written description of the editing,[62] and contrasts 'film-originals' with 'films translated from the theatrical and literary language'.[63] This was a point of principle, as Svilova makes clear:

> The film was constructed with no voice-over, so we never had to rely on explanatory material: the images were set out so that the author's ideas could be discerned clearly and distinctly.
>
> We experienced incredible and incomparable delight when this or that episode could be understood without voice-over.[64]

In this manner the film disrupted the primacy of the spoken word. Vertov sees the film as entering the spectator's mind directly, needing no 'translation' into words. A voice-over would make the spectator into a listener. This would be acceptable only if the material was of a low standard and could not be made sense of without commentary, but this is a Vertov film.[65] The spoken word here is that of the interviewees or Lenin: voices that have value as documentary recordings. They do not occupy the privileged position of a voice-over, even if Lenin's words are repeated to underline the revolution's original international promise. As with *Man with a Movie Camera* and *Enthusiasm*, with *Three Songs of Lenin* Vertov felt he had succeeded in articulating a universally accessible 'image-language', and saw H.G. Wells's praise for the film's clarity without translation as proof of success.[66]

A further factor enabling Vertov to dispense with voice-over is his use of intertitles. While sometimes seen as a shortcoming,[67] or indicative of an aesthetic that 'straddles the boundaries between sound and silence',[68] in fact the intertitles are intrinsic to the film's international aspirations and exploration of distance and difference. With their Russian quotations from the song lyrics the intertitles introduce the issue of translation, a further marker of geographical and cultural distance, where the more conventional voice-over translation would have drowned out their sound, stripping them of their characteristic flavour.[69] If the film is to contain documentary recordings of songs, then intertitles are appropriate. But to what extent is this film a documentary, and how does it relate to what passed for documentary in 1934?

Three Songs of Lenin as Prototype for Stalinist Documentary

It has been claimed that *Three Songs of Lenin* became a prototype for Soviet documentary film in the 1930s and beyond.[70] In fact, a brief comparison with subsequent Soviet documentaries confirms that the film had little influence and few imitators in the Soviet Union. Certainly, it was not typical of the film-song genre as it developed later that decade, and stands head and shoulders above other Stalin-era documentaries on the Lenin theme. An indicative example of such films is *Lenin*, a 1938 full-length feature by Vertov's former protégé, Ilya Kopalin. As with all films of this genre, including Vertov's own, *Lenin* has to solve the problem posed by the dearth of actual archive footage. The film begins promisingly by concentrating on the revolution and employs much of the footage of Lenin used by Vertov and Shub, although here it is shown to undistinguished musical accompaniment. After taking only half a reel to reach 1924 and Lenin's death, the rest of the first reel is taken up with Stalin's interpretation of Lenin's legacy. The remaining five reels are devoted to the achievements of Stalin's Russia in the subsequent 14 years. This is presented in strident voice-over, with occasional synchronised speeches by Stalin and his closest associates.

Mikhail Romm's 1949 film *Vladimir Ilich Lenin* is a similarly unbalanced documentary treatment of the theme. While it is like *Lenin* in its linear chronological structure, this film treats the whole of Lenin's life, and thus he survives until reel seven of an 11-reel film. Even so, over a third of the film treats Stalin and the accomplishments of the Soviet Union after Lenin's death. The film's historical sweep informs its use of oil paintings to portray scenes from Lenin's early life not captured in photographs or on film, but soon manipulates these images to show Stalin by Lenin's side at crucial moments, thus presenting a misleading sense of Stalin's prominence in the pre-Revolutionary Party and the October Revolution. This kind of misuse of painting became common in Stalin-era documentaries.[71]

While Svilova successfully sought out fresh footage of Lenin for the film,[72] *Three Songs of Lenin* does not simply compensate for the paucity of footage by extending the chronology beyond his death. It is not concerned primarily to demonstrate the continuity between Lenin and Stalin. Rather, it starts in a vaguely defined Central Asia at an ambiguous time and sets about illustrating the liberating effect Lenin had on Moslem women. The first song is a kind of allegory of revolution. Only then are we presented with images of Lenin, at the end of the first song and in the second. These come in the form of a flashback to Lenin's life from within the flashback to his funeral. The whole of the second song's evocation of Lenin is presented as a kind of memorial meeting whereby events are recalled by modern-day Central Asian women. The result is a refracted image of Lenin as inspiration and metaphor for revolution and freedom: not so much Lenin as legitimisation of the state and anointer of Stalin, but tributes to him and perceptions of him. The film explicitly thematises the distance of contemporary Soviet citizens from Lenin, and the loss of him, rather than promising Lenin and giving Stalin. Care is taken to resist the image of a unique and mystically wise Lenin but, rather, delicately to balance his exceptional status and his accessibility.[73] This is far from a 'fascistic' vision of people and leader.[74] In fact, Vertov's vision of Lenin's continuity was a problematic one, since Stalin's role is peripheral even in the original film, and was a probable reason for its difficult reception in Russia.[75]

This issue is, of course, clouded by textology: altered before release so that already in 1934 the film no longer existed in its 'author's original version',[76] a silent edition was then produced in 1935, and both films were then re-edited in 1938 so as to insert more footage of Stalin in the third song.[77] The 1938 silent version in particular corresponds to this shift in portrayals of historical subject matter, with Stalin dominating the third song, and uses an oil painting of Fanny Kaplan's assassination attempt on Lenin as a historical document in the film's new preface. However, the version most widely available today is a restoration released in 1970, which cuts out all references to Stalin, even those present in the original, so that even the synchronised recordings are edited because two of the speakers praise Stalin. Furthermore, it retains material from the 1938 version, such as the Spanish Communist orator Dolores Ibarruri (La Pasionaria) and female combatants from the Spanish Civil War.[78]

While it was always possible to re-edit a documentary, its capacity to project the mythic and Stalinist vision of history would still be hampered by its unfortunate reliance on actual recordings.[79] This is the weakness of the documentaries of Kopalin and Romm, and largely explains their marginality in Stalinist culture. For all Vertov's brilliance in reworking documents,[80] a major reason *Three Songs of Lenin* failed to give due prominence to Stalin was the simple fact that there exists little footage of him with Lenin. As Peter Kenez puts it: '[D]ocumentaries, however remotely, ultimately depend on reality.'[81] No matter how hard they tried to stage and falsify, they were never quite as good at it as acted historical films, which were completely free to delete and invent.[82] These, and not documentaries, were the key cultic films establishing the Stalinist version of Lenin, and Stalin's discipleship. *Three Songs of Lenin* retains some commitment to film as record, and was no less of an affront to the cinema establishment than Vertov's. Documentaries were marginalised by the stress upon historical films, which were given the lion's share of resources.[83]

Yet the truth claims both of documentary film and historical reconstructions depended on a climate of voices corroborating them. The unanimous acclaim for *Lenin in October* [Lenin v oktiabre, 1937] contrasts sharply with reactions to Eisenstein's *October* [Oktiabr', 1927], which may be considered the first attempt on film to portray Lenin using an actor.[84] Here there was widespread condemnation, and reflection upon the rights and wrongs of the whole enterprise. Osip Brik argues:

Eisenstein...resorted to the most disgraceful method, one of profound vulgarity: he got someone who looked like Lenin to play the role of Lenin. The result is a disgraceful forgery, which is believeable only for people completely insensitive to historical truth.[85]

Shub agreed:

A historical fact cannot be staged, because staging distorts fact. Vladimir Ilich cannot be replaced by an actor's performance and someone who looks like Vladimir Ilich. [...]

In these things what is needed is the historical truth, the facts, the document, and the greatest possible rigour in execution. What is needed is newsreel.[86]

Even Sergei Tretiakov, Eisenstein's one-time collaborator, warned prophetically of the dangers of 'staged newsreel':

[C]ounterfeit newsreel, no matter how good it is, will only encourage the growth of those vulgar interests of the spectator and weaken the resistance of the spectator to fictional falsification.[87]

By the 1930s such resistance was all but non-existent, as is clear from one worker's reaction to Mikhail Romm's *Lenin in October*: 'I never saw Lenin, but I am convinced that is precisely how he must have been.'[88] This view is not challenged by critics as naïve or ill-informed but treated as authoritative. Unlike Vertov's or Eisenstein's 1920s Lenin films, *Lenin in October* was a film for the new generation, who could not remember Lenin. The film created the illusion of presence, as *Chapaev* had. Partly this was due to the realist veneer of the film, praised for being un-obtrusive and invisible.[89] This serves to deny the spectator's distance from the Lenin era, in precisely the opposite way to Vertov's thematisation of contemporary distance from it.

Reviewers universally proclaim *Lenin in October* to be historically accurate. One commentator talks of 'the documentarily verified sequence of events occurring in the film, and the historical accuracy of every detail'.[90] Not a single voice breaks ranks to point out the outrageous distortions of the film, such as the omission of Trotsky, or the undue prominence of Stalin.[91] *Pravda* similarly stresses the 'documentary truthfulness' of Boris Shchukin's performance as Lenin.[92] Only one of a number of reviews to use the words 'truthful' and 'accurate', this is of course complete nonsense: the film is, in fact, an outrageous fabrication, but, as with *Chapaev*, what is unusual about the Soviet historical film as opposed to, for example, Hollywood films is that the films are hailed as an accurate historical record, and the factual distortions passed over in silence. Rather, the film is treated as painstakingly accurate. No critics claimed westerns to be accurate reconstructions of historical events: 'The genre's main thrust has always been to fictionalise, to break free from history, first into legend, then swiftly, as it gathered cultural gravitas, to enter the imagination of both American and European readers as myth.'[93] As this comparison shows, in presenting mythified images, Soviet cinema is essentially doing the same as Hollywood, but the crucial difference is the way in which these images are indexed, the way in which their critical reception defines them as actually occurring. A purely textual analysis of these films is incapable of enabling us to understand this. We can grasp this important point only by considering their critical reception. As André Bazin puts it: '[T]he only difference between Stalin and Tarzan is that the films devoted to the latter do not claim to be rigorous documentaries.'[94]

Yet, if Tarzan films never claimed to be documentary, Lenin and Stalin films strove to entertain. While stressing *Lenin in October*'s faultless historical accuracy, reviewers also insist it is superior to the 'craven empiricism', or 'photographic naturalism', of documentary in its engaging form and sense of the deeper meaning of events. Writing in 1938, S. Tsimbal in particular is clearly polemicising with Vertov as he stresses the inadmissibility of documentary for a film about Lenin:

> In working on a film about Vladimir Ilich Lenin the arbitrary treatment of facts and any kind of historical inaccuracies for the sake of the plot composition and structure of the film would have been equally unthinkable and impermissible. But just as unforgivable here would be the detached, anaemic pedantry, the cold arrogance of collectors of facts and documents content with 'the fact as such', with dry documentation as proof of the reliability of the film's account.[95]

According to Tsimbal, *Lenin in October* successfully avoids both of these pitfalls. What is fascinating here is the fact that, in praising this historical film, he argues that documentary is inadequate for the representation of the Lenin theme.[96]

> [Soviet spectators] greedily seized upon the small number, and unfortunately, inadequate newsreel shots recording the image of the living Lenin. But spectators were not satisfied with these shots. They wanted to see, and not only see but also hear Lenin, to recognise in his cinema image all of his fascination, to get a complete and true picture of him. And for this newsreel was no use. It took an artist to reconstruct the image of Lenin, to present it to spectators as hundreds of millions of people preserve it in their hearts.[97]

Only dramatic reconstructions can create an image of Lenin that corresponds to how people feel about him. Documentary is incapable of successfully combining entertainment and ideology to do this.[98] Indeed, this had been required of Soviet documentary no less than of Soviet fiction film since the 1928 conference. These attitudes explain why *Three Songs of Lenin* was received in a lukewarm manner, and why Vertov found it increasingly difficult to make films. Documentaries were simply superfluous, since acted reconstructions could do the same thing better and more quickly.[99]

Nevertheless, if documentary and fiction were to be judged according to the same criteria, did this point to a slippage between the two categories?

One of the foremost cultural historians of the Stalin era, Katerina Clark, has argued that the distinction between fiction and fact in this era became increasingly difficult to maintain:

> The distinctions between ordinary reality and fiction lost the crucial importance they have in other philosophical systems.
>
> At this time, as at no other, the boundaries between fiction and fact became blurred. In all areas of public life…the difference between fiction and fact, between theater and political event, between literary plot and factual reporting, all became somewhat hazy.[100]

This demand for dramatic reworking and entertainment was, effectively, extended to real life. The theatrical effect of the show trials was not only scripted but rehearsed, and we cannot be entirely sure which version was recorded: the rehearsal or the final performance.[101] These highly performative political events can even be analysed according to the prescriptions of melodrama.[102] Life was a spectacle. Documentary as a distinct category was doomed.

7

Years of Sound and Silence: *Lullaby*

In the stifling and hostile atmosphere of the Soviet 1930s Vertov became an ever more marginal figure. His kind of documentary was a threateningly good example of the true possibilities of the medium now traduced. Until recently discussions of Vertov's work passed over this last period in silence, either because of its perceived lesser stature or because it involved considering Vertov's contribution to the Stalin cult, a difficult subject for Soviet and Western enthusiasts alike.[1] Nevertheless, between finishing *Three Songs of Lenin* and the end of World War II Vertov was able to make a number of films that deserve to be seen as a distinct final phase of his film-making career. While these works usually stand out from the typical films of the period, *Lullaby* alone bears comparison with his greatest achievements. However, these final films are punctuated by longer intervening periods of creative silence.

The Films not Made

At the 1935 All-Union Conference of Creative Workers in Cinema the new Soviet cinema was said to be characterised by 'optimism, heroism and theatricality'. While the conference spent a great deal of time criticising the old guard of directors, especially Eisenstein, Vertov was largely ignored.[2] The debate about documentary film was already considered resolved. However, the term 'documentalism' was still occasionally invoked in discussions of Soviet film as an example of an unacceptable commitment to documentary as recording. A good example of this came in Boris Shumiatsky's programmatically entitled book 'A Cinema for the Millions', in which *Three Songs of Lenin* is praised precisely for its supposed renunciation of documentalism.

Meanwhile, Vertov was busy convincing himself his persecution was over.[3] He seemed never to grasp that acted films were being elevated as the new truth, and that documentaries were playing an ever more subservient role. Instead, he continued to maintain the distinction between documentary and acted film,[4] arguing that *Chapaev* and *Three Songs of Lenin* represented the respective paths of development for newsreel and acted film, and kept clamouring for more attention and respect to be shown his work, and that of documentary and newsreel in general. To make and maintain the distinction between acted film and newsreel or documentary was to expose the fakery of the staged films. Consequently, Vertov found it increasingly difficult to make films, completing only three feature-length films in the period 1935–1941. However, this was not inactivity but, rather, the inability to get his proposals funded or accepted. Failing to adapt to new conditions in which scope for individuality was minimal, Vertov repeatedly demanded to make films with complete creative freedom.[5] Other directors with fewer pretensions and less talent prospered, but Vertov found himself repeatedly stymied.[6] Mezhrabpom, who had produced *Three Songs of Lenin,* closed down in June 1936, while he was preparing his next film, *Lullaby.*[7] Vertov succeeded in completing the film only after writing a number of letters to Soviet cinema boss Boris Shumiatsky.[8] The effort was sapping his mental strength, draining the incredible reserves of energy and optimism that had sustained him for so long.[9]

The Birth of *Lullaby*

The genesis of *Lullaby* dates back to a 1933 proposal for a film about a composer writing a symphony contrasting the position of women under capitalism and socialism.[10] If this initial conception of the film relates to the period when Vertov was filming *Three Songs of Lenin, Lullaby* is also similar to that film in its exploration of an international theme primarily through images of Soviet Far Eastern women. Initially, the film was to dwell a great deal more on the pre-Revolutionary and foreign repression of women, especially prostitution and the sexual exploitation of women more generally, which was in turn to be associated with sexualised images in Western films, epitomised by the Hollywood star Mae West.[11] This made the nature of the exploitation less exclusively Islamic and more universalised, giving it something of the internationalist perspective of *A Sixth Part of the World.* The completed film shifted focus towards the Soviet Union and the present day.

Moreover, like *Three Songs of Lenin*, *Lullaby* is also about women, but this time with a shift towards motherhood and children. As we saw in Chapter 4, this change dates back to *Man with a Movie Camera*. There may be personal reasons for this: although Vertov and Svilova were childless, Svilova had a miscarriage sometime between 1924 and 1926, after which references to childbirth, children and the adoption of a female perspective steadily increase in the films and unrealised proposals.[12]

An alternative explanation for the shift is that Vertov adopts a female persona as a reaction to the suffering, powerless role forced upon him by cinema's authorities.[13] If, earlier in his career, he idealised the masculine world of work, demolition and physical strength, increasingly Vertov's focus is upon a feminine sensibility and less aggressive forms of self-realisation. Yet it seems likely that it is not just Vertov adopting a female perspective but that Vertov and Svilova become an ever closer creative partnership, as Svilova outgrows her role simply as editor, or 'editing assistant'. This seems to be corroborated by the fact that she becomes increasingly prominent in film credits: the pair appear as co-directors in the credits for *Lullaby* and *In Memory of Sergo Ordzhonikidze*, and Svilova is listed as co-author of the scenario in *Three Heroines*. By the end of the war she is offered more work than Vertov. Vertov adopts something of a female point of view, but Svilova expresses her view through Vertov, and gains ever greater influence over the writing and directing of the films. In this last period, even more than earlier, it becomes increasingly difficult to distinguish Vertov and Svilova.

Lullaby: An Analysis

Lullaby poses the question: what is happiness? Its responses are motherhood and October, shown as opening up all paths to women's development. In order to convince us of this not terribly self-evident association, the film uses a range of means to associate joyous motherhood with the revolution. In essence, the method employed is a development of the earlier documentary approach. The ongoing importance of documentary reference for the film is clear from the many drafts for the scenario, where initially the main characters had real prototypes and were named.[14] However, this was increasingly allied to the idea of the film as a song.[15] One version of the scenario describes the film in the following terms:

> The plan I am submitting
> is the plan for a musical

and poetical
and graphic
and documentary
work.[16]

The words of the eponymous song sung by Soviet mothers to their children are the first and most straightforward way of linking motherhood and October:

Joy in October rose above the Earth.
Sleep, my little girl, sleep.
Joy is rocking with you in the cradle.
Sleep, my little girl, sleep.

The use of songs also adopts an ostensibly documentary strategy. However, whereas Vertov claimed that *Lullaby* was his 'fourth song based on folk material',[17] it seems unlikely that there were original folkloric sources for it. Certainly, there are not even the snippets of original recorded materials we hear in *Three Songs of Lenin*. Similarly, the music and words are original compositions by Daniel and Dmitri Pokrass and by Vasili Lebedev-Kumach (lyricist for Grigori Alexandrov's *Circus* [Tsirk, 1936] and *Volga-Volga* [1938]).[18] *Lullaby* was close in conception to a 'film-song'. By now these were, typically, five-minute films such as *Higher and Higher* [Vse vyshe, 1940], a film-song which features a white dot bouncing over the lyrics, karaoke-style, to help the audience sing along.[19] This film showed pictures of airmen flying over the Arctic and singing *The Aviators' March*, a much-reprised celebration of airmen's heroism, and general ability to make fairy tales come true. Similarly, *Lullaby* puts the songs in the mouths of the women.

In this film, though, presenting the song as sung by the mothers is less a genuine claim to a profilmic model and more a narrative strategy, one long employed in, for example, the art of the novel, where a frame narrator claims to have heard the tale or found the memoir which forms the central story of the work. Again, here, the distinct nature of documentary has been accommodated to the structure and representational approach characteristic of realism, and has become indistinguishable from art, whereas in *Three Songs of Lenin* the songs truly were found, and had real referents that pre-existed the making of the film. Vertov, like a folklorist, records them. In *Lullaby*, the claim to have discovered a found object is a fiction, a device intended to endow the art work with the aura of the real.

However, in its photography *Lullaby* employs more convincingly documentary methods to press home its central message. There is a consistent attempt to photograph unactable states: notably, we see shots of the main subject laughing in a very spontaneous and carefree way with a friend at a demonstration, or the women walking down the street who laugh when they see the camera, as well as a whole succession of children laughing. Through their laughter the women and children provide a concrete example of happiness, and serve to give concrete life to the notion of motherhood as joyful. Likewise, we also see a large number of shots of women breastfeeding their babies. In each case these are authentic, unactable states that are being recorded as part of a powerful, highly emotive rendering of childhood and motherhood.

Vertov's documentary approach is again evident in the decision to shoot most of the film outside, as he had almost exclusively in his earlier works.[20] In particular, the children are often photographed swinging in hammocks bathed in sunlight. However, for all their authenticity, nowhere here does Vertov appear to be employing hidden or caught off-guard photography. In *Lullaby* Vertov again returns to the theme of the Soviet Far East, and again uses the notion of the lifting of the veil employed in *Three Songs of Lenin*. Indeed, in this film the image serves to underpin the film's core association of motherhood and October, since the Soviet woman's happiness is defined by the fact that she is free of the veil. Just as in *Three Songs of Lenin*, the Soviet woman of the Far East is made an image of liberated vision, only here it is a liberation that is far in the past. In addition to which, through the notion of childbirth, Vertov's women are now doubly associated with creativity: the mother is the film-maker or artist. This is a masked reflexive theme. While in earlier films the lifting of the veil sequence sometimes looked incongruously staged, here this is the dominant aesthetic. The veil-lifting is one of a number of very obviously posed scenes, in which Vertov has the subject standing next to a bust of Lenin or reading a book while standing next to a window. Moreover, the scenes from Red Square, from congresses and the shots of Stalin are by their very nature highly theatrical. This is presumably why it is sometimes said of Vertov that his final films are staged: 'It is, with its highly posed subjects and staged events, little more than a propaganda piece.'[21]

However, we need to consider what staging means in this context. Certainly, this film uses little hidden camera or caught off-guard filming. Nevertheless, many of these instances can still be treated as reconstruction. For all the posed nature of these scenes, they are not rehearsed or scripted, or at least not by Vertov, and there is little or no studio photography.

In its use of sound *Lullaby* shows a similar commitment to documentary, but not without further accommodation to prevailing norms. This compromise is particularly evident, as we have seen, in his use of

song, which is markedly less documentary than in *Three Songs of Lenin*. However, Vertov uses an incredible quantity of synchronous sound recording compared with other documentary films of the time, and his subjects rarely speak scripted words, apart from speeches at congresses, which are effectively scripted anyway. For films of the late 1930s and early 1940s this was a strong and coherent reformulation of documentary principles for sound.

While the vitality and ingenuity of sound in Soviet documentary films of the early 1930s gave way during the late 1930s and 1940s to the impersonal, authoritative 'voice of God' commentary and the occasional dubbed sound effect, *Lullaby* at least succeeds in avoiding voice-over commentary. While this was not completely outlandish or unusual for 1937, it was indicative of a resistance that held out essentially for as long as Vertov was able to control the films he made. Avoiding the sound voice-over commentary in favour of silent-style intertitles is clearly a choice motivated by a desire not to disturb the visual integrity of the film by making voice the generator of meaning.

Beyond the specialised recordings of dances, ensembles and songs, the few synchronised sequences were typically speeches interpolated in films dominated by the voice-over. The unwieldy nature of sound recording equipment meant that as late as 1960 Soviet documentary film-makers still divided their shooting plan up into sound and silent sequences, and had more silent cameramen than sound operators to a ratio of 1:10. The ratio of sound to silent sequences was similar.[22] Those synchronised sequences permitted are typically at the ideological heart of the film: one of the film's most significant moments. For Karmen's *Moscow–Kara-Kum–Moscow* it is a tribute to Stalin, and even in Yuli Raizman's *Berlin* [1945] it is the voice of General Helmuth Weidling conceding Germany's defeat. Vertov's synchronised sequences stand out in this context, in that they record the voice of relatively simple people: a concrete worker (*Three Songs of Lenin*) and a parachutist (*Lullaby*). Sometimes heroic in their way, certainly, but simple, accessible, part of the mass at the same time. They are not scripted or politically the central point of the film. This is Vertov's way of maintaining his dedication to the cause of recording, to the indexical mission of documentary. It was as if synchronous sound's potential for introducing the unexpected was at odds with Stalinist film.[23]

Discussion of sound in *Lullaby* tends to concentrate, with great justification, on the interview with the female parachutist. Truly, this is a remarkable sequence, in that she comes across in a completely natural way; we even see her pick her nose. Moreover, we can hear the voice of the film-maker (presumably Vertov) asking her questions about how she felt when she completed the parachute jump. She even expresses fear and weakness: 'If I thought about it I wouldn't have jumped,' she says, and laughs. Somewhere in the background we hear a hen clucking, and from time to time she looks at the camera. The effect is incredibly fresh and spontaneous. Comparisons are sometimes made with the Maria Belik interview in *Three Songs of Lenin*. There are good reasons for such comparisons, although the parachutist gives far more of a genuine interview, which is much more revealing of the person.

Reel two of *Lullaby* provides an excellent example of Vertov's skilful use of synchronised sound. This section seeks to show the wealth of opportunities available to the Soviet child and uses a whole range of synchronised sequences. What is particularly noteworthy here is the clever use of the sound bridge to link scenes, so that, even though the sound is recorded on location, it may be used to accompany another shot. The first shot of the reel shows a girl in shorts running out of her house, something of a literalisation of the previous intertitle, the last shot of the first reel: 'All paths are open before you.' The sound accompanying this image is that of someone playing the piano, and the film then cuts to a small girl practising the piano, before cutting to Pioneers hiking, children painting and a rose budding, all to the same piece of music. In this sequence Vertov brilliantly demonstrates his commitment to the location recording of sound, while at the same time avoiding the tedious trap of forcing sound to illustrate the image. As a result we have a musical image of learning the piano, which becomes an image of creativity interacting with the images of painting, flowering and the journey, before ultimately returning to the title song of the film. Vertov uses similar sound bridges, such as that of machine sounds to accompany other scenes of work, or that of a child singing to accompany images of a woman preparing for a parachute jump. In Vertov's hands the sound bridge has become an instrument of montage, a way of linking together images to suggest associations or concepts.

It may be argued that the film, in particular the first two reels, is very much still a montage film, a sense enhanced by the lack of a voice-over. The expressive nature of the montage is clear particularly at the beginning of the film, where the question 'what is happiness?' is answered by an extreme close-up of the woman's eyes. An intertitle then says '...you thought about the answer for a long time', and we see the woman standing next to her friend looking pensive. The next intertitle, '...and you answered', cues a montage sequence beginning with a close-up of the woman marching at a demonstration with her eyes lowered, before cutting to a close-up of her face next to a bust of Lenin in the background. The same two women are then shown at demonstration, laughing and smiling with eyes clearly visible, before switching to a shot of the first woman

reading next to a window. The music and pace of the shots reach a crescendo as we see a shot of a child next to a Communist banner and a woman next to babies in a hospital.

This is a montage sequence which would not look out of place in Vertov's 1920s films. Its purpose is to show a process of thought about happiness covering friendship, educational opportunity and political activism, and culminating in motherhood. These themes are all characteristic of happiness, the sequence seems to suggest, but motherhood, a motherhood made free and fulfilling by the revolution, is the greatest happiness of all.

The images of flowering, learning and of life's journey ultimately lead to Moscow and to Stalin. This is very much in keeping with the official Stalin cult, and the film has been duly condemned for its hagiographical portrayal perpetuating the myth of Stalin the sole masculine stimulus for a female nation, the father of 140 million Soviet 'daughters'.[24] However, it is worth considering the images of Stalin in the wider context of such portrayals, especially in newsreel and documentary. Vertov shows Stalin from a high angle, not the more accepted low angle, and we see a huge number of images of women and children embracing him and giving him flowers. Vertov seems to be attempting to use his, and Svilova's, skill in collating and editing archive footage to assemble and present an image of Stalin as more human and more approachable than is the norm in portrayals of him. There is even an extreme close-up in reel three in which the pockmarks on his face are quite clearly visible. *Lullaby* is conceived as a contribution to the Stalin myth, but Vertov's commitment to documentary and his striving, as a film-maker, to finding unusual angles and images results in it presenting a somewhat original image of Stalin. But Stalin does not succeed in pushing aside the opening theme of motherhood and happiness,[25] or, indeed, the film's engaging formal qualities. There are undoubtedly many jarring, incongruous elements to the combination Vertov is attempting in this film. As one critic has put it, Vertov unsuccessfully attempted to combine a Stalinist message with a Formalist style.[26] While not exactly Formalist, the style of the film does not represent a significant break with his earlier work. It can rightly be called the last echo of modernism.[27] But was this ambiguity really the reason for the film's strange fate?[28]

Why was *Lullaby* Removed?

Lullaby was released on 1 November 1937, in a number of lesser Moscow cinemas. Despite generally positive reviews, it was removed from Moscow screens on 6 November.[29] Although not banned, why was it taken off so soon?

There are a number of possible explanations.[30] One problem with the film may have been the expectations Shumiatsky in particular had of it. Clearly supportive of Vertov's film-song, as is evident from Vertov's appeals to him,[31] Shumiatsky imagined it would launch the eponymous song, giving it unprecedented popularity as *Circus* had for 'Song of the Motherland'.[32] Shumiatsky spelt out his hopes for the film at a speech before a preliminary screening:

> In this film together with the directors, with the author, we set ourselves...the task of producing a song that would be good for mobilising the masses, and at the same time would be ideologically targeted, which would come down from the screen and pass through territories, through spaces, and would enter the everyday life of our country and through the foreign tours of our wonderful light orchestras, through popular word of mouth would be transmitted to toiling masses abroad.
>
> We are sure, and I personally am very sure, that in this film, as an essential element entering and comprising it organically, we have created such a song.[33]

Effectively, Shumiatsky staked his reputation on the success of the film. But the film that really impressed at this anniversary was *Lenin in October*. Its success was literally a fatal blow to Shumiatsky, since it was completed so quickly, in contrast to so many of the other works he supervised. *Lullaby*, promoted by the outgoing Shumiatsky, was tainted by his patronage.

Whether or not Shumiatsky's demise was behind *Lullaby*'s disappearance, the scenario in itself illustrates the petrifying atmosphere of fear that pervaded the Soviet film industry at this time. Fear of putting a foot wrong was slowing down the whole cinematic process, with bureaucrats obstructing films so as neither to permit or ban them.[34] The first major documentary about Stalin was a prospect that simultaneously attracted and paralysed those in charge at Soviet newsreel studios for these reasons, and their reaction may well have been to kill the film softly.[35] This was like the Hollywood genre system, but with the added element of physical, not financial, fear. To innovate was to run the risk not of ruin but of arrest, torture and death. Indeed, the terror caused the film to be re-edited to remove images of people who had been arrested. Later head of secret police Nikolai Yezhov too was edited out: he had since been shot and replaced by Lavrenti Beria. But these were relatively minor changes to the film that would present no bar to its distribution.[36]

The absence of a review in *Pravda* supports the rumour that Stalin himself had indicated his displeasure at the film.[37] It appears Stalin did not appreciate documentary film in general,[38] and was particularly worried about appearing in photographs and films, leading to *Pravda* representing him exclusively in paintings.[39] It is instructive here to compare *Lullaby* with a successful Ukrainian treatment of the Stalin theme, *Song of Stalin* [Pesnia o Staline, 1938], directed by Iosif Poselsky, which appears to adopt elements of its panegyric to a distant leader from Vertov's own *Three Songs of Lenin*. This film concentrates almost exclusively on popular tributes, such as portraits, songs, tapestries and paintings devoted to the theme of Stalin. Stalin himself appears only briefly at the end, watching the villagers dancing from the mausoleum in Red Square. By rationing his presence the intention is to create a sense of timelessness and permanence, of Stalin as above history, beyond the democratising medium of photography.[40] This is, of course, directly paralleled by the use of actors to play Stalin in historical-revolutionary films. If Stalin is to appear in a feature film, it must be in a reconstruction where someone tall and handsome can play him. The fact that *Lullaby* and *Lenin in October* came out at the same time is significant: Vertov's film seemed to attempt the same elevation of Stalin, but the historical staging achieved a similar purpose a great deal more satisfactorily. *Lenin in October* was the first of this cultic genre.

Consequently, Vertov is criticised in reviews of *Lenin in October*, and at least one review of *Lullaby* criticised its 'documentalism'.[41] The most extended documentary treatment of Stalin in the pre-war period, *Lullaby*'s failure may simply be a consequence of its genre. It was still too committed to the path of recording. It was still a documentary film.

In Memory of Sergo Ordzhonikidze (1938)

It is quite possible that, after *Lullaby*, those in power in the USSR felt that they would never get precisely what they asked for from Vertov.[42] This is why he barely made another film again. Supposedly, he was told not to submit any more proposals as they would be neither read nor discussed.[43] Of those that he did submit, *A Day of the World* is typical. This was a proposal based upon an article by his long-standing acquaintance, Mikhail Koltsov, which would show various aspects of the world on a single day. Vertov proposed a trip abroad, and stressed the need to include foreign material, since, without it, 'Where is the criterion for judging what's good and what's bad?'[44] While true, this comment could be made of most Soviet documentary films, which presented a self-contained, self-proclaimed world of perfection. This was the model followed when the film was made in 1940 by Roman Karmen and Mikhail Slutsky as *A Day of the New World*, containing exclusively Soviet material.

It is claimed that Vertov's last feature-length films were indistinguishable from the mass of informational newsreel of the time.[45] As we shall see, the film usually referred to as *In Memory of Sergo Ordzhonikidze* is still very much a Dziga Vertov work. Released in February 1938, it sported the catchy title *In Memory of Sergo Ordzhonikidzhe, Ardent Fighter for the Cause of the Working Class, for the Cause of Communism, Fearless Leninist-Bolshevik, Friend and Comrade-in-Arms of Stalin the Great.* Here Vertov was co-director with Iakov Bliokh, and Svilova was an assistant director. Once again this was a 'film-song', like Vertov's previous two completed works. This time the music was by the composer and librettist team of Isaak Dunaevsky and Vasili Lebedev-Kumach, who had collaborated incredibly successfully on *Circus*.

Like *Lullaby*, this film is engaging in its use of synchronised sound. The whole first reel of the film is taken up with Sergo Ordzhonikidze making a speech at a congress, in his capacity as People's Commissar for Heavy Industry. However, rather than simply remaining on the initial shot of Ordzhonikidze speaking, the film cuts to images of various industrial processes, which accompany, and, give visual form to, his words. While some of the shots, such as those of tanks, simply illustrate the speech, others, such as those of trucks and tractors, are edited for visual effect so as to contrast movement in different directions. Photographing industrial machinery as well as editing such shots dynamically was, of course, something Vertov had been doing effectively since the early 1920s. As we shall see, this continued to be seen as his and Svilova's speciality even when they were relegated to newsreel editing towards the end of the war.

Throughout the rest of the film Vertov uses a great number of synchronised sequences; he also introduces the song, a powerful song sung by a passionate off-screen male voice. The music and words combine feelings of loss with a sense of ultimate victory, epitomised by the refrain 'No, it will not grow cold, a heart such as this is present in every victory'.

As is the case with many 'film-songs', the finale presents the words of the song line by line so as to help the audience sing along. However, in this film, Vertov employs a voice-over commentary to a greater extent than ever before, although even then he does so sparingly, and primarily for continuity, to identify locations such as Ordzhonikidze's flat or the funeral hall. Instead, the sound of the film is dominated by the song and a range of synchronised speeches, both by Ordzhonikidze and in memory of him. Indeed, when we consider the ten-to-one ratio of synchronised to non-synchronised sound normal in this period, then here, as with the rest of his sound film, Vertov succeeds in making this work distinctly his own. Nevertheless, its subject, a leader whose suicide was covered up, ensured the film could never be very successful.

Three Heroines (1938)

In the years before the Nazi invasion of the Soviet Union, in 1941, Vertov continued to submit scenarios for a range of films on the themes of women and children, and of aviation. The most colourful of these was *A Giant's Tale*, a kind of educational *Honey, I Shrunk the Kids*. These themes came together in *Three Heroines*. Here, for the first time, Vertov and Svilova were co-directors; there was no hierarchy whatsoever established by the credits. Moreover, as with *Lullaby*, the music was composed by the Pokrass brothers, and the text of the songs written by Lebedev-Kumach. This is a further indication as to just how seriously he takes the role of music and songs in these films. *Three Heroines* employs no voice-over commentary at all, and uses a great deal of synchronised sound. As with *Lullaby* and *Sergo Ordzhonikidze*, the device of the sound bridge is used extensively, such as in an early sequence in which the voice of a man on the telephone at the control room in Moscow accompanies shots (a model) of the plane 'Rodina' flying, and an animated map of its path.

However, the merit of this use of synchronised sound must be tempered by the fact that this is a film which employs a great deal of staging – indeed, it seems to follow a script, and large parts appear to have been reconstructed in a studio. Nevertheless, it does contain some more effective synchronised sound sequences, such as an episode where the women pilots speak to their children on the telephone. We see both the women and the children, and, despite the fact that both the women and their children clearly act up in the presence of the cameras, there is a certain unfalsified tenderness here harking back to *Lullaby*. More predictable are the following extended scenes of speeches by the women to a gathering in Khabarovsk in synchronised sound. In sum, this a film that continues the film-song idea, and further demonstrates Vertov's commitment to synchronised sound as part of documentary, but it employs the studio, a written dialogue script and staging to a far greater extent than any previous Vertov film.

Once again, the song is not a found document, but written specially for the film. In its staging and use of the song, *Three Heroines* marks a further step back from a commitment to documentary. Despite these efforts to adapt, *Three Heroines* was never released.[46]

The Great Patriotic War

While in the context of the Nazi invasion, newsreel and documentary film truly came to the fore once again,[47] it was logistically impossible for a director to retain creative control over cameramen at the front. Soviet film-making in the war was a collective endeavour, with one or two notable exceptions. Vertov was one of the last to evacuate Moscow during the German advance on the city in October 1941. In Alma-Ata, where the rest of the Soviet film industry had long since relocated, Vertov was still regarded as too problematic a figure to be trusted. Moreover, he persisted in trying to make films over which he would retain artistic control. Against considerable hostility, in 1942 he succeeded in making his last feature-length film, *For You at the Front!*

Like the greater part of Vertov's previous sound films, *For You at the Front!* also bears the hallmarks of the film-song genre. Indeed, it harks back to *Three Songs of Lenin* and *Lullaby* in its use of pseudo-folklore: the beginning of the film introduces a Kazakh musician, who begins to play his lute-like stringed instrument and sing a song. This is a well-known folk singer, Nurpeis Baiganin.[48] Indeed, an earlier working title for the film had been 'Song of Saule' [Pesnia Saule].[49] Intertitles explain that this is a song about Saule intended to inspire the war effort of all the republics of the USSR. The whole film is, as it were, a song sung by this Kazakh bard. For the most part the film is conventionally narrative, but a song plays a substantial role, and towards the end the words come up in the approved film-song manner. The attraction here, as with *Three Songs of Lenin,* is not simply that the song heightens the film's expressive power but also that the story itself is not invented, it is not the creation of Vertov's imagination, but a found object, an authentic artefact. This was something of a fiction with regard to *Three Songs of Lenin*, and it is probably even more of a fiction here. What is more significant is that Vertov appears to require this mediation almost as a last vestige of documentary authenticity.

However, this *is* a vestige, because, ultimately, this is a highly scripted, highly staged film. That the main characters are not professional actors is something we can take only on trust, since stylistically the film resembles an acted, scripted film more than it resembles Vertov's documentaries of the 1920s, for example. Here, as with *Three Heroines*, we have named heroes. The difference is that we are not sure whether they are fictional or real.

One respect in which the film remains true to Vertov's vision is that it uses voice-over very sparingly, and even plays around with its conventions. We hear what initially we take to be a voice-over, but the heroine, Saule, comes out of the mine and hears what we hear: a voice announcing that her lover, Dzhamil, has accomplished heroic deeds at the front. We realise now that this is in fact a radio announcement on a loud speaker placed outside the mine. She smiles, the miners all smile and embrace her. In response, she writes a letter to Dzhamil at the front.

This device enables Vertov to display his skills in portraying industrial production to present a huge number of shots of Kazakh agriculture and industry, with particularly effective sequences portraying mining, trucks laden with coal, furnaces being stoked and metal being smelted. This may have been a war film, but Vertov remained even here firmly associated with the industrial theme. His attachment to this subject matter is possibly one reason why, in contrast to Medvedkin or to Kopalin, he did not flourish in the war's frenetic and dangerous, but ultimately favourable, conditions for Soviet documentary.[50] It is worth noting here that Vertov's greatest works had been filmed under his direct supervision, or that of his closest associates. This kind of film-making was suitable for films of industry, but not for battle conditions, where directors were rarely allowed to the front, and cameramen sent footage in to be edited at the studios.[51]

Nevertheless, it is not entirely true that Vertov made no war films about war: his 1941 short film *Blood for Blood* depicted enemy atrocities, and called on Soviet troops to avenge them. Yet this is very much the exception. Even his 1944 three-reel film *The Oath of Youth* concentrates more on the Young Communists' efforts on the home front than in battle. Indeed its most effective sequences by far are of industry: the first is a synchronised voice bridge in which a factory supervisor's voice becomes a voice-over describing the work done by each member of his shift. The second is a slow dissolve of two close-ups of cotton weaving briefly creating a double exposure in a beautiful criss-cross pattern. A poignant reminder of *Man with a Movie Camera*, Vertov and Svilova were occasionally to include slow dissolves in their final treatments of industrial themes.

For whatever reason, *For You at the Front!* was badly received by the authorities and received a third distribution category, and after several screenings at the studio did not even make it to cinemas.[52] Despite as many as 13 script proposals, this was to be Vertov's last feature-length film, after which, once newsreels turned to the subject of reconstruction, he turned exclusively to editing and made a handful of issues of *News of the Day* per year.[53]

'Creative Starvation': Final Newsreels

With such landmarks in film form as Alexander Dovzhenko's *Battle for Our Soviet Ukraine* [Bitva za nashu sovetskuiu Ukrainu, 1943] and Yuli Raizman's *Berlin*, World War II was a highpoint in Soviet film. The post-war years represented a nadir. While documentary did not suffer Soviet fiction film's fall in output, its quality suffered no less.[54] There were very few ambitious or accomplished documentaries. Typically, longer films were stylistically undistinguished recordings of particular events. In this context it was difficult if not impossible to retain a distinctive style or artistic vision. If this was true for feature-length documentaries, it was even more the case for the *News of the Day* [Novosti dnia] newsreel series. All the *News of the Day* newsreel series have a strident but solemn male voice-over accompanied by equally strident martial music, and frequently contain no synchronised recordings at all: 'The viewer was to feel that "History" was talking to him, rather than a mere mortal.'[55]

With the exception of occasional special issues (e.g. Winston Churchill's visit to Moscow in *News of the Day* no. 11, October 1944) they contain a number of subjects, sometimes as many as 12. Typically the subjects would be authored by a different cameraman from around the Soviet Union and Soviet-controlled Eastern Europe, and edited by a single 'director-editor' in Moscow.

Some editions of this series are quite effective pieces of film-making, but it is difficult to detect anything approaching a distinct authorial coherence, and most discussions of this period in Vertov's work take the generally plausible line that they are indistinguishable from the rest.[56] Nevertheless, in Vertov's and in Svilova's work it is at times possible to detect certain biases in theme and device. In particular, they are far more likely than their fellow newsreel editor-directors to conduct synchronised recordings. They are also far more likely to explore the industrial theme,

and when doing so may edit in an interesting way. An example of this is an issue edited by Svilova (*News of the Day* no. 3, January 1945) in which she uses a slow dissolve, creating a momentary double exposure of contrasting motion in shots of the construction of a turbine destined for a hydroelectric dam. This shot echoes *The Eleventh Year* strongly.

There are also faint echoes of the 1928 film in *News of the Day* no. 6 (January 1947), which explores the reconstruction of the Volkhov hydroelectric dam. Here too, slow dissolves of the dam remind the attentive viewer of the earlier work. For the most part, however, these films evoke earlier masterpieces in theme but not technique: *News of the Day* no. 43 (June 1947) has a piece about Lenin hiding in the summer of 1917. Instead of Vertov's earlier archive footage and simple testimony, statues and paintings dominate, as is typical of this era's treatments of Lenin.

As for Vertov and Svilova's greater use of synchronised sound, this is evident from probably one of the last noteworthy Soviet films of the period: Roman Karmen's *The Peoples' Court* [Sud narodov, 1946], on which Svilova worked as editor. Devoted to the Nuremburg process, this film displays many examples of Svilova's virtuoso editing, and uses a great many synchronised recordings, in particular of the indictments of the American and Russian prosecutors. Similarly, *News of the Day* no. 2 (January 1946) directed by Vertov, includes three synchronised sound speeches in treating the theme of elections for the Supreme Soviet, and in *News of the Day* no. 3 (January 1945), directed by Svilova, there is a great deal of synchronous sound recording of a meeting commemorating the twenty-first anniversary of Lenin's death. This item, the first in the issue, completely eschews voice-over commentary. When one considers that many issues of *News of the Day* contained no synchronous sound then, clearly, Vertov and Svilova were still associated with this, a final reminder of what documentary had once meant.

Even this humble newsreel work was not quite Vertov's nadir. In March 1949, in the repressive backlash against leading artists and writers, and particularly against Jews, Vertov was denounced at a special open Party meeting at the Central Documentary Film Studios. *Man with a Movie Camera* in particular was condemned for 'propagandising views that have nothing in common with the views of the Soviet people'.[57] In an autobiography written a couple of months later, Vertov deliberately omitted *Man with a Movie Camera*, knowing that its mention would do little to enhance his reputation in the Soviet Union.[58] His work on *News of the Day* slowed to a trickle. Physical death followed in February 1954. Only now, with its creator in his grave, would his masterpiece receive due acclaim, as Vertov himself achieved recognition as a seminal figure in documentary film.

8

Forward, Dziga! Foreign and Posthumous Reception

While some of Vertov's earlier newsreels and compilation films may have been shown abroad, the first foreign showing associated with his name was probably at the 1925 Paris Exposition internationale des arts décoratifs, where it seems that an excerpt from *Cine-Eye* was shown. As a result Vertov received a prize,[1] but made little immediate impact and exerted little direct influence on Western film-makers.[2] The few aware of his work were typically visitors to the Soviet Union, such as Léon Moussinac.[3]

Given the acclaim of Eisenstein and Vsevolod Pudovkin in the West, it seems Vertov was surprised to discover on his trip to Germany in 1929 that he was virtually unknown.[4] He quickly set about trying to remedy the situation, giving lectures and screenings of *Man with a Movie Camera* and excerpts from earlier works, especially *The Eleventh Year*, in at least ten German cities and in Paris, generating a great deal of press coverage. While Vertov returned to Russia at the end of July, *Man with a Movie Camera* was exhibited in New York in September, where it generated mixed reviews as 'an interesting and amusing experience'[5] and a 'hodge-podge'.[6]

If the film was not seen widely by large audiences it nevertheless left a deep impression upon a small group of intellectuals serious about film, and inspired a number of imitations.[7] In Germany the famous critic Siegfried Kracauer wrote an insightful review, which has rarely been surpassed to this day.[8] In New York *Man with a Movie Camera* was the first Soviet film seen by the future film historian and practitioner Jay Leyda. It changed him for ever.[9]

The influential London film journal *Close-Up* published reactions to the 1929 Paris and Stuttgart screenings of *Man with a Movie Camera* which already refer to Vertov's legendary status, encouraging readers to fight to see the film. Yet, despite the efforts of Ivor Montagu of the Film Society, it was not shown in Britain until January 1931.[10] The delay created a palpable sense of anticipation, which soon turned into a disappointed sense that this had been done before. The time gap made Vertov seem to be responding to Walter Ruttmann or Eisenstein. This masterpiece, the summit of achievement of silent film, a letter to the future, was seen as derivative: '[L]ess effective than "Berlin", which it naturally recalls.'[11]

Ivor Montagu treats Vertov as an errant student of Eisenstein elevating documentary into a false religion:

> Forgetting that Eisenstein and Pudovkin used real people and real things, not because they are more 'true' than actors or stage properties, but simply because they are more effective for a given arbitrary purpose, he also forgot the purpose. The real ingredient per se is good, he proclaimed, anything but the real ingredient–meretricious. Presenting a false picture.[12]

The most interesting reaction was from the 'founder of documentary film', John Grierson, whose anxiety is palpable: 'Some of us have been hearing a great deal about Kino-Eye and it has worried us considerably.'[13] Grierson's worry may well mask a hostility to Vertov's alternative vision of documentary, and a fear that it might take the form in a different direction. While recognising Vertov's use of real locations, Grierson too sees this as pre-empted by Ruttmann,[14] and objects to the film's form as 'a snapshot album. There is no story, no dramatic structure.'[15] For Grierson, Vertov's film is all record and no art. Therefore, in his terms, it is not documentary. The British documentary film-makers were more influenced by acted films such as *The Battleship 'Potemkin'* and *Earth* than by than Vertov.[16]

The Coming of Sound: *Enthusiasm* Abroad

The fact that Vertov's next film, *Enthusiasm,* was one of the first Soviet sound films presented a golden opportunity to demonstrate Soviet technical achievement. In July 1931 Vertov set out on a second trip abroad, taking in numerous towns in Germany, including Hanover, Frankfurt, Hamburg and Breslau. Vertov himself believed that sound presented documentary with an opportunity to enhance the international character of cinema, enabling 'proletarians of all nations, all countries, to see, hear and understand one another'.[17] Aided by superior Western sound facilities, enabling foreign filmgoers to hear the film better than those at home, the international reception of *Enthusiasm* seemed to vindicate Vertov's expectations.[18] In Germany's polarised political atmosphere the film attracted large audiences, most notably in Hamburg, and considerable interest, before being one of the first films banned in October under President Hindenburg's Emergency Decrees. This gained the film a certain notoriety, provoking a storm of protest, including an open letter to the government signed by numerous prominent figures in German cultural life, such as artist László Moholy-Nagy and composer Hans Eisler.[19]

Unable to show the film in Germany any more, Vertov organised screenings in Austria and Switzerland, where once more it created political scandal. After further screenings generating more publicity and acclaim in Paris, Amsterdam and Rotterdam,[20] Vertov arrived in London in November, where the Film Society screened the film. In sharp contrast to Germany, this elite British audience acclaimed Vertov's film for its aesthetic merits far more than its politics. Thus, while the Communist *Daily Worker* ignored the film, it was the papers of the British establishment, such as *The Morning Post* ('The Empire's Senior Daily'), that were most vocal in their praise: '"Enthusiasm" has very considerable importance as an advanced example of screen art…one of the most interesting experiments in…sound technique yet made.'[21] Even the hysterically anti-left *Daily Mail* (whose banner read 'For King and Empire') agreed:

[A]s a demonstration of the art of the sound film, it is the most significant talking picture yet seen in this country.

Technically, 'Enthusiasm' is a thrilling achievement which must fascinate all students of cinematography.[22]

The Liberal *Manchester Guardian* was particularly hostile to the film's politics, but recognised its technical accomplishments:

[I]n the silent films so now with sound the Russians can lead the way in imaginative technique…in one bound Vertov in 'Enthusiasm' has done things with camera and microphone that not only have never been done, but never attempted before.[23]

Close-Up took essentially the same view:

Vertov's first sound-film. The newest thing in sound films. Like a bright sports-model, bristling with gadgets. Like a new car, leaves the rest nowhere. It used sound as it should be used. It welded it with picture as it should be. Sound was image-sound, picture was equally image. Technically it was, adult, intelligent, on our level. It was the nearest approach to what could be done that has been done.[24]

While for Grierson, and fellow British director Anthony Asquith, the film's technical brilliance meant that it was disparaged as an occasionally striking but structureless film for film-makers, the glowing reviews clearly intrigued Charlie Chaplin, generally hostile to sound film. The day after the screening of *Enthusiasm* at the Film Society, Chaplin requested Vertov show him the film privately which he duly did.[25] After the screening Chaplin gave Vertov the famous letter:

> Never had I known that these mechanical sounds could be arranged to sound so beautiful. I regard it as one of the most exhilarating symphonies I have heard. Mr. Dziga Vertov is a musician. The professors should learn from him, not quarrel with him.
>   Congratulations.[26]

Chaplin's lavish praise for the film is all the more strange in that it celebrates the kind of industrial Fordism condemned as dehumanising in *Modern Times* [USA, 1936].

Nevertheless, in a 1932 article Vertov refers extensively to Chaplin's comments and the film's reception abroad to counter mounting Soviet criticism of him and his documentary approach.[27] The editors of *Proletarskoe kino* respond in the same issue, arguing that the reputation of the USSR ensured a positive reception for Vertov's film, not any qualities of Vertov's film or any alleged 'talent'.[28] A growing if belated international reputation was Vertov's last hope of outflanking his opponents. Unfortunately, as the international economic and political situation deteriorated, the world itself became more inward-looking.

Three Songs of Lenin

During his lifetime *Three Songs of Lenin* was probably the most widely seen of Vertov's films, although this is more true of its reception abroad than in the Soviet Union. Indeed, the film seems to have been made with half an eye on international distribution, as is evident both from its internationalist message and the fact of its being financed by Workers International Relief (Mezhrabpom).[29] However, it appeared on foreign screens, as on those of Moscow, only after persistent petitioning. The film was sent to the Venice Film Festival, in August 1934, only after the poet Alexander Bezymensky had written articles in the press demanding it be sent, yet it was part of a highly acclaimed Soviet programme.[30] It seems likely that it was this success at Venice that prompted the Soviet authorities to organise the first Moscow Film Festival the following year, where they could ensure that *Chapaev* won the main prize, thus indicating the preferred path for Soviet film, while apparently bestowing a little of the kudos that came with foreign acclaim.

With the German market now closed to Soviet films, efforts were focused on America, where the film's 6 November showing in New York was incorrectly advertised as its 'world premiere'.[31] Adverts in *The Daily Worker* intoned 'Hear Lenin's Own Voice!'[32] and it was the leftist critics who were the most enthusiastic for the film. It served as an inspiration for Samuel Brody, a prominent figure in an influential domestic school of left documentary.[33] Brody's review was published by *The Daily Worker.*

> I predict that this film is destined to become one of the most talked of since 'Potemkin'...
>
> ...when a film utilizing exclusively material recorded in reality can reach the emotional and lyrical heights of 'Three Songs,' then indeed we are dealing with a real revolution in the artistic form of the revolutionary cinema.
>
> ...ask yourself when a passage in any acted film has so affected you. Vertov is the new giant of Soviet cinema and infinitely more important than any other single director, inasmuch as his work has influenced and will continue to influence the whole course of Soviet production.[34]

This acclaim was far from universal even among critics from the left. *New Republic* wrote:

> In Vertov's 'Three Songs about Lenin' the Soviets come forward to bury the great leader in Westminster Abbey, with something of the atmosphere of Patriots' Day. Objectively, it is an attempt to idolize, not so much a man as his concepts; it is thus rather limited in appeal... when Lenin tots up a column of figures to give some of the Eastern peoples economic freedom, what are you going to do about it in terms of pictures?... on the whole it seems poorly melted newsreel material with a poetic cast...[35]

While the *New York Herald Tribune* recognised the film's striking photography and 'crusading zeal', it agreed that 'it is virtually counter-revolutionary in the mystic, devotional way in which it goes in for ecstatic and religious worship of its great hero'.[36]

This bifurcation between those who praised the film as revolutionary and those who were concerned by its quasi-religious treatment of the Lenin theme was widespread.[37] Thus H. G. Wells saw the film as typifying Soviet Russia's replacement of religion with an equally harmful secular piety:

> In Moscow I was shown one evening Dziga Vertov's new film: *Three Songs for Lenin*. This is a very fine and moving apotheosis of Lenin. It is Passion Music for Lenin and he has become a Messiah. One must see

and hear it to realize how the queer Russian mind has emotionalized Socialism and subordinated it to the personal worship of its prophets, and how necessary it is that the west wind should blow through this land afresh.[38]

By contrast, for Walter Benjamin, *Three Songs of Lenin* typified the tendencies of documentary, and of Soviet cinema, towards a democratisation of representation and the portrayal by people of themselves in their own work process, as opposed to the illusion and spectacle of Western cinema.[39] The paradox is that Soviet cinema itself was beginning to adopt a very similar aesthetic of illusion and spectacle.

Three Songs of Lenin reached London in October 1935, nearly a year after its Moscow and New York screenings, and over six months after a successful Paris run.[40] The print used contained intertitles prepared with the help of W. H. Auden. Once again, *The Manchester Guardian* is most vocal in its praise:

> It can take its place among the great Soviet films of the past, not as a return to the spirit of those films but as a carrying forward... 'Three Songs of Lenin' is documentary in form, but it is a new kind of documentary... Every resource of photography and sound is used with the sure touch of a master, and not once does the film falter...[41]

The discerning voice of *Sight and Sound* is clearly intrigued by the film's 'complicated interposition and accumulation of loosely-related shots and ideas, given a combined value by general reference to the same underlying theme' held together by emotional intensity rather than neat continuity.[42] Elsewhere, the same reviewer praises the film for its 'absence of commentary, and the interspersion instead of sub-titles as links'.[43]

In general, though, British critics resent the film as propaganda so far as to be blind to its technical merits. Thus the *New Statesman and Nation* review describes it as 'fine propaganda and not particularly good art',[44] and resorts to ridiculing the left-wing audience's reaction to the then obligatory performance of the national anthem: 'The wistful refrain of this proletarian triumph was: "If Lenin could see our country now..." If too, he could have seen this England at one moment fervently acclaiming him, at the next rigidly quiet for God Save the King, he would surely have found such dexterity – or stolidity – both puzzling and perfidious.'[45]

British censors similarly objected to the film's overt politics, and demanded the removal of Lenin's words 'The power of the landlords and the capitalists is broken in Russia and will be throughout the whole world'.[46] Subsequently, the film was screened more by leftist groups than by film buffs.[47]

Once again, Vertov himself was greatly encouraged by reports of the film's success abroad,[48] but if Vertov hoped to bolster his domestic position with foreign success he need only recall reactions to the acclaim of *Enthusiasm*: all success could be attributed to the prestige of the USSR and not to any intrinsic merit of the film. His fall from grace continued, and *Three Songs of Lenin* was to be Vertov's last film distributed abroad. Even so big an enthusiast as Leyda was unable to see *Lullaby*, and consequently the last period of Vertov's work has often been condemned out of ignorance. A 1948 overview of Soviet documentary by Roman Karmen concludes a brief history of Vertov's work with a mention that Vertov is alive and working, so as to surprise Western readers.[49] In truth, Vertov may as well have been dead for the Western spectator, for whom his death passed unnoticed.

In short, the three Vertov films to have made a lasting direct impact in the West were those distributed abroad soon after their release: *Man with a Movie Camera*, *Enthusiasm* and *Three Songs of Lenin*. Three of his greatest films, *Forward, Soviet!*, *A Sixth Part of the World* and *The Eleventh Year*, were barely known in the West during Vertov's lifetime, despite *The Eleventh Year* apparently being shown in Germany before its Moscow release.[50] Indeed, the situation has improved little since. The early part of Vertov's work is known anachronistically through its influence on other Soviet film-makers such as Eisenstein, and through the efforts of Western visitors to the Soviet Union or, more recently, through Russian visitors to the West.

Vertov and Western Documentary

In his lifetime, Vertov's influence upon newsreel and documentary film-makers in the West was typically unacknowledged or indirect. As cameraman on Jean Vigo's *À Propos de Nice* [France, 1930], Boris Kaufman appears to have attempted to apply Vertov's concept of 'life off-guard':

> Conscious behavior cannot be tolerated, character must be surprised by the camera if the whole 'documentary' value of this kind of cinema is to be achieved...
>
> The method was to take by surprise facts, actions, attitudes, expressions, and to stop shooting as soon as the subject became conscious of being photographed.[51]

Nevertheless, Vertov's younger brother rarely admitted to Vertov's influence, and never in public. Other Western film-makers reinvent or do without wheels long since patented by Vertov. Communists in the West began to develop 'workers newsreel' from 1928, but without any apparent knowledge of Vertov, as is evident from their stylistic similarity to conventional newsreel forms of the time, with the recording of sport and royalty replaced by strikes and demonstrations with little attempt to articulate an argument.[52] By the time Vertov arrived with *Man with a Movie Camera*, the West was making its first tentative efforts in worker newsreel, while he had already reinvented and abandoned the form.

Newsreel in general did not reach the level to which Vertov had taken it until well into the sound era. The arrival of sound meant that newsreel became much more significant than it had been previously. With the coming of sound the big newspaper proprietors extended their reach to film.[53]

Newsreel-dedicated cinemas sprung up in a host of big cities, especially in train stations. *The March of Time* newsreel series was seen as truly innovative for its conscious attempt to edit newsreel footage thematically to articulate a certain point of view. Graham Greene, reviewing the first issue to hit Britain in November 1935, wrote: 'No attempt has ever been made over here really to edit news films.' As a result newsreels were 'scraps of unimportant material ... flung together without arrangement on to the screen'.[54] '[*The March of Time*] fortnightly programmes can be compared with an authoritative article by a special correspondent rather than with a haphazard page of photographs from the *Daily Mirror*.'[55] It seems incredible that, over ten years after Vertov's achievements with *Leninist Cine-Pravda*, the editing together of newsreel to construct an argument should seem so novel.

In retrospect it seems that a major reason for Vertov's isolation stemmed from the fact that he took newsreel seriously in the silent era, which required a revolution in cinematic expression to make the images persuade. This fed his purist attitude to documentary, and further isolated him. By contrast, *The March of Time* used studio reconstructions widely, as well as voice-over commentary. The aim of the series may have been similar to Vertov's, interpretive journalism rather than mere chronicling of events, but Vertov's implacable commitment to film as an unstaged visual medium set him apart from this new tendency in newsreel, abroad no less than at home.

Equally, as we have seen with the attitudes of Grierson, it made him appear less relevant than Eisenstein to British documentary film-makers. In 1930s US, documentary film debates ranged between those who stressed the need to stage and reconstruct, on the one hand, and those who invoked the name of Vertov as representing a distinct anti-staging tendency.[56] Joris Ivens had recently arrived from the Soviet Union, where the Vertov tendency had been defeated. His own films, such as the Soviet-produced *Song of Heroes* [Pesnia o geroiakh, 1932], represented the dominant Soviet mode, which comprised narrative, identifiable characters, scripting and *mise en scène*.[57] At the same time, it is probably no accident that we see a number of the motifs of Vertov's films entering the vocabulary of documentary film-making in America through the films of Ivens. This is particularly true of images of irrigation in *Spanish Earth* [USA, 1937] that are at least faintly reminiscent of the scenes of dam-building in Vertov's *Eleventh Year*. Vertov himself had also shown such images of irrigation in *Three Songs of Lenin*.[58] Dams became a major theme in American documentary of the 1930s, but Vertov's pioneering of this theme was seldom if ever acknowledged.

Ultimately, Vertov's method had lost out to other approaches to documentary. However, it was precisely this marginal position which ensured that, when the *cinéma-vérité* and direct cinema movements reacted against the stagnant mainstream of the form, Vertov appeared far more relevant, and less dated than any of his contemporaries.

Life after Death

Vertov himself outlived Stalin by less than a year. Soon Soviet documentary awoke from its long stylistic slumber, and from the absolute dominance of the voice-over in documentary. Vertov was the key figure to whom film-makers could turn as a trailbreaker in the art of synchronous recording and the conversation with the protagonist or interview. The interview had been extremely marginal in Soviet documentary film: it was seen as 'shameful' for one of the camera crew to enter the frame or be heard asking questions, potentially introducing the film-maker in the film, and thus an element of chance and of improvisation. The possibility of the interviewee saying something inadvertently revealing was at odds with the very nature of Stalinist documentary.[59] In this atmosphere, Vertov suddenly seemed a contemporary in that he had, even with the incredibly limited technology available to him in the 1930s, striven towards the kinds of film-making that suddenly became dominant in the 1960s. O. Podgoretskaya (who had worked with Mikhail Slutsky in the 1930s and 1940s) refers to Vertov as synonymous with brilliant synchronic sound sequences.[60] She sees the new approach to sound as the 'new Spring' in Soviet documentary film.[61] Nevertheless, the more traditional style of the Stalin era was still employed by the old guard: Karmen's 1965 documentary *The Great Patriotic War* [Velikaia otechestvennaia] has just three synchronised sound sequences – Stalin's speech of 3 July 1941, a speech by Hitler and a partisan's oath.

Post-Stalin Soviet documentary film-makers were also inspired by the Vertov ideal of 'life caught off-guard', and now strove towards hidden cameras, or filming people at their place of work without interrupting them.[62] Similarly, L. Derbysheva, who herself worked with Vertov on some of his final newsreels, talks about 'phenomenal' shots: where subjects are unaware of the camera.[63] Some of the most striking examples of this technique can be found in the contemporary sequences of the most influential Soviet documentary of the 1960s, Mikhail Romm's 1965 *Ordinary Fascism* [Obyknovennyi fashizm], although personal antipathies prevented any public recognition of this debt.[64]

While Soviet film-makers were rediscovering the relevance of Vertov's films, Russian scholars were also uncovering Vertov's legacy. Nikolai Abramov's 1962 book marks a crucial stage in this process. It was preceded by an evening devoted to Vertov at the House of Cinema in 1959, at which Kopalin, Abramov and Shklovsky spoke. Sergei Drobashenko's publication of an (albeit contentiously selective) edition of Vertov's writings in 1966 was a further milestone. In a sure sign of official recognition, in 1967 Vertov's remains were moved to the Novodevichy cemetery and a marble headstone erected on his grave. This was followed by a film about Vertov in which excerpts from the films are combined with excerpts from his diaries (L. Makhnach, *World With No Play* [Mir bez igry, 1968]), and by the restoration of *Three Songs of Lenin* in time for the 1970 centenary of Lenin's birth.[65] In the USSR the film had come to be seen as Vertov's masterpiece, and it played a pivotal role in the process of rebuilding his reputation.[66] It is this belated acclaim that has misled some into proclaiming it an unqualified triumph on its initial release and others to conclude that the film was therefore conformist.[67]

As more written materials and films became available in Russia, this facilitated and strengthened a renewed interest from the West from the early 1960s onwards. Here, too, the impetus came in part from a change in attitudes to documentary film that resulted in Vertov's increasing relevance to two major strands of post-war film-making: *cinéma-vérité* and direct cinema. The very attributes of reflexiveness, rigour in recording and explicit politics that made Vertov so antipathetic to documentary film-makers of the 1930s and 1940s made him relevant to a new generation in the 1960s. Moreover, the hidden camera and the interview were both techniques little employed not only in Stalinist cinema but also in the mainstream of Western documentary. As Georges Sadoul puts it, Vertov's cinema and ideas were a bit like Jules Verne's tales of submarines and trips to the Moon. They seemed fantastic at the time, but anticipated future developments.[68]

As the objective, impartial stance of the Griersonian tradition came to be reassessed in favour of an open acknowledgement of bias, Vertov became relevant once more. As far back as 1957 the Robert Flaherty Film Seminar, a crucial impetus for documentary film in America, was heralding the heritage of Vertov as a theorisation for the new impulses in documentary that would become direct cinema.[69] In the early 1960s Jean Rouch was one of the first Western film-makers who explicitly drew inspiration from Vertov: 'When Edgar Morin and I decided to make *Chronicle of a Summer* [Chronique d'un été, France, 1961] a new experiment in 'cinéma vérité', our sole intention was a homage to Dziga Vertov.'[70] 'I'm one of the people responsible for this phrase [cinéma-vérité] and it's really in homage to Dziga Vertov, who completely invented the kind of film we do today.'[71]

In particular, Rouch appreciated Vertov's partisan approach to documentary, insisting that film is subjective. Moreover, Rouch attributes a special sense to Vertov's idea of the camera's privileged position of knowledge (i.e. Cine-Eye), seeing the process of recording someone as a 'psychoanalytic stimulant' with the capacity to reveal. As evidence of this he cites an example from his own work of an interview conducted with a concentration camp survivor recorded while walking down the street.[72] Thus, for Rouch, it was important to find ways to obviate rehearsal and staging:

> The one thing I want to say about *cinéma-vérité* is that it would be better to call it cinema-sincerity, if you like. That is, that you ask the audience to have confidence in the evidence, to say to the audience, 'This is what I saw. I didn't fake it, this is what happened. I didn't pay anyone to fight, I didn't change anyone's behaviour. I looked at what happened with my subjective eye and this is what I believe took place.'[73]

As in Russia, scholarship went hand in hand with the efforts of film-makers: the work of French film historian Sadoul enabled Rouch and Morin to employ an already sophisticated language with which to describe and discuss their more reflexive form of documentary; to draw upon this vibrant tradition represented by Vertov.[74] Indeed, the very phrase 'cinéma-vérité' was a direct translation of 'kinopravda' (i.e. Cine-Pravda) by Sadoul, whose 1948 first edition of *Histoire du cinéma* made the phrase emblematic of Vertov's whole approach. Sometimes shortened to 'vérité', it is now virtually synonymous, even in the English language, with documentary itself.

Curiously, though, when Rouch's use of the term became internationally adopted, Sadoul realised that, through lack of access to the wider body of Vertov's writings, he had mistakenly made 'cinéma-vérité' synonymous with Vertov's theories as a whole. Originally the term 'Cine-Pravda' had been applied only by analogy to the Bolshevik daily, and not as a concept of cinema. As Sadoul admits, the sense taken by Rouch is nearer to Vertov's notion of Cine-Eye, which encapsulated his whole approach to documentary.[75]

Vertov's ostracisation by the Stalinist elite, and his patchy reception abroad, meant that he was less tainted than his contemporaries in the eyes of 1960s and 1970s radicals conscious of the shortcomings of the Soviet Union's brand of socialism. The French New Wave, including makers of fiction films, was also attracted by Vertov. The increasingly political character of 1960s film-making and scholarship found their agenda vindicated in Vertov's attitudes to art and politics. In Jean-Luc Godard's 'Groupe Dziga Vertov', the stress was upon political film-making that was not a reflection of reality, and the sense of film as a collective enterprise. In particular, Godard seems inspired by Vertov's rejection of the concept of art.[76] Consequently, the aspect of Vertov's technique that seems to have been most important to these directors was Vertov's striving to reveal the process by which his films were made.

Nevertheless, Godard also claimed that the choice of Vertov as inspiration is also informed less by a desire to apply his programme and more by a sense that Eisenstein had already been appropriated by the mainstream.[77] Thus Godard saw the 1972 French translation of Vertov's works as a cinematic equivalent of Chairman Mao's 'little red book': an inspirational text to the French hard left of the late 1960s and early 1970s in their battle with the insufficiently radical Moscow-oriented Communist Party.[78] Godard was later to admit that this emphasis was for polemical purposes above all else.[79] Or, as Colin McCabe puts it, this was 'a deliberate provocation' in a period when Vertov was a highly marginal figure compared to Eisenstein.[80]

Before long, though, French leftists did battle not just between Vertov and Eisenstein but even between different interpretations and works by Vertov: the Maoist film journal *Cinéthique* criticised French television for showing *Man with a Movie Camera*, 'the only one of Vertov's films that has always been appreciated by the bourgeois cultural tradition', and not, for example, *Enthusiasm*.[81] Now it was not Vertov's opponents but his supporters who were contesting his entry into the museum of culture. A broad swathe of radical film-makers of the 1960s and 1970s were treating Vertov as the main progenitor of their approach to film-making, as is clear by the equal prominence given to Vertov and

Godard in the first issue of the short-lived British radical film journal *Afterimage* in 1970.[82]

Aesthetic radicals too were increasingly drawn to Vertov, with the film-making avant-garde adopting him as their own. The Anthology Film Archive and other film libraries in America were increasingly collecting and exhibiting Vertov's films, often alongside the American avant-garde, such as Maya Deren, Kenneth Anger and Stan Brakhage.[83] In Russia too, over the last ten years, Vertov has been recognised and hailed as an avant-garde artist, with *Man with a Movie Camera* ousting *Three Songs of Lenin* as Vertov's masterpiece, a fact acknowledged by its release on DVD. This shift was marked most powerfully in a brilliant, award-winning documentary by Evgeny Tsymbal, *Dziga and his Brothers* [Dziga i ego brat´ia, 2002].

However, all too often those inspired by Vertov in the West were familiar with *Man with a Movie Camera* and little else. This is particularly true of the scholarship: there are now two books and a wealth of articles in the English language on *Man with a Movie Camera*, but no monograph covering the whole or even most of Vertov's career.[84] Part of the problem is the availability of these films: even Georges Sadoul, probably one of the Western critics with the deepest knowledge of Vertov at the time, who later wrote a book about him, saw *A Sixth Part of the World* for the first time in Moscow in 1959.[85] While there may have been some film clubs that showed this film,[86] along with *Forward, Soviet!* and *The Eleventh Year* they are seen very rarely outside a few archives in Europe and America. Similarly, very few editions of *Cine-Pravda* have been screened outside the confines of the Krasnogorsk Archive in Russia. Before Vertov can occupy his rightful place in the history of cinema as more than the director of a single brilliant work, a more representative body of his work needs to become readily available beyond the festivals and retrospectives of Pordenone or Cambridge.

By contrast, most of Vertov's theoretical works are easily available. The desire to understand the motives behind *cinéma-vérité* demanded translations of these texts. The early 1960s saw excerpts of Vertov's writings published in a number of languages, including French, German and English. These were followed by book-length collections based on Drobashenko's 1966 edition, such as Annette Michelson and Kevin O'Brien's *Kino-Eye* (1984). Yet this translation is based upon a selection, in which there have been politically motivated deletions (such as mentions of Stalin and Trotsky) and other dubious editorial decisions. Moreover, our knowledge of Vertov, in both Russia and the West has moved on since 1966 and 1984, and a more comprehensive and rigorous edition of Vertov's works in translation would hopefully reflect this.

Rather than simply replacing the misleading terms 'caught unawares' with 'caught off-guard' and 'artistic film' with 'fiction film', there needs to be some gloss as to the practices that lay behind these terms.

Russian scholarship more than any other has been gaining pace in recent years: from the cautious trickle of publications by Viktor Listov and Lev Roshal in the 1970s and 1980s, since the 1990s there has been a tidal wave of new material being published, particularly by Alexander Deriabin. Barely an issue passes of the film journal *Kinovedcheskie zapiski* without something new from Vertov's archive or about Vertov. This has culminated in Deriabin's *Dramaturgical Experiments* and Yuri Tsivian's *Lines of Resistance*, both released to coincide with the 2004 Vertov retrospective at the Pordenone silent film festival. However, the lack of proper funding in Russia for this kind of research will probably mean that it is many years before we have anything like a complete edition of Vertov's writings, in any case a mammoth task.

This growth in new Russian scholarship, and a growing acquaintance with the whole corpus of Vertov's films, enable us to move beyond the simplistic clichés of Vertov the film poet and Vertov the embodiment of the Russian avant-garde. We can now see more of the Soviet context around him, the critical, industrial and political climate which he moulded and was moulded by. At the same time, there is still a need to demonstrate Vertov's ongoing relevance to wider film-making practices and to film-making today. This book has attempted to respond to both challenges, by showing how he developed and defined a distinct and incredibly powerful variant of documentary film.

Digital imagery seems to herald a new scepticism towards documentary as an objective register, further weakening the Griersonian realist tradition. Vertov's explicitly partisan exhortation, as well as his scepticism towards the image and recording process, echo central themes of the digital age. Indeed, it has been argued that his search for non-narrative solutions to the organisation of material anticipates those of the database.[87] Yet, for all his relevance to these themes, Vertov's revelation of the persuasive power of images was ultimately rooted in record.

Notes

Introduction

1 Vlada Petrić, *Constructivism in Film: The Man with the Movie Camera: A Cinematic Analysis*, Cambridge, 1987, pp. 1–21; Oksana Bulgakova, 'LEF i kino', *Kinovedcheskie zapiski*, no. 18, 1993, pp. 165–187; Graham Roberts, *Forward Soviet! History and Non-fiction Film in the USSR*, London, New York, 1999, p. 23.

2 Brian Winston, *Lies, Damned Lies and Documentaries*, London, 2000, p. 18.

3 Older Soviet commentaries briefly assert a the link between Vertov and Bolshevik journalism. See N. P. Abramov, *Dziga Vertov*, Moscow, 1962, pp. 10, 24, 27; E. I. Vertova-Svilova and A. L. Vinogradova (eds), *Dziga Vertov v vospominaniiakh sovremennikov*, Moscow, 1976, pp. 45, 58, 172; Sergei Iutkevich, 'Razmyshleniia o kinopravde i kinolzhi', *Iskusstvo kino*, no. 1, 1964, p. 75.

4 Vlada Petrić, 'Dziga Vertov as Theorist', *Cinema Journal*, vol. 18 no. 1, 1978, p. 30.

5 Denise J. Youngblood, *Soviet Cinema in the Silent Era, 1918–1935*, Ann Arbor, MI, 1985, p. 139. Youngblood praises an article by Viktor Shklovskii discussed in Chapter 3.

6 '*Fahrenheit 9/11* is many things, but for pity's sake let's not call it a documentary. To do so abuses the word and shames the good and balanced work done by film-makers...' Ty Burr, *Boston Globe*, 3 June 2004. http://www.boston.com/movies/display?display=movie&id=7054 (last visited 05/02/05).

7 Judith Mayne, 'Ideologies of Metacinema', unpublished PhD thesis, State University of New York, Buffalo, 1975, p. 65.

8 Roberts typifies this view: Roberts, *Forward Soviet!*, p. 23. Also see V. S. Listov, 'Vertov: odnazhdy i vsegda', *Kinovedcheskie zapiski*, no. 18, 1993, p. 128.

9 Seth Feldman, '"Peace Between Man and Machine": Dziga Vertov's *The Man with a Movie Camera*', in Barry Keith Grant and Jeanette Sloniowski (eds), *Documenting the Documentary: Close Readings of Documentary Film and Video*, Detroit, MI, 1998, pp. 41–42.

10 This was a comment apparently made by Philip Rosen, at the Pordenone Film Festival, October 2004.

11 Brian Winston, *Claiming the Real: The Documentary Film Revisited*, London, 1995, p. 166. Bill Nichols sees Vertov primarily as a reflexive film-maker,

but he is the only example of this approach in a period Nichols elsewhere sees as characterised by expository documentary. Bill Nichols, *Representing Reality: Issues and Concepts in Documentary*, Bloomington and Indianapolis, IN, 1991, pp. 33–35.

Chapter 1

1　Even Vertov's name has been the subject of disagreement. For example until 1993 all works on him claimed Vertov's name was Denis Arkadievich. This was in fact a russified name adopted in the context of intense anti-Semitism. A 1918 questionnaire proves he was in fact born David Abelevich. See V. M. Magidov, 'Iz arkhiva Vertova', *Kinovedcheskie zapiski*, no. 18, 1993, p. 162. Many commentators outside Russia appear unaware of this discovery. For more about Vertov's biography, see Listov, 'Vertov: odnazhdy i vsegda', pp. 121–143. Also see the excellent documentary film by Evgeny Tsymbal, *Dziga and his Brothers* [Dziga i ego brat´ia, 2002].

2　The town, now in Poland, was then called Belostok, and was part of the Russian Empire.

3　There is much debate over the meaning of the pseudonym 'Dziga Vertov', with suggestions that 'Dziga' refers to the whirring sound of a film camera. See Seth Feldman, *Dziga Vertov: A Guide to References and Resources*, Boston, MA, 1979, pp. 1–2. Roshal´ claims he was called 'Dziga', the Ukrainian word for spinning top, by a Ukrainian nanny in response to his constant fidgeting as a child. Since 'Vertov' refers to the same notion, the nickname would thus simply be 'spinning top'. See L. M. Roshal´, 'Stikhi kinopoeta', *Kinovedcheskie zapiski*, no. 21, 1994, p. 86. Another version is provided by Mikhail Kaufman in his final interview: Vertov was a reference to the spinning of the wheel on an editing table and Dziga the whirring of film through it. Mikhail Kaufman, 'Poslednee interv'iu Mikhaila Kaufmana', *Kinovedcheskie zapiski*, no. 18, 1993, p. 143.

4　For example, Svilova claims in *LEF* in 1924 that no one had previously thought of editing newsreel footage. E. Svilova, 'U kinokov', *LEF*, no. 4, 1924, p. 220.

5　See, for example, Drankov's *Cine Journal* [Kinozhurnal, 1910].

6　Then also known as Lemberg, now as Lviv.

7　See, for example, *Russian Military Newsreel*, Series 2 (1914).

8　Roberts, *Forward Soviet!*, p. 16.

9　Roberts, *Forward Soviet!*, p. 17.

10　Seth Feldman argues that Vertov's influence can first be detected slightly later, in *Cine Week* no. 30, 10 January 1919. See Seth Feldman, *Evolution of Style in the Early Work of Dziga Vertov*, New York, 1975, pp. 47–48. Vertov himself denied this series constituted anything of a departure: Dziga Vertov, *Stat´i, dnevniki, zamysly*, ed. S. Drobashenko, Moscow, 1966, p. 76; Dziga Vertov, *Kino-Eye: The Writings of Dziga Vertov*, trans. Kevin O'Brien, ed. with an introduction by Annette Michelson, Berkeley, CA, 1984, p. 42. Sergei Drobashenko also stresses the 'passive descriptive' nature of *Cine Week*. Sergei Drobashenko, *Istoriia sovetskogo dokumental'nogo kino. Uchebno-metodicheskoe posobie*, Moscow, 1980, p. 6.

11 Seth Feldman, *Dziga Vertov: A Guide to References*, pp. 5–6. For evidence of the popularity of this film and newsreel in general during the civil war, see: Dziga Vertov, 'Cine-Eye and the Struggle for Newsreel' (1926), RGALI 2091/2/161.

12 Evan Mawdsley argues that terror 'came from the logic of the October uprising'. Evan Mawdsley, *The Russian Civil War*, 2nd edn revised, Edinburgh, 2000, p. 81.

13 Vertova-Svilova and Vinogradova, *Dziga Vertov v vospominaniiakh sovremennikov*, p. 66.

14 Listov, 'Vertov: odnazhdy i vsegda', p. 125.

15 Nichols, *Representing Reality*, pp. 34–38.

16 Vertova-Svilova and Vinogradova, *Dziga Vertov v vospominaniiakh sovremennikov*, p. 70. A number of Soviet film historians note the Communists' intention to use cinema for agitation and propaganda rather than simply for informing. See, for example, Drobashenko, *Istoriia sovetskogo dokumental'nogo kino*, p. 5.

17 L. A. Molchanov, *Gazetnaia pressa Rossii v gody revoliutsii i grazhdanskoi voiny (okt. 1917–1920 gg.)*, Moscow, 2002, p. 14.

18 Peter Kenez, *The Birth of the Propaganda State: Soviet Methods of Mass Mobilisation, 1917–1929*, Cambridge, 1985, p. 21.

19 See Mawdsley, *The Russian Civil War*, p. 211: 'One of the major White weaknesses was a failure to match the scale and quality of Bolshevik propaganda'; Roger Pethybridge, *One Step Backwards Two Steps Forward: Soviet Society and Politics in the New Economic Policy*, Oxford, 1990, p. 121; Molchanov, *Gazetnaia pressa Rossii, passim*.

20 V. I. Lenin, *Collected Works*, trans. Jane Finberg and George Hanna, ed. Victor Jerome, 4th edn, Moscow, 1975 [1961], vol. 5, p. 22.

21 Kenez, *Birth of the Propaganda State*, p. 36; even in his 1905 'Party Organisation and Party Literature' Lenin derides notions of freedom of speech: Lenin, *Collected Works*, vol. 10, p. 48. Also see Jeffrey Brooks, 'The Press and its Message: Images of America in the 1920s and 1930s', in Sheila Fitzpatrick et al. (eds), *Russia in the Era of NEP: Explorations in Soviet Society and Culture*, Bloomington, IN, 1991, p. 231; Jeffrey Brooks, *Thank You, Comrade Stalin! Soviet Public Culture from Revolution to Cold War*, Princeton, NJ, 2000, p. 8.

22 Kenez, *Birth of the Propaganda State*, p. 35.

23 I am thinking in particular of Kenez, *Birth of the Propaganda State*.

24 The term 'interpretive' belongs to Brooks: Brooks, *Thank You, Comrade Stalin!*, p. 6.

25 Svilova, 'U kinokov', p. 221.

26 Vertova-Svilova and Vinogradova, *Dziga Vertov v vospominaniiakh sovremennikov*, p. 70.

27 Abramov, *Dziga Vertov*, p. 51.

28 Vertova-Svilova and Vinogradova, *Dziga Vertov v vospominaniiakh sovremennikov*, p. 61. As a result he faced criticism from what remained of the world of cinema. Vertova-Svilova and Vinogradova, *Dziga Vertov v vospominaniiakh sovremennikov*, p. 84. Abramov, *Dziga Vertov*, p. 6.

29 Aleksandr Rubashkin, *Mikhail Kol'tsov. Kritiko-biograficheskii ocherk*, Leningrad, 1971, p. 34.

30 While in the 1920s themed issues were characteristic of the weeklies, by the 1930s there were themed editions of dailies, such as the 1933 issue of *Krest'ianskaia gazeta* devoted to Stalin. See Brooks, *Thank You, Comrade Stalin!*, pp. 61, 63.

31 Listov mentions this link between Kol'tsov's *ocherk* and Vertov's film; see V. S. Listov, 'Mikhail Kol'tsov i "Desiataia muza"', *Kinovedcheskie zapiski*, no. 5, 1990, pp. 50–51. Listov also briefly analyses Vertov's later reworking of this sequence in *Three Songs of Lenin*; see Listov, 'Vertov: odnazhdy i vsegda', p. 128.

32 Mikhail Kol'tsov, *Izbrannye proizvedeniia*, 3 vols, Moscow, 1957, vol. 1, p. 74.

33 The term 'iconic' is being used here in the semiotic sense of an image which resembles what it represents. See Peter Wollen, *Signs and Meaning in the Cinema*, 3rd edn revised and enlarged, London, 1979, p. 122.

34 Nina Tumarkin, *Lenin Lives! The Lenin Cult in Soviet Russia*, 2nd edn enlarged, Cambridge, MA, and London, 1997, p. 165.

35 Drobashenko, *Istoriia sovetskogo dokumental'nogo kino*, pp. 11, 13.

36 See Yuri Tsivian (ed. and introduction), *Lines of Resistance: Dziga Vertov and the Twenties*, trans. Julian Graffy, Gemona, 2004, pp. 2–3.

37 Dziga Vertov, 'On i ia', *Kino-fot*, no. 2, 1922, p. 11.

38 Dziga Vertov, 'On the Significance of Non-Acted Cinema' (1923), *Kino-Eye*, p. 51; *Stat'i*, p. 83.

39 See Roberts, *Forward Soviet!*; also see Valeriya Selunskaya and Maria Zezina, 'Documentary Films – A Soviet Source for Soviet Historians', in Richard Taylor and Derek Spring (eds), *Stalinism and Soviet Cinema*, London, 1993, p. 180. By the end of the 1930s few films were complete without such parades.

40 Listov, 'Vertov: odnazhdy i vsegda', p. 127.

41 E.g. Khrisanf Khersonskii, 'Kino-Glaz', *Izvestiia*, 15 October 1924, p. 7.

42 In 1925 *Cine-Eye* allegedly received a diploma of honour at the International Exhibition in Paris; see Listov, 'Vertov: odnazhdy i vsegda', p. 129. However, Feldman notes that it was not his first film to be seen abroad, since *Godovshchina revoliutsii* [1919] had been exported; see Feldman, *Dziga Vertov: A Guide to References*, p. 21. Also see below, Chapter 8.

43 Listov, 'Vertov: odnazhdy i vsegda', p. 128. Roberts does not argue this of *Cine-Eye*, but sees this as the general trajectory of Vertov's career. Roberts, *Forward Soviet!*, pp. 23, 28.

44 Vertov dates the beginning of the Cine-Eyes as a broad movement beyond a few disciples as starting from 1925; Dziga Vertov, 'From Cine-Eye to Radio-Eye' (1929), *Kino-Eye*, p. 87; *Stat'i*, p. 111. Critics have typically missed this

shift to the Cine-Eyes as a mass movement, instead seeing them purely as a term for 'the three film-makers'; Roberts, *Forward Soviet!*, p. 22.

45 Dziga Vertov, 'Cine-Pravda' (1923), *Kino-Eye*, p. 33; *Stat'i*, p. 68. *The Film Factory: Russian and Soviet Cinema in Documents*, ed. and trans. Richard Taylor, co-ed. with an introduction by Ian Christie, Cambridge, MA, 1988, p. 84. I have used Taylor's translation (with slight changes).

46 Roberts, *Forward Soviet!*, p. 28

47 Molchanov, *Gazetnaia pressa Rossii*, pp. 21–27, 58–61. In fact, some pre-Revolutionary journalists stayed to work on the Bol'shevik press; see O. Litovskii, *Tak i bylo. Ocherki, ospominaniia, vstrechi*, Moscow, 1958, pp. 7–8.

48 Litovskii, *Tak i bylo*, pp. 12–13, 15–16.

49 Jeffrey Brooks, 'Public and Private Values in the Soviet Press, 1921–1925', *Slavic Review*, vol. 48 no. 1, 1989, p. 18.

50 A number of other commentators have remarked upon this distinctive feature of Soviet journalism of the time: Molchanov, *Gazetnaia pressa Rossii*, pp. 64–67. *Bednota* in particular published huge numbers of readers' letters, and responded to them. Litovskii, *Tak i bylo*, pp. 57–59. Brooks 'The Press and its Message', p. 234; *Thank You, Comrade Stalin!*, p. 6.

51 Needless to say, as the 1920s progressed, letter-writers were encouraged to be more constructive in their criticism. Their purpose became less about informing the centre about the periphery, and more about expounding the centre's views.

52 The terms 'interactive' and 'participatory' belong to Brooks: Brooks, 'The Press and its Message', p. 234; *Thank You, Comrade Stalin!*, p. 6.

53 It has even been claimed that Vertov showed some of his early films to Maria Il'ichna, who in turn showed them to Lenin. Aleksandr Lemberg, 'Dziga Vertov prikhodit v kino', *Iz istorii kino*, no. 7, Moscow, 1968, p. 47. Curiously, this claim is absent from the book version of Lemberg's memoir.

54 N. Bukharin, 'Dva slova o nekotorykh osobennostiakh rabkorovskoi raboty', *Rabochii korrespondent*, nos 3–4, 1924, p. 15.

55 'Oko' is not 'a playful colloquial alternative' to the word 'glaz', Roberts, *Forward Soviet!*, p. 22.

56 For example, B. Nebyletskii wrote to Vertov asking to become a cine-correspondent [kino-korrespondent] in 1926. Vertova-Svilova and Vinogradova, *Dziga Vertov v vospominaniiakh sovremennikov*, pp. 128–133.

57 Vertov suggests avoiding the term '*kinorabkor*' since it could easily be confused with worker correspondents who write reviews of films. Dziga Vertov, 'The Essence of Cine-Eye' (1925), *Kino-Eye*, p. 49; *Stat'i*, p. 81.

58 Abramov, *Dziga Vertov*, pp. 45–46.

59 According to some estimates 75–80% of worker correspondents wrote exclusively for wall newspapers: L. Leonidov, 'Na vernom puti (k itogam raionnykh knoferentsii rabkorov Moskvy)', *Raboche-krest'ianskii korrespondent*, no. 4, 1925, p. 15.

60 Dziga Vertov, 'Tvorcheskaia kartochka 1917–1947',·*Kinovedcheskie zapiski*, no. 30, 1996, p. 163. While compiled in 1947, this document comprises quotations from earlier documents in Vertov's own archive.
61 Vertov, 'Tvorcheskaia kartochka', p. 166.
62 Roberts, *Forward Soviet!*, p. 26.
63 Dziga Vertov, 'Cine-Eye' (1925), RGALI 2091/2/157.
64 Petrić sees the film as being purely an illustration of method: Petrić, *Constructivism in Film*, p. 29.
65 Vertov, 'Tvorcheskaia kartochka', p. 166.
66 Vertov, 'Cine-Eye' (1926), *Kino-Eye*, p. 72; *Stat'i*, p. 95.
67 Vertov, 'Cine-Eye' (1926), *Kino-Eye*, p. 67; *Stat'i*, p. 93.
68 See Michelson's thought-provoking reading of the image of the magician in *Cine-Eye*: Annette Michelson, 'From Magician to Epistemologist: Vertov's *The Man with a Movie Camera*', in P. Adams Sitney (ed.), *The Essential Cinema: Essays on Films in The Collection of Anthology Film Archives*, New York, 1975, vol. 1, p. 104.
69 Vertov, 'Tvorcheskaia kartochka', p. 166.
70 Vertov, 'Cine-Eye' (1926), *Kino-Eye*, pp. 70–71; *Stat'i*, p. 96.
71 Vertov, 'Cine-Eye' (1926), *Kino-Eye*, p. 75; *Stat'i*, pp. 99–100.
72 Listov, 'Vertov: odnazhdy i vsegda', p. 130.
73 Dziga Vertov, 'The Cine-Platform "Cine-Eye"' (1925), RGALI 2091/2/158.
74 For example, Vertov believed peasants prefer documentary to fiction film, and would be a willing audience for works of the Cine-Eyes. Dziga Vertov, 'To the Cine-Eyes of the South' (1925), *Kino-Eye*, p. 51; *Stat'i*, p. 83.
75 Vertov, 'The Essence of Cine-Eye' (1925), *Kino-Eye*, p. 49; *Stat'i*, p. 81.

Chapter 2

1 See Chapter 8.
2 Roberts refers to 'life caught unawares' as key; Roberts, *Forward Soviet!*, p. 2.
3 Petrić, 'Dziga Vertov as Theorist', p. 31. This is the best treatment of Vertov's theories.
4 *Kino-Eye*, p. 338. Michelson also states that the Vertov group adopted 'candid camera' techniques from the period 1923–1924. She seems to imply this was the only method adopted. *Kino-Eye*, p. xxiv. Petrić makes the distinction between hidden camera and *zhizn' vrasplokh*. However, he does not explore the issues of intervention and performance this raises. Petrić, 'Dziga Vertov as Theorist', p. 32. Elsewhere in the book O'Brien translates 'zhizn' vrasplokh' (in the filmography) as 'life unrehearsed'. This is a better translation in many respects, suggesting unpractised performance, but nevertheless performance. However, its potential is not explored in the book's introduction. *Kino-Eye*, p. 332.
5 Dziga Vertov, 'From the History of the Cine-Eyes' (1929), *Kino-Eye*, p. 94; *Stat'i*, p. 116.

6 This translation seems to originate with Samuel Brody in the early 1930s; see Tsivian, *Lines of Resistance*, p. 353.

7 Stella Bruzzi, *New Documentary: A Critical Introduction*, London and New York, 2000, p. 90.

8 Bruzzi, *New Documentary*, p. 8.

9 Bruzzi, *New Documentary*, p. 74.

10 Winston, *Lies, Damned Lies and Documentaries*, p. 106.

11 Tsivian, *Lines of Resistance*, p. 384. Yuri Tsivian credits Julian Graffy with this translation. However, the translations themselves, and the book's index, persist with the translation 'life caught unawares'. Tsivian, *Lines of Resistance*, pp. 104, 418.

12 *Kino-Eye*, p. 162; *Stat´i*, p. 164.

13 Dictionary definitions of the word 'vrasplokh' give near-synonyms such as 'unexpectedly' and 'suddenly', and examples relating to ambushing and catching the enemy by surprise, unprepared or off-guard. See, for example, A. Evgen´eva (ed.), *Slovar´ russkogo iazyka*, 4 vols, 2nd edn revised, Moscow, 1981, vol. 1, s.v. 'vrasplokh'.

14 *Kino-Eye*, pp. 162–163; *Stat´i*, p. 164.

15 Winston, *Claiming the Real*, p. 6.

16 *Kino-Eye*, p. 168; *Stat´i*, p. 170.

17 Feldman quotes this passage and then argues that it related to a prior period in Vertov's film-making that predated *Cine-Eye*, and to difficulties ultimately overcome by Mikhail Kaufman's use of hidden camera; Feldman, *Evolution of Style*, p. 131. As I hope to have shown, this is not a convincing interpretation.

18 Feldman, *Evolution of Style*, p. 132.

19 Oksana Bulgakova rightly sees Vertov's concentration on objects as the flip side of 'zhizn´ vrasplokh': Bulgakova, 'LEF i kino', pp. 187–188. Feldman also refers to this: Feldman, *Evolution of Style*, p. 130.

20 *Kino-Eye*, p. 147; *Stat´i*, p. 154.

21 Vladimir Erofeev, 'Kino-Glaz', *Kino*, 21 October 1924, in Tsivian, *Lines of Resistance*, p. 105.

22 Dziga Vertov, 'On the Film Known as "Cine-Eye"' (1923), *Kino-Eye*, p. 34; *Stat´i*, p. 68.

23 Kaufman, 'Poslednee interv´iu Mikhaila Kaufmana', p. 148.

24 Winston, *Lies, Damned Lies and Documentaries*, p. 146.

25 Roberts describes this moment as an example of staging: Roberts, *Forward Soviet!*, p. 27.

26 Roberts, *Forward Soviet!*, p. 21.

27 Vertov, 'The Essence of Cine-Eye' (1925), *Kino-Eye*, p. 49; *Stat´i*, p. 81.

28 Dziga Vertov, Notebooks, Diaries (1924), *Kino-Eye*, p. 161; *Stat´i*, p. 163.

29 Michelson, 'From Magician to Epistemologist', p. 110.

30 Vertov, 'Cine-Eye' (1926), *Kino-Eye*, pp. 72–73; *Stat´i*, pp. 97–98.

31 Vertov, 'The Essence of Cine-Eye' (1925), *Kino-Eye*, p. 50; *Stat´i*, pp. 82–83.

32 Vertov-Svilova and Vinogradova, *Dziga Vertov v vospominaniiakh sovremennikov*, p. 126.

33 'Cine-Eye (A Newsreel in Six Parts)' (1924), Kino-Eye, p. 39; Stat'i, p. 73. For the comparison of the camera with the telescope, see Vertov, 'Cine-Eye' (1926), Kino-Eye, p. 67; Stat'i, 94.

34 Dziga Vertov, 'The Birth of Cine-Eye' (1924), Kino-Eye, p. 41; Stat'i, p. 75.

35 Roshal', 'Stikhi kinopoeta', p. 90. Roshal' argues these poems were written around the beginning of 1927.

36 Sergei Tret'iakov, 'Stenogramma soveshchaniia', Novyi LEF, nos 11–12, 1927, p. 54. Tamara Selezneva quotes Tret'iakov's view as the concluding point in the debate on documentary cinema: T. F. Selezneva, Kinomysl' 1920-kh godov, Leningrad, 1972, p. 55. This is not strictly accurate.

37 This is implicit in Grierson's concept of the 'original (or native) actor'; John Grierson, Grierson on Documentary, ed. with an introduction by Forsyth Hardy, Boston, MA, and London, 1979, p. 37. An element of acting, and the directing of non-professional actors, are assumed to be irreducible.

38 G. Boltianskii, 'Teoriia i praktika kinokov', Sovetskoe kino, nos 4–5, 1926, p. 12.

39 Boltianskii, 'Teoriia i praktika kinokov', p. 12.

40 Dziga Vertov, Notebooks, Diaries (1936), Kino-Eye, pp. 197–198; Stat'i, pp. 197–198.

41 For an exploration of these issues, see David Lyon, The Electronic Eye: The Rise of the Surveillance Society, Cambridge, 1994, pp. 60–66.

42 Vertov, 'Cine-Eye' (1925), RGALI 2091/2/158.

43 Petrić, Constructivism in Film, pp. 81–82.

44 Dziga Vertov, 'From the Book "Cine-Eyes: A Revolution"' (c. 1925), RGALI 2091/2/155.

45 E.g. Feldman, Dziga Vertov: A Guide to References, pp. 37–38; also Evolution of Style, p. 133. Nevertheless, Feldman deserves credit for being the only major commentator on Vertov to comment at any length on Vertov's proposals for a grassroots cinematography movement.

46 Vertov, 'Tvorcheskaia kartochka', p. 166.

47 Vertov, 'Tvorcheskaia kartochka', pp. 166–167. The finished film in fact comprises five reports.

48 Boltianskii, 'Teoriia i praktika kinokov', p. 12. The dictionary gives a typical usage for 'donesenie' as 'To find out enemy positions through the reports [donesenie] of spies'. S. I. Ozhegov, Slovar' russkogo iazyka, 9th edn revised, Moscow, 1972, s.v. 'donesenie'.

49 Vertov, 'Cine-Eye' (1926), Kino-Eye, p. 69; Stat'i, p. 95.

50 Dziga Vertov, 'Itinerary Plans for Shooting D. A. Vertov film "The Eleventh Year"' (c. 1930), RGALI 2091/1/22.

51 Kino-Eye, p. 185; Stat'i, p. 186.

52 When advising his followers in the Southern branch of LEF about permission to shoot, Vertov advises them to contact Goskino or Sovkino; Vertov, 'To the Cine-Eyes of the South' (1925), RGALI 2091/2/157.

53 Sheila Fitzpatrick, Everyday Stalinism: Ordinary Life in Extraordinary Times: Soviet Russia in the 1930s, New York and Oxford, 1999, pp. 164–177.

54 Fitzpatrick, Everyday Stalinism, p. 168.

Chapter 3

1 V. Zhemchuzhnyi, 'Kino-khronika', *Sovetskoe kino*, nos 4–5, 1926, p. 9; V. Maiakovskii, 'Karaul', *Novyi LEF*, no. 2, 1927, p. 24; Lev Roshal´, *Dziga Vertov*, Moscow, 1982, p. 124.

2 G. Boltianskii, 'Kino-khronika za 10 let', *Sovetskoe kino*, no. 7, 1927, p. 14. Similarly, newspapers, free during the civil war but sold under the NEP, faced falling circulations.

3 Only 50,000 metres had been made in the years since 1922, whereas 150,000 metres were made in the civil war. Boltianskii, 'Kino-khronika za 10 let', p. 15.

4 One such example is Vertov's 1924 film *Soviet Toys* [Sovetskie igrushki], which justifies the Soviet use of advertising. See the discussion of Vertov's animated adverts in Aleksandr Deriabin, '"Plod sozrel i ego nado sniat´." K istokam vertovskogo shedevra', *Kinovedcheskie zapiski*, no. 49, 2000, p. 193.

5 This work was written in 1923. Dziga Vertov, 'The Cinema Advert', in *Almanakh Proletkul´ta*, Moscow, 1925, pp. 131–136. The dated manuscript can be found in RGALI 2091/2/156.

6 Vertov, 'The Cinema Advert' (1923), RGALI 2091/2/156.

7 Winston, *Claiming the Real*, p. 134.

8 Viktor Shklovskii, 'Where is Dziga Vertov Striding?' (1926), in Taylor, *The Film Factory*, p. 152.

9 This point is well made by Yuri Tsivian in his notes to the film in *Le Giornate del cinema muto 2004. 23rd Pordenone Silent Film Festival Catalogue*, Pordenone, 2004, p. 50. That these were the generic expectations is clear from contemporary responses to the film. See Vladimir Blium, 'Forward, Soviet!' (1926), in Tsivian, *Lines of Resistance*, p. 157.

10 Lev Monovich, 'Database as Symbolic Form', *Millennium Film Journal*, no. 34, Fall 1999, p. 41.

11 For example, see *Cine Week* nos 22, 29, October 1918; Trotsky speaks to Czechoslovak legionnaires who have come over to the revolution.

12 *Literaturno-instruktorskii agit-parokhod VTsIK 'Krasnaia zvezda'* [1919]. The speaker is an agitator called Voznesensky.

13 See, for example, *Cine-Pravda* nos 13 and 14.

14 Tsivian, *23rd Pordenone Silent Film Festival Catalogue*, pp. 54–55.

15 Viktor Listov sees *A Sixth Part of the World* as marking a turning point, after which all Vertov's films are poetic and no longer oriented towards journalism and verifiable fact; Listov, 'Vertov: odnazhdy i vsegda', p. 132. Lev Roshal´ sees the film as founding the genre of poetic documentary; Roshal´, *Dziga Vertov*, p. 158.

16 Viktor Shklovskii, 'Poeziia i proza v kinematografii' (1927), in *Za 60 let, Raboty o kino*, Moscow, 1985, p. 37.

17 Nichols, *Representing Reality*, p. 57.

18 See Roshal´, *Dziga Vertov*, p. 154; Ben Singer, 'Connoisseurs of Chaos', *Literature/Film Quarterly*, vol. 15 no. 4, 1987, p. 248; Vertov, Notebooks, Diaries (1941), *Kino-Eye*, p. 235; *Stat´i*, p. 234. There is a wealth of evidence

for Vertov's familiarity with the works of and personal acquaintance with Maiakovskii.

19 See, for example, the 1855 preface to 'Leaves of Grass', Walt Whitman, *The Portable Walt Whitman*, ed. Michael Warner, London, 2004, p. 332.

20 Vertov plucks isolated half-sentences from a long speech. This is clear from the online Russian edition of Stalin's works: http://www.hrono.ru/libris/stalin/1-1.html (last visited 22/08/05). Vertov's intermediate version of these intertitles contains fewer paraphrases. See 'D. A. Vertov's Director's Scenario for *A Sixth Part of the World*. Rough Drafts' (c. 1925), RGALI 2091/1/10. Vertov insisted he had checked every letter of the intertitles against Stalin's XIV Congress speech: 'Reports and Declarations by D. A. Vertov to Kul´tkino, Goskino, Sovkino and Glavrepertkom as to Shooting, Editing and Publicity for *A Sixth Part of the World*' (1925–1926), RGALI 2091/1/15.

21 E.g. 'Song of Myself', *The Portable Walt Whitman*, p. 5.

22 Roman Jakobson, 'The Speech Event and Functions of Language', in Roman Jakobson, *On Language*, ed. Linda R. Waugh and Monique Monville-Burston, Cambridge, MA, and London, 1990, p. 76.

23 See Mayne, 'Ideologies of Metacinema'.

24 Shklovskii, 'Poeziia i proza v kinematografii', pp. 37–38. Pier Pasolini too sees an opposition between prose and poetic cinema, where the former is narrative in structure and the latter metaphoric; Naomi Greene, *Pier Paolo Pasolini: Cinema as Heresy*, Princeton, NJ, 1990, p. 112. Essentially the same distinction is made by Carl Plantinga's category of the 'poetic nonfiction film', where aesthetic function rather than argument or assertion is the 'primary organisational principle'; Carl R. Plantinga, *Rhetoric and Representation in Nonfiction Film*, Cambridge, 1997, p. 103.

25 Singer, 'Connoisseurs of Chaos', p. 248.

26 See, for example, James Perrin Warren, *Walt Whitman's Language Experiment*, University Park, PA, and London, 1990, *passim*.

27 It should be noted that Whitman was a journalist for most of his life, and thought that poetry should 'give ultimate vivifaction to facts'; *The Portable Walt Whitman*, p. 381.

28 Singer, 'Connoisseurs of Chaos', p. 250.

29 Richard Barsam, *The Vision of Robert Flaherty: The Artist as Myth and Filmmaker*, Bloomington and Indianapolis, IN, 1988, p. 27.

30 Emma Widdis, *Visions of a New Land: Soviet Film from the Revolution to the Second World War*, New Haven, CT, and London, 2003, p. 110. Martin Stollery is closer to the mark in arguing that the film presents the diverse peoples as 'a spectacle for and possession of the Russian proletariat'; Martin Stollery, *Alternative Empires: European Modernist Cinemas and Cultures of Imperialism*, Exeter, 2000, p. 111.

31 Graham Roberts, *The Man with the Movie Camera*, London and New York, 2000, p. 26.

32 When combined with issues of transport, industrialisation was the second most important theme in photographs used in the paper in this year. By

1929 it was the leading topic in *Pravda* by a long way, with over a quarter of all images in the leading national daily treating this subject. Rosalinde Sartorti, *Pressfotographie und Industrialisierung in der Sowjetunion: die Pravda, 1925–1933*, Berlin and Wiesbaden, 1981, pp. 86–87.

33 Dziga Vertov, 'Critique of the Critics. Some Thoughts' (1931), RGALI 2091/2/176.

34 This is clear from a wide swathe of reviews, such as Boris Gusman's review of *Cine-Eye* in *Pravda*, 15 October 1924, p. 7. Also see dictionary definitions of the words chronicle and 'khronika': 'a continuous register of events in order of their occurence', H. W. Fowler and F. G. Fowler (eds), *The Concise Oxford Dictionary of Current English*, 9th edn, ed. Della Thompson, Oxford, 1995, s.v. 'chronicle'; 'a record of events in chronological order', Ozhegov, *Slovar' russkogo iazyka*, s.v. 'khronika'. Also see Evgen'eva et al. (eds), *Slovar' russkogo iazyka*, s.v. 'khronika', where 'khronika' is also defined as 'a documentary film recording events chronologically'.

35 Viktor Shklovskii, 'Po povodu kartiny Esfiri Shub', *Novyi LEF*, nos 8–9, 1927, p. 54.

36 Vertov-Svilova and Vinogradova, *Dziga Vertov v vospominaniiakh sovremennikov*, p. 81.

37 Dziga Vertov, Diary (1927), *Kino-eye*, p. 166; *Stat'i*, p. 168. According to Roshal', the original contains a number of expletives; Roshal', *Dziga Vertov*, p. 164.

38 This is an expansion of Lev Roshal''s argument; see Roshal', *Dziga Vertov*, pp. 160–161. Curiously similar criticisms have been levelled at the flawed chronology in Michael Moore's *Roger and Me*; see John Corner, *The Art of Record: A Critical Introduction to Documentary*, Manchester, 1996, pp. 166–168.

39 Gr, '*A Sixth Part of the World*' (1927), in Tsivian, *Lines of Resistance*, pp. 206–207.

40 Vertov, Notebooks, Diaries (1924), *Kino-Eye*, p. 161; *Stat'i*, p. 163. Vertov states: 'We take a stand against the artistic [*khudozhestvennyi*] cinema'. The word translated as 'artistic' cinema should here be 'fiction', in the sense of 'khudozhestvennyi fil'm' or fiction film.

41 Aleksandr Lemberg says the decision by Vertov to employ the term 'director' for these early non-fiction films was a bold and innovative one, disapproved of by directors of fiction films. Vertov-Svilova and Vinogradova, *Dziga Vertov v vospominaniiakh sovremennikov*, pp. 80–81.

42 In *Cine-Eye* he called himself 'cine-scout'; *Cine-Pravda* no. 17 is subtitled 'An experiment in newsreel by Cine-Eye Dziga Vertov'; *Cine-Pravda* nos 18 and 20, for example, are attributed to him simply as his 'cine-work', whereas for *Forward, Soviet!* and *Man with a Movie Camera* he is credited as 'supervisor' (others such as Kopalin are called 'scouts'). In *A Sixth Part of the World* he is credited as 'author-supervisor'. For *The Eleventh Year*, *Enthusiasm* and *Three Songs of Lenin* Vertov is credited as 'author-director'.

43 D. Lianov, 'Koe-chto o soderzhanii sovetskikh kartin', *Sovetskoe kino*, no. 1, 1925, p. 29.

44 Mikhail Levidov, 'The Strategist and his Soldiers (*A Sixth Part of the World* – A Film by Vertov)' (1926), in Tsivian, *Lines of Resistance*, p. 202.

45 Sergei Eisenstein, *Selected Works*, vol. 1: *Writings, 1922–1934*, ed. and trans. Richard Taylor, London, Bloomington and Indianapolis, IN, 1988, p. 64.

46 V. Fefer, 'Shagai, sovet!', *Sovetskoe kino*, no. 2, 1926, p. 12.

47 Izmail Urazov, '*Forward, Soviet!*' (1926), in Tsivian, *Lines of Resistance*, p. 163.

48 Vladimir Blium, 'A New Victory for Soviet Cinema' (1926), in Tsivian, *Lines of Resistance*, p. 250. The translation renders 'neigrovaia', literally 'unplayed', as 'non-fiction'.

49 G. Osipov, '*Forward, Soviet!*' (1926), in Tsivian, *Lines of Resistance*, p. 165.

50 Fefer, 'Shagai, sovet!', p. 13.

51 Vitalii Zhemchuzhnyi, '*A Sixth Part of the World*' (1926), in Tsivian, *Lines of Resistance*, p. 198.

52 Anon, '*Forward, Soviet!* Has Been Released' (1926), in Tsivian, *Lines of Resistance*, p. 179.

53 Roshal´ claims *A Sixth Part of the World* was shown in the majority of Moscow cinemas and in the workers' clubs at the end of December 1926; Roshal´, *Dziga Vertov*, p. 172. Vertov refers to 13 successful days at a first-run cinema; Vertov, 'On the Cusp Between 1926 and 1927, at the Start of the Tenth Anniversary of the October Revolution' (1927), in Tsivian, *Lines of Resistance*, p. 193. According to Ippolit Sokolov, however, it was not a commercial success; Ippolit Sokolov, 'On the Film *A Sixth Part of the World*: A Letter to the Editor' (1927), in Tsivian, *Lines of Resistance*, p. 239. Yet this is to judge the film by the same criteria as commercial cinema.

54 Its critical acclaim equalled its popularity. Pudovkin, for example, calls it 'the first proper newsreel': V. Pudovkin, 'Anketa', *Sovetskoe kino*, nos 8–9, 1927, pp. 6–7. Oksana Sarkisova sees the reactions to Shub's film as pivotal; see Oksana Sarkisova, 'Envisioned Communities: Representations of Nationalities in Non-Fiction Cinema in Soviet Russia, 1923–1935', unpublished PhD dissertation, Central European University, Budapest, 2004, pp. 8–9.

55 Roshal´, *Dziga Vertov*, p. 170.

56 Youngblood, *Soviet Cinema in the Silent Era*, p. 139.

57 Sokolov claimed Vertov shot 26,000 metres and used only 1140 of this footage. Ippolit Sokolov, 'On the Film *A Sixth Part of the World*', pp. 237, 241. This is to leave aside for the moment the issue of Vertov's method of shooting for his own library of film material; see Vertov, 'A Letter to the Editor' (1927), in Tsivian, *Lines of Resistance*, p. 239.

58 Esfir´ Shub, *Zhizn´ moia – kinematograf. Krupnym planom. Stat´i, vystupleniia. Neosushchestvlennye zamysly. Perepiska*, ed. L. Poznanskaia, Moscow, 1972, p. 282.

Chapter 4

1 Zhemchuzhnyi commented in 1926 that Vertov and the Cine-Eyes should be used to improve the quality of Soviet newsreel. Vitalii Zhemchuzhnyi, 'Kino-khronika', *Sovetskoe kino*, nos 4–5, 1926, p. 9.

2 Known as *The Defeat of German Armies near Moscow* in the UK. Vertov claims that those Cine-Eyes who stayed in Moscow were able to prevent documentary from reverting to the state of Pathé. In particular, he mentions Kopalin, Ivan Beliakov, Petr Zotov and Irina Setkina. Dziga Vertov, 'Cine-Eye, Radio-Eye and So-Called "Documentalism"', *Proletarskoe kino*, no. 4, 1931, p. 15.

3 Sokolov, 'On the Film *A Sixth Part of the World*', pp. 235–236; Shklovskii, 'Kinoki i nadpisi', *Kino*, no. 44, 1926, p. 3.

4 Tsivian insists that *Man with a Movie Camera* in particular was a response to this criticism. See Yuri Tsivian, 'Homeless Images: D. W. Griffith in the Eye of Soviet Filmmakers', *Griffithiana*, vol. 20 nos 60–61, 1997, p. 67.

5 This reaction was not entirely unique to him: at the same time in Germany, an admirer of his, Albrecht Victor Blum, made *Hands: A Study* [Hände: Eine Studie, 1928–1929], a film entirely without intertitles.

6 Aleksei Gan, '"Bolezn′ moia inogo poriadka" Pis′ma Alekseia Gana Esfiri Shub', *Kinovedcheskie zapiski*, no. 49, 2000, p. 223.

7 Vertov, 'The Battle Continues' (1926), in Tsivian, *Lines of Resistance*, p. 260.

8 Vitalii Zhemchuzhnyi, 'The Eleventh Year', (1928), in Tsivian, *Lines of Resistance*, p. 302.

9 Dziga Vertov, Mikhail Kaufman, Elizaveta Svilova, 'Cine-Eyes' Letter to the Editor Repudiating Osip Brik's Review of *The Eleventh Year*', in Tsivian, *Lines of Resistance*, p. 316.

10 Dziga Vertov, 'Speech at a Discussion of the Film *The Eleventh Year* at the ARK', in Tsivian, *Lines of Resistance*, p. 290.

11 Vertov, 'Itinerary Plans for Shooting D. A. Vertov's film *The Eleventh Year*' (c. 1928), RGALI 2091/1/22.

12 Dziga Vertov, 'List of Items Shot for D. A. Vertov's Film *The Eleventh Year*' (c. 1928), RGALI 2091/1/21.

13 Tsivian, *Lines of Resistance*, p. 291.

14 Roberts claims Vertov had use of his library of film from Moscow. While, clearly, he uses this material in *Man with a Movie Camera*, there is little sign of it in *The Eleventh Year*. Roberts, *The Man with the Movie Camera*, p. 32. Moreover, Vertov had complained before leaving Moscow that he was denied access to archive material for this film, then conceived as 'Ten Years'. Dziga Vertov, Letter dated 28/01/1927, RGALI 2091/2/164.

15 The Scythians were an ancient people who lived in what is now Southern Russia and Ukraine.

16 Tsivian discusses images of washing in his commentary to the British Film Institute (BFI) DVD. Roberts argues that the imagery of water, washing and cleaning connote political purging; Roberts, *The Man with the Movie Camera*,

pp. 59, 73, 77. Vertov would have been far from the only artist to play upon such associations. Vladimir Maiakovskii had recently written a play, *The Bathhouse*, exploring the same metaphor.

17 Osip Brik, 'Vertov's *The Eleventh Year*' (1928), in Tsivian, *Lines of Resistance*, p. 311.

18 Drobashenko, *Istoriia sovetskogo dokumental'nogo kino*, p. 17.

19 Kazimir Malevich, 'Pictorial Laws in Cinematic Problems' (1929), in Tsivian, *Lines of Resistance*, p. 344.

20 Elizaveta Svilova, 'Where is *The Eleventh Year*?' (1928), in Tsivian, *Lines of Resistance*, p. 294.

21 L. Shatov, 'The Eleventh Year' (1928), in Tsivian, *Lines of Resistance*, pp. 298–299.

22 Zhemchuzhnyi, '*The Eleventh Year*', p. 301.

23 Erofeev advocated the term after a 1925 trip when he noted the popularity in Germany of the expeditionary form of *Kulturfilm*. Quoted in A. S. Deriabin, '"Nasha psikhologiia i ikh psikhologiia – sovershenno raznye veshchi". "Afganistan" Vladimira Erofeeva i sovetskii kul'turfil'm dvadtsatykh godov', *Kinovedcheskie zapiski*, no. 54, 2001, p. 56.

24 In 1924 Nikolai Lebedev was also advocating the *Kulturfilm* rather than films of entertainment to show the countryside. Quoted in Youngblood, *Soviet Cinema in the Silent Era*, p. 29. Lebedev was particularly fond of the term and was even preparing a book on the subject. See Nikolai Lebedev, 'Kul'turfil'ma na zapade i u nas. Glava iz neizdannoi knigi', *Kinovedcheskie zapiski*, no. 58, 2002, pp. 382–406.

25 Taylor, *The Film Factory*, p. 191.

26 Taylor, *The Film Factory*, p. 194; Sarkisova, 'Envisioned Communities', pp. 12–13; Youngblood, *Soviet Cinema in the Silent Era*, pp. 160–161.

27 Sarkisova, 'Envisioned Communities', pp. 12–13. This is by far the most extensive discussion of the term *Kulturfilm* in English.

28 Indicative of the term's indeterminacy is the fact that a major book on the subject is split between articles advocating acting and others rejecting it. K. I. Shutko (ed.), *Kul'turfil'ma. Politiko-prosvetitel'naia fil'ma*, Moscow, 1929.

29 Esfir' Shub, 'Neigrovaia fil'ma' (1929), in *Zhizn' moia – kinematograf*, p. 263. Erofeev too ultimately rejects the term, as is clear from comments made during a 1929 visit to Germany: '"Tam ia uvidel neobychainye veshchi," Sovetskie kinematografisty o svoikh poezdkakh v Germanii (ARK, 1928–1929)', ed. Aleksandr Deriabin, *Kinovedcheskie zapiski*, no. 58, 2002, p. 279.

30 Dziga Vertov, Untitled (c.1926), RGALI 2091/2/164. Vertov continued to voice this criticism through to 1931. See Vertov, 'Cine-Eye, Radio-Eye and So-Called "Documentalism"', p. 15. Also see Vertov, 'Point of View' (1931), RGALI 2091/2/176.

31 Although some critics and film administrators kept to the notion of *Kulturfilm*, arguing for its profitability under the conditions of rational production and distribution. Sarkisova, 'Envisioned Communities', p. 13.

32 Youngblood, *Soviet Cinema in the Silent Era*, pp. 214–215.
33 'Iz istorii rozhdeniia "Cheloveka s kinoapparatom"', ed. Aleksandr Deriabin, *Kinovedcheskie zapiski*, no. 49, 2000, p. 203.
34 'Iz istorii rozhdeniia', p. 204.
35 'Party Cinema Conference Resolution: The Results of Cinema Construction in the USSR and the tasks of Soviet Cinema' (1928), in Taylor, *The Film Factory*, p. 212.
36 Roshal', *Dziga Vertov*, p. 179.
37 Vertov, Untitled (c.1926), RGALI 2091/2/164.
38 Brik, 'Vertov's *The Eleventh Year*', p. 310.
39 Vertov, Kaufman and Svilova, 'Cine-Eyes' Letter to the Editor…', p. 316.
40 Gilles Deleuze, *The Movement Image*, trans. Hugh Tomlinson and Barbara Habberjam, Minneapolis, MN, 1986, pp. 38–40, 80–84.
41 Michelson, 'From Magician to Epistemologist', p. 110.
42 Roberts, *The Man with the Movie Camera*, pp. 103–104.
43 Monovich, 'Database as Symbolic Form', p. 41.
44 Also see Carsten Strathausen, 'Uncanny Spaces: The City in Ruttmann and Vertov', in Mark Shiel and Tony Fitzmaurice (eds), *Screening the City*, London and New York, 2003, pp. 15–40.
45 Joseph Schaub, 'Presenting the Cyborg's Futurist Past: An Analysis of Dziga Vertov's Kino-Eye', *Postmodern Culture*, vol. 8 no. 2, 1998, 27 paras (para. 26).
46 Judith Mayne, *Kino and the Woman Question: Feminism and Silent Film*, Columbus, OH, 1989, p. 182.
47 Kazimir Malevich, 'Painterly Laws in the Problems of Cinema', trans. Cathy Young, in Margarita Tupitsyn, *Malevich and Film*, London and New Haven, CT, 2002, p. 156.
48 Feldman enthusiastically accepts the claim that this was a Formalist film, since it is 'not only aware of its own structure but composed of nothing else'; Feldman, '"Peace Between Man and Machine"', p. 49.
49 Petrić, *Constructivism in Film*, p. 17.
50 Roberts, *The Man with the Movie Camera*, p. 93.
51 Roberts, *The Man with the Movie Camera*, p. xiii. Similarly, Michelson insists that the film 'stands alone' in Vertov's *oeuvre*; Annette Michelson, 'The Kinetic Icon in the Work of Mourning: Prolegomena to the Analysis of a Textual System', *October*, no. 52, 1990, p. 19, although Michelson is principally referring to a sense that it was not commissioned by a specific agency for a specific end.
52 Nevertheless, the following analysis of the film does not pretend to the kind of exhaustivity attained in the monographs of Petrić and Roberts.
53 Roberts, *The Man with the Movie Camera*, p. xiii. This is an insight Roberts fails to expand upon.
54 Lynne Kirby, 'From Marinetti to Vertov: Woman on the Track of Avant-Garde Representation', *Quarterly Review of Film Studies*, vol. 10 no. 4, 1989, p. 314.
55 As Pearl Latteier notes, the most prominent studies by Feldman and Petrić fail to explore this theme. Pearl Latteier, 'Gender and the Modern Body:

Men, Women, and Machines in Vertov's *Man with a Movie Camera*', *Post Script*, vol. 22 no. 1, 2002, pp. 23–24.

56   Russian has no article so translators are free to decide whether *Man and Movie Camera* have 'a', 'the' or no article. Petrić, Roberts and Tsivian, among others, are drawn to **The** Man with **the** Movie Camera, presumably because it echoes the popular title 'The Man with the...'. Yuri Tsivian, 'Man with a Movie Camera, Reel One', *Film Studies*, no. 2, 2000, p. 51. I have opted for *Man with a Movie Camera* because its suggestions of an allegory of relations between humanity and machine are richer.

57   Tsivian, commentary to BFI DVD.

58   Kirby, 'From Marinetti to Vertov', pp. 313–314.

59   Tsivian, 'Man with a Movie Camera, Reel One', p. 58.

60   Vertov, 'Cine-Eye' (1925), RGALI 2091/2/160.

61   Jay Leyda, *Kino: A History of the Russian and Soviet Film. A Study of the Development of Russian Cinema, from 1896 to the Present*, London, 1983, p. 251; Roberts, *The Man with the Movie Camera*, pp. 22, 36; Michelson, 'From Magician to Epistemologist', p. 103.

62   Patricia R. Zimmermann, 'Reconstructing Vertov; Soviet Film Theory and American Radical Documentary', *Journal of Film and Video*, vol. 44 nos 1–2, 1992, p. 81.

63   This was the title for the initial proposal: Dziga Vertov, '*Man with a Movie Camera: A Visual Symphony*' (1928), *Kino-Eye*, p. 283; *Stat'i*, p. 277. Later, accused of imitating Ruttman, Vertov referred back to this notion of the symphony: 'Letter from Berlin' (1929), *Kino-Eye*, p. 102; *Stat'i*, p. 121.

64   Dziga Vertov, 'About Love for the Living Person' (1958), *Kino-Eye*, p. 155; *Stat'i*, p. 158. I have corrected the translation from 'They are *as* essential as a pledge of future victories'.

65   Zimmermann, 'Reconstructing Vertov', pp. 86–87.

66   Vertov, Notebooks (1927), *Kino-Eye*, p. 166; *Stat'i*, p. 168.

67   'Iz istorii rozhdeniia', p. 203.

68   V. Fefer, 'Operator khroniki, smelost', smert'', *Sovetskoe kino*, nos 6–7, 1926, p. 14.

69   'Iz istorii rozhdeniia', p. 204.

70   Vertov, 'About Love for the Living Person' (1958), *Kino-Eye*, p. 154; *Stat'i*, p. 158.

71   Kaufman, 'Poslednee interv'iu Mikhaila Kaufmana', p. 146.

72   Dziga Vertov, 'Dziga Vertov's Letter to Mikhail Kaufman Requesting He Repudiate Brik's Review of *The Eleventh Year*' (1928), in Tsivian, *Lines of Resistance*, pp. 311–312.

73   Mikhail Kaufman, 'Film Analysis' (1931), in Tsivian, *Lines of Resistance*, p. 391. Kaufman's commitment to this approach is evident from his accomplished 1934 single-reel film, *Aviamarsh*, which also employs no intertitles.

74   Khrisanf Khersonskii, '*Man with a Movie Camera*' (1929), in Tsivian, *Lines of Resistance*, p. 329.

75   Shub, 'Neigrovaia fil´ma', p. 266. She also stresses that this is a product of Kaufman's talent; p. 207.

76   Feldman, '"Peace Between Man and Machine"', p. 40.

77   Strathausen, 'Uncanny Spaces', *passim*; Schaub, 'Presenting the Cyborg's Futurist Past', *passim.*

78   His later writings attempted to represent his earlier work as exploring character through a 'a gallery of emotionally expressed portraits'; Vertov, 'Tvorcheskaia kartochka', p. 167.

79   See anon, 'Why Dziga Vertov has been Dismissed from Sovkino' (1927), in Tsivian, *Lines of Resistance*, pp. 254–255. *Man with a Movie Camera* was, Vertov claims, already half finished when he left in 1927, but had been cut up and spread around other films; Dziga Vertov, Untitled (1927), RGALI 2091/2/164.

80   G. Lenobl, 'Man with a Movie Camera' (1929), in Tsivian, *Lines of Resistance*, p. 337.

81   Roberts, *The Man with the Movie Camera*, p. 50.

82   Feldman, '"Peace Between Man and Machine"', p. 47. Mayne notes that this is virtually the only private space in the film; Mayne, *Kino and the Woman Question*, p. 176.

83   Yuri Tsivian, 'Notes to Vertov Exhibition', Sacile, October 2004. Similarly, Roberts comments that Vertov's goal was 'All must look; all must be seen'; Roberts, *The Man with the Movie Camera*, p. 53

84   Lenobl, '*Man with a Movie Camera*' (1929), in Tsivian, *Lines of Resistance*, p. 340.

85   Khersonskii, '*Man with a Movie Camera*' (1929), in Tsivian, '*Lines of Resistance*, p. 328.

86   See, for example, A. Mikhailov, 'O fil´me "Krest´iane"', *Sovetskoe kino*, no. 5, 1935, p. 33.

Chapter 5

1   Eric Rhode, *A History of the Cinema from its Origins to 1970*, New York, 1976, p. 262. The shift to sound even in America was not overnight; Fox Movietone News had been in sound since April 1927.

2   Jay Leyda, *Films Beget Films*, London, 1964, p. 36.

3   Christie refers to 1936 as the final year of Soviet silent film, but is apparently referring to fiction films alone. See Ian Christie, 'Making Sense of Early Soviet Sound', in Richard Taylor and Ian Christie (eds), *Inside the Film Factory: New Approaches to Russian and Soviet Cinema*, London and New York, 1991, p. 177.

4   The term belongs to Harvey Denkin. Harvey Denkin, 'Linguistic Models in Early Soviet Cinema', *Cinema Journal*, vol. 17 no. 1, Fall 1977, p. 7.

5   Dziga Vertov, 'Man with a Movie Camera, Absolute Kinography, and Radio-Eye' (1928), in Tsivian, *Lines of Resistance*, p. 319.

6   Vertov, 'From Cine-Eye to Radio-Eye' (1929), *Kino-Eye*, p. 91; *Stat´i*, p. 115. For Vertov's further discussion of implicit sound in *The Eleventh Year*, see Vertov, 'From the History of the Cine-Eyes' (1929), *Kino-Eye*, p. 98; *Stat´i*, p. 119.

7   Dziga Vertov, 'First Steps' (1931), *Kino-Eye*, p. 112; *Stat'i*, p. 128.
8   See Roshal', *Dziga Vertov*, pp. 18–19.
9   Dziga Vertov, *Kino-Eye*, p. 20; *Stat'i*, p. 57. For other anticipations of sound newsreel, also see Dziga Vertov, 'Cine-Pravda and Radio-Pravda' (1925), *Kino-Eye*, pp. 52–56; *Stat'i*, pp. 84–86.
10   Taylor, *Film Factory*, pp. 234–235. Also see Christie's discussion of this: Christie, 'Making Sense of Early Soviet Sound', pp. 180–183.
11   A. Gol'dman, 'Kadry v kinopiatiletke', *Kino i zhizn'*, no. 22, 1930, pp. 3–4; quoted in Youngblood, *Soviet Cinema in the Silent Era*, p. 222.
12   Dziga Vertov, 'Speech to First All-Union Conference on Sound Cinema' (1930), in Taylor, *Film Factory*, p. 302.
13   Roshal', *Dziga Vertov*, p. 211.
14   Taylor, *Film Factory*, p. 301. Shub took broadly the same attitude: Shub, *Zhizn' moia – kinematograf*, p. 270.
15   *Puti sovetskoi kinokhroniki*, ed. V. S. Iosilevich, Moscow, 1933, p. 52.
16   Dziga Vertov, 'Reports and Declarations by D. A. Vertov to directors of Kiev Studio of VUFKU and others on the shooting and sound for the film *Enthusiasm*' (1930–1931), RGALI 2091/1/42.
17   Dziga Vertov, '*Enthusiasm*' (1931), RGALI 2091/2/176.
18   Vertov, 'Reports and Declarations...' (1931), RGALI 2091/1/42.
19   Vertov, 'Reports and Declarations...' (1931), RGALI 2091/1/42; '*Enthusiasm*' (1931), RGALI 2091/2/176.
20   Vertov, 'Reports and Declarations...' (1931), RGALI 2091/1/42.
21   Dziga Vertov, 'Speech to First All-Union Conference on Sound Cinema' (1930), in Taylor, *Film Factory*, p. 302.
22   Vertov, 'First Steps' (1931), *Kino-Eye*, p. 114; *Stat'i*, p. 129.
23   Abramov, *Dziga Vertov*, p. 123; Roshal', *Dziga Vertov*, pp. 215–218; John McKay, 'Disorganized Noise: *Enthusiasm* and the Ear of the Collective, 3. Cacophony of the Donbass', pp. 1–7, www.kinokultura.com/articles (last visited 27/07/05).
24   Note that McKay argues the film has no narrative, a feature it shares with inherently anti-narrative utopian tendencies; McKay, 'Cacophony of the Donbass', p. 4.
25   There are apparently two prints in circulation: one circulated by Gosfil'mofond, which is shorter and in which the sound is not synchronised; the other has synchronised sound, restored by Peter Kubelka for the Austrian Film Museum and Anthology Film Archives. In this analysis I refer to this version, also available on video and DVD.
26   Lucy Fischer, '*Enthusiasm*: From Kino-Eye to Radio-Eye', *Film Quarterly*, vol. 31 no. 2, Winter 1977–1978, p. 28.
27   Fischer argues that the woman sculpting a bust of Lenin is the erstwhile radio operator, thus signalling her emergence from passive listening to active creation; Fischer, '*Enthusiasm*', p. 29.
28   Roshal', *Dziga Vertov*, p, 174.
29   As Fischer argues, '[I]t is impossible ever to reconstruct the geography of the settings we are in'; Fischer, '*Enthusiasm*', p. 31.

30 For Fischer this is about disorienting the spectator; Fischer, '*Enthusiasm*', p. 31.
31 McKay, 'Cacophony of the Donbass', p. 1.
32 Fischer, '*Enthusiasm*', p. 30.
33 Fischer, '*Enthusiasm*', pp. 30–31.
34 Fischer, '*Enthusiasm*', p. 30.
35 Liudmila Dzhulai, *Dokumental'nyi illiuzion. Otechestvennyi kinodokumentalizm – opyty sotsial'nogo tvorchestva*, Moscow, 2001, p. 23.
36 Fischer treats such moments of synchronous sound as so isolated as to shock the viewer; Fischer, '*Enthusiasm*', p. 32.
37 Dziga Vertov, 'Notebook with Plans and Schemas for Sound in *Enthusiasm*' (1929–1930), RGALI 2091/2/239.
38 Vertov, 'Speech to First All-Union Conference on Sound Cinema' (1930), in Taylor, *Film Factory*, p. 303.
39 Vertov, 'Speech to First All-Union Conference on Sound Cinema' (1930), in Taylor, *Film Factory*, p. 303.
40 Dzhulai argues it is a hidden polemic with Vertov; see Dzhulai, *Dokumental'nyi illiuzion*, p. 23.
41 Taylor, *Film Factory*, p. 235.
42 Vertov, '*Enthusiasm*' (1931), RGALI 2091/2/176. Also see Dziga Vertov, 'Replies to Questions' (1930), *Kino-Eye*, pp. 105–106; *Stat'i*, p. 124.
43 Christie, 'Making Sense of Early Soviet Sound', p. 178.
44 Dziga Vertov, 'We: Variant of a Manifesto' (1922), *Kino-Eye*, p. 7; *Stat'i*, p. 46.
45 Christie, 'Making Sense of Early Soviet Sound', p. 178.
46 Dziga Vertov, 'D. A. Vertov's Literary and Director's scenario for *Enthusiasm (A Symphony of the Donbas)*' (1928), RGALI 2091/1/35. The *subbotnik* was the practice of voluntarily working on a day off.
47 Vertov, 'Notebook with Plans and Schemas for Sound in *Enthusiasm*' (1929–1930), RGALI 2091/2/239.
48 '*Enthusiasm*' (1931), RGALI 2091/2/176.
49 In this sense Tret'iakov was right when he referred to Vertov's method as 'flagrant' filming: all too often his intention is to catch 'in flagrante', in the act of committing an offence. Sergei Tret'iakov in Bulgakova, 'LEF i kino', p. 52.
50 Vertov, 'First Steps' (1931), *Kino-Eye*, p. 114; *Stat'i*, p. 128.
51 G. Zosimov, 'Kinokhronika na ekrane. Obzor produktsii soiuzkinokhroniki za 1932 g.', *Sovetskoe kino*, no. 8, 1933, p. 39. Also see Ansel'm Bogorov, 'Leningradskie kinokhronikery', *Iz istorii kino. Materialy i dokumenty*, no. 9, 1974, p. 159.
52 Dzhulai, *Dokumental'nyi illiuzion*, p. 26.
53 Selunskaya and Zezina, 'Documentary Films', in Taylor and Spring, *Stalinism and Soviet Cinema*, p. 179; Taylor, *Film Factory*, p. 194.
54 Noel Burch, *To the Distant Observer: Form and Meaning in the Japanese Cinema*, ed. and revised by Annette Michelson, London, 1979, p. 147.
55 In a 1932 response to a questionnaire, Vertov refers to his Lenin film (i.e. what would become *Three Songs of Lenin*) as 'sound newsreel [khronika],

aimed at a mass audience', but refers to his own work as 'khronikal'naia dokumental'naia fil'ma'. See Dziga Vertov, 'Cinema Workers, Use All Your Powers and Creative Experience in the Realisation of the Decisions of the 17th Party Conference', *Proletarskoe kino*, no. 4, 1932, pp. 5–6. In 1931 Vertov is already using the term 'documentary' as a synomym for 'neigrovoe' and 'kinoglaz'; Vertov, 'Cine-Eye, Radio-Eye and So-Called "Documentalism,"' p. 13. Boris Tseitlin also refers to *Symphony of the Donbas* as a sound documentary; B. Tseitlin, 'Dokumental'naia zvukovaia', *Kino i zhizn'*, no. 25, 1930, p. 16. The film credits for *Enthusiasm* refer to its 'audio-visual documentary material'.

56 Winston, *Claiming the Real*, p. 9.

57 For example, Sutyrin, an editor of *Proletarskoe kino*, refers to documentary as a synonym of 'unplayed'; V. Sutyrin, 'O sotsialisticheskoi rekonstruktsii kinematografii', *Proletarskoe kino*, no. 1, 1931, p. 14. Similarly, in 1931 Erofeev stresses that 'documentary', 'newsreel' and 'unplayed' all refer to different aspects of the same phenomenon, but mentions 'documentary' as being the most widely used term; V. Erofeev, 'Tekhnicheskoe novatorstvo dokumental'noi fil'my', *Proletarskoe kino*, nos 2–3, 1931, p. 6.

58 Bogorov, 'Leningradskie kinokhronikery', p. 172.

59 A. Zorich, in *Gudok* (1927), quoted in Dziga Vertov, 'The Complete Capitulation of Nikolai Lebedev', *Proletarskoe kino*, no. 5, 1932, p. 16.

60 The Russian term 'dokumentalizm' is variously translated as 'documentarism' (*Film Factory*, p. 321) and as 'documentalism' (Roberts, *Forward Soviet!*, pp. 100–103). It is not a term in widespread use, although Sergei Drobashenko employs it to refer to documentary film-making: Drobashenko, *Istoriia sovetskogo dokumental'nogo kino*, p. 3. It was also incorrectly associated with factography; Zosimov, 'Kinokhronika na ekrane', p. 40.

61 Al. Borisov, 'Dokumentalisty v zvukovom kino', *Proletarskoe kino*, nos 5–6, 1931, p. 33.

62 Vertov, 'Cinema Workers, Use All Your Powers', p. 6.

63 Dziga Vertov, 'Documentary Film and Documentalism' (1931), RGALI, 2091/2/174.

64 Dziga Vertov, 'Once More about So-Called Documentalism', *Proletarskoe kino*, no. 3, 1932, p. 46.

65 Roberts, *Forward Soviet!*, p. 101.

66 Dziga Vertov, RGALI 2091/2/174.

67 V. Sutyrin, 'Vol ili liagushka', *Proletarskoe kino*, no. 4, 1932, p. 14.

68 Taylor, *Film Factory*, p. 322.

69 V. Sutyrin, 'Vol ili liagushka (prodolzhenie)', *Proletarskoe kino*, no. 5, 1932, p. 11.

70 For a classic statement of this position, see Jacques Aumont, A. Bergala, M. Marie and M. Vernet, *Esthétique du film*, Paris, 1983, p. 71. Also see Winston, *Claiming the Real*, pp. 122, 247–253.

71 Sutyrin, 'Vol ili liagushka (prodolzhenie)', p. 6. This argument goes back to Voronskii, a literary critic relentlessly criticised by the Proletarians in the 1920s, but not before they had plagiarised his theories.

72 Sutyrin, 'Vol ili liagushka (prodolzhenie)', p. 6.
73 *Puti sovetskoi kinokhroniki*, pp. 7–8.
74 Zosimov, 'Kinokhronika na ekrane', p. 40.
75 Nikolai Lebedev, 'Za proletarskuiu kinopublitsistiku', *Proletarskoe kino*, no. 12, 1931, p. 20.
76 Lebedev, 'Za proletarskuiu kinopublitsistiku', p. 23. Sutyrin makes the same argument: Sutyrin, 'Vol ili liagushka (prodolzhenie)', p. 5.
77 Lebedev, 'Za proletarskuiu kinopublitsistiku', p. 23
78 Roberts condemns the debates over 'documentalism' as a trivial distraction. In fact, what is being attacked is the very existence of documentary as a distinct category, enabling both a shift in documentary and a shift towards acted reconstructions. Roberts, *Forward Soviet!*, p. 92.
79 *Puti sovetskoi kinokhroniki*, p. 59.
80 *Puti sovetskoi kinokhroniki*, pp. 51–52.
81 *Sovetskaia kinokhronika* (Tvorchesko-proizvodstvennye i tekhnicheskie voprosy), *Sbornik pervyi*, Moscow, 1934, p. 52.
82 This is particularly evident in Shumiatskii's speech to the First Conference of Newsreel Workers; *Puti sovetskoi kinokhroniki*, pp. 5–6.
83 V. Golovnia, 'Nekotorye itogi i perspektivy', *Sovremennyi dokumental'nyi fil'm. Kriticheskie zametki. Problemy teorii. Iz sobstvenogo opyta*, Moscow, 1970, p. 18.
84 *Puti sovetskoi kinokhroniki*, p. 38.
85 *Kino*, 4 March 1934; quoted in Dzhulai, *Dokumental'nyi illiuzion*, p. 65.
86 Drobashenko, *Istoriia sovetskogo dokumental'nogo kino*, p. 48.
87 *Puti sovetskoi kinokhroniki*, p. 11.
88 N. Kolin (ed.), *Zapiski kinooperatorov*, Moscow, 1938, p. 113.
89 *Zapiski kinooperatorov*, p. 113.
90 *Sovetskaia kinokhronika*, p. 14.
91 *Sovetskaia kinokhronika*, p. 14; Drobashenko, *Istoriia sovetskogo dokumental'nogo kino*, p. 48.
92 *Puti sovetskoi kinokhroniki*, p. 59.
93 *Puti sovetskoi kinokhroniki*, p. 96.
94 *Puti sovetskoi kinokhroniki*, p. 60.
95 *Puti sovetskoi kinokhroniki*, p. 41.
96 *Sovetskaia kinokhronika*, p. 36.
97 *Puti sovetskoi kinokhroniki*, p. 38.
98 *Puti sovetskoi kinokhroniki*, p. 57.
99 *Puti sovetskoi kinokhroniki*, pp. 88–89.
100 *Puti sovetskoi kinokhroniki*, p. 70.
101 *Puti sovetskoi kinokhroniki*, p. 72.
102 Bogorov, 'Leningradskie kinokhronikery', pp. 159–160.
103 *Puti sovetskoi kinokhroniki*, p. 54.
104 Robert, *The Man with the Movie Camera*, p. 26. Although Vertov claimed he intended to make other Cine-Eye films from this footage, nevertheless it would still be far higher than these ratios.
105 Shub, *Zhizn' moia – kinematograf*, p. 282.

106 *Zapiski kinooperatorov*, p. 47.
107 *Sovetskaia kinokhronika*, p. 40.

Chapter 6

1   Dziga Vertov, *'Leninist Cine-Pravda'* (1924), RGALI 2091/2/157.
2   Roberts, *Forward Soviet!*, p. 123.
3   Michelson, 'The Kinetic Icon in the Work of Mourning', p. 38.
4   Michelson claims that *Three Songs of Lenin* was the only one of Vertov's films granted 'immediate, unanimous and enduring approval ... within the Soviet Union'; Michelson, 'The Kinetic Icon in the Work of Mourning', p.18. See below, Chapter 8 for a discussion of the film's fluctuating domestic reputation.
5   Feldman, '"Peace Between Man and Machine"', p. 51.
6   Stollery reviews the spectrum of positions engagingly; Stollery, *Alternative Empires*, pp. 117–119.
7   Leyda, *Kino*, p. 312.
8   Vlada Petrić, 'Vertov, Lenin, and Perestroika: The Cinematic Transposition of Reality', *Historical Journal of Film, Radio, and Television*, vol. 15 no. 1, 1995, p. 4.
9   Selunskaya and Zezina, 'Documentary Films', in Taylor and Spring, *Stalinism and Soviet Cinema*, p. 178. Widdis praises its 'unsettling energy' but also comments on the film's 'strikingly slow' pace; Widdis, *Visions of a New Land*, pp. 218, 162.
10 Richard Taylor, *Film Propaganda: Soviet Russia and Nazi Germany*, 2nd edn revised, London and New York, 1998, p. 76.
11 Leyda, *Kino*, p. 313.
12 Dziga Vertov, Notebooks, Diaries 'On My Illness' (1934), *Kino-Eye*, p. 188; *Stat'i*, p. 189.
13 Vertov, Notebooks, Diaries 'On My Illness' (1934), *Kino-Eye*, p. 188; *Stat'i*, p. 189.
14 *Sovetskaia torgovlia*, 4 November 1934; quoted in Roshal', *Dziga Vertov*, p. 227.
15 Dziga Vertov, untitled (1936), *Tri pesni o Lenine*, ed. E. I. Vertova-Svilova and V. I. Furtichev, Moscow, 1972, p. 120.
16 Dziga Vertov, Notebooks, Diaries (1934), *Kino-Eye*, pp. 178–179; *Stat'i*, pp. 181–182.
17 K. Iukov, 'Iubileinyi god kinoiskusstva', *Sovetskoe kino*, nos 11–12, 1934, p. 24.
18 Aleksandr Deriabin (ed.), '"A driani podobno 'Garmon'' bol'she ne stavite?" Zapiski besed B. Z. Shumiatskogo s I. V. Stalinym posle kinoprosmotrov, 1934g.', *Kinovedcheskie zapiski*, no. 61, 2002, p. 319.
19 *Pravda*, 26 January 1934, p. 1. Also see *Pravda*, 10 April, 1934, p. 1; reproduced in Sartorti, *Pressfotographie und Industrialisierung*, p. 259. For analysis of the shifting representations of the two leaders, see Sartorti,

Pressfotographie und Industrialisierung, p. 257. Also see Tumarkin, *Lenin Lives!*, p. 246.

20 See, for example, D. Velikorodnyi, '"Chapaev" podarok 15-letnego iubiliara', *Sovetskoe kino*, nos 11–12, 1934, p. 110.

21 Dziga Vertov, 'My Latest Experiment' (1935), *Kino-Eye*, p. 137; *Stat'i*, p. 145.

22 Drobashenko, *Istoriia sovetskogo dokumental'nogo kino*, p. 40. Roshal´ similarly argues that the choice of women as central themes for Vertov's last works was due to his seeing the liberation of the women of the East as the greatest achievement of Soviet power; Lev Roshal´, 'Vertov i Stalin', *Iskusstvo kino*, no. 1, 1994, p. 108.

23 Stollery, *Alternative Empires*, p. 137.

24 Stollery, *Alternative Empires*, p. 124.

25 This appeared only in the 1970 and 1938 versions of the film, and is a quotation from Stalin.

26 Taylor, *Film Propaganda*, p. 83.

27 Stollery, *Alternative Empires*, p. 124.

28 Both of these intertitles appear in the restored 1970 version, but are not present in certain other prints. See 'Intertitles to *Three Songs of Lenin*, 1934', *October*, no. 52, 1990, pp. 40–51. This appears to be based on the 1934 print.

29 Petrić, 'Vertov, Lenin, and Perestroika', p. 9; also see Roberts, *Forward Soviet!*, p. 124.

30 Deriabin, '"Plod sozrel i ego nado sniat´..."', pp. 196–197; Aleksandr Deriabin, '"Kolybel'naia" Dzigi Vertova: zamysel-voploshchenie-ekrannaia sud'ba', *Kinovedcheskie zapiski*, no. 51, 2001, p. 31.

31 Stollery, *Alternative Empires*, pp. 137–138.

32 Stollery, *Alternative Empires*, p. 138.

33 Vertov, 'Cine-Eye' (1925), RGALI, 2091/2/160.

34 *Zapiski kinooperatorov*, pp. 95–96.

35 For this earlier variant of the film, see Dziga Vertov, *Iz naslediia: Dramaturgicheskie opyty*, ed. Aleksandr Deriabin, Moscow, 2004, pp. 141–161.

36 Elizaveta Svilova-Vertova, untitled (n.d.), *Tri pesni o Lenine*, p. 107. Vertov also stresses the unexpected nature of the discovery of the folk songs: Dziga Vertov, 'I Wish to Share My Experience' (1934), *Kino-Eye*, p. 122; *Stat'i*, p. 136.

37 Vertov, Notebooks, Diaries (1936), *Kino-Eye*, p. 196; *Stat'i*, p. 196

38 Vertov, 'My Latest Experiment' (1935), *Kino-Eye*, p. 135; *Stat'i*, p. 144. This could be better translated as 'documents of popular creative art'.

39 See Frank J. Miller, *Folklore for Stalin: Russian Folklore and Pseudofolklore of the Stalin Era*, Armonk, NY, and London, 1990, pp. 10–11.

40 Vertov, Notebooks, Diaries (1934), *Kino-Eye*, p. 178; *Stat'i*, p. 181. I have altered O'Brien's translation from 'subtitles' for 'nadpisi'.

41 Vertov, 'My Latest Experiment' (1935), *Kino-Eye*, p. 135; *Stat'i*, p. 144.

42 Dziga Vertov, Notebooks, Diaries (1933), *Kino-Eye*, p. 171; *Stat'i*, p. 174.

43 Roshal´, *Dziga Vertov*, p. 226.

44 As Vertov comments in his 1936 diary on the surge in interest in folklore in Soviet art, he had collected songs back in 1933, before this kind of thing became fashionable; *Kino-Eye*, p. 196; *Stat'i*, p. 196. For Gor'kii's endorsement of folklore, see *Soviet Writers' Congress 1934. The Debate on Socialist Realism and Modernism in the Soviet Union*, London, 1977, pp. 35–36. Also see Régine Robin, *Socialist Realism: An Impossible Aesthetic*, trans. C. Porter, Stanford, CA, 1992, pp. 53–54.

45 Dzhulai, *Dokumental'nyi illiuzion*, p. 42.

46 V. I. Fomin, *Pravda skazki. Kino i traditsii fol'klora*, Moscow, 2001, p. 100.

47 Fomin, *Pravda skazki*, pp. 103–107. A clear example of this was the criticism of Dem'ian Bednyi's comic opera based on folkloric material, *Bogatyri*, in 1936.

48 Michelson, 'The Kinetic Icon in the Work of Mourning', pp. 32, 38; Oksana Bulgakova, 'Prostranstvennye figury sovetskogo kino 30-kh godov', *Kinovedcheskie zapiski*, no. 29, 1996, pp. 51–55.

49 Dziga Vertov, '*Three Songs of Lenin* and Cine-Eye' (1934), *Kino-Eye*, p. 125; *Stat'i*, p.139.

50 Stollery, *Alternative Empires*, p. 132.

51 Vertov, Notebooks, Diaries (1934), *Kino-Eye*, pp. 193–194; *Stat'i*, p. 194.

52 For a brief history of the newspaper interview, see Winston, *Lies, Damn Lies and Documentaries*, p. 121.

53 Dziga Vertov, Rough Notes (1932), *Tri pesni o Lenine*, p. 111.

54 Dziga Vertov, 'Cine-Pravda' (1934), *Kino-Eye*, p. 132; *Stat'i*, p. 143.

55 Vertov, '*Three Songs of Lenin* and Cine-Eye' (1934), *Kino-Eye*, p. 124; *Stat'i*, p. 138.

56 Dziga Vertov, 'About Love for the Living Person' (1958), *Kino-Eye*, pp. 147–148; *Stat'i*, p. 154.

57 Dziga Vertov, Notebooks (1934), *Tri pesni o Lenine*, p. 115.

58 Roshal', 'Vertov i Stalin', p. 107; Drobashenko, *Istoriia sovetskogo dokumental'nogo kino*, p. 41; Petrić, 'Vertov, Lenin, and Perestroika', p. 9.

59 Drobashenko claims it is the first interview. Jay Leyda claims the first newsreel interview was with Maxim Litvinov on his way to Geneva on 26 January 1932. Roman Karmen recalls his first sound interview, of H. G. Wells, in July 1934. Drobashenko, *Istoriia sovetskogo dokumental'nogo kino*, p. 41; Leyda, *Kino*, p. 285; Roman Karmen, *No Pasaran!*, Moscow, 1972, p. 214.

60 Winston, *Claiming the Real*, p. 43. As Winston points out, this was a technique already widely exploited in radio.

61 Thomas Waugh, 'Joris Ivens' *The Spanish Earth*: Committed Documentary and the Popular Front', in Thomas Waugh (ed.), *'Show us Life': Towards a History and Aesthetics of the Committed Documentary*, Metuchen, NJ, and London, 1984, p. 125

62 Dziga Vertov, 'From a Memorandom to the Directors of "Mezhrabpomfil'm"' (1934), *Tri pesni o Lenine*, p. 113.

63 Vertov, 'My Latest Experiment' (1935), *Kino-Eye*, p. 137; *Stat'i*, p. 145.

64 Vertova-Svilova, untitled (n.d.), *Tri pesni o Lenine*, p. 114.

65 Dziga Vertov, Diary (n.d.), *Tri pesni o Lenine*, p. 117.
66 Dziga Vertov, 'Without Words' (1934), *Kino-Eye*, p. 118; *Stat'i*, p.132.
67 Roberts comments on the large number of intertitles in the film; Roberts, *Forward Soviet!*, p. 166, n. 8.
68 Michelson, 'The Kinetic Icon in the Work of Mourning', p. 20.
69 Roshal', *Dziga Vertov*, p. 231.
70 '*Three Songs of Lenin* is typical of what the Soviet "documentary" would become.' Youngblood, *Soviet Cinema in the Silent Era*, p. 230.
71 Shub later denounced it; Shub, 'Vsevolod Vishnevskii' (1958), *Zhizn' moia – kinematograf*, p.177.
72 Apparently, one of Svilova's functions in the creative aspect of their partnership was indexing and tracking down footage: see Vertov, 'About Love for the Living Person' (1958), *Kino-Eye*, p. 153; *Stat'i*, p. 158.
73 Stollery, *Alternative Empires*, p. 126.
74 Youngblood, *Soviet Cinema in the Silent Era*, p. 230.
75 Roberts, *Forward Soviet!*, p. 123.
76 Vertov, Notebooks, Diaries (1934), *Kino-Eye*, p. 186; *Stat'i*, p. 187.
77 300 metres of film were added; Deriabin, '"Kolybel'naia" Dzigi Vertova', p. 42.
78 This is the version used in the currently available DVD: *Three Songs about Lenin*, Kino International/Image-Entertainment, 1999.
79 A. Ia. Kletskin, 'Dziga Vertov i Robert Flaherty', *Kinovedcheskie zapiski*, no. 16, 1992, p. 98.
80 Leyda sees the compilation sequences in *Three Songs of Lenin* as so effective as to have changed that form permanently; Leyda, *Films Beget Films*, p. 42.
81 Peter Kenez, 'Black and White: The War on Film', in Richard Stites (ed.), *Culture and Entertainment in Wartime Russia*, Bloomington and Indianapolis, IN, 1995, p. 161. Curiously, Stalin seems to take a similar view: see '"A driani podobno 'Garmon'' bol'she ne stavite?"', p. 300.
82 Roberts, *Forward Soviet!*, p. 133.
83 Shub sees this as a shift away from the recording of the present; Shub, Letter to Mosfil'm (1941), *Zhizn' moia – kinematograf*, p. 193.
84 Rostislav Yurenev, 'Art and Ideology: The Soviet Historical Film', *Culture*, vol. 2 no. 1, 1974, p. 62.
85 Osip Brik, 'Ring LEFa – Tovarishchi sshibaetes' mneniami', *Novyi LEF*, no. 4, 1928, p. 30.
86 Shub, 'Eta robota krichit' (1928), *Zhizn' moia – kinematograf*, pp. 256–257.
87 S. Tret'iakov, 'Kino k iubileiu', *Novyi LEF*, no. 10, 1927, p. 28.
88 Quoted in I. Vaisfel'd, 'Zamechatel'nyi fil'm', in P. Poluianov (ed.), *Lenin v Oktiabre*, Moscow, 1938, p. v.
89 S. Tsimbal, 'Obraz Lenina v kino', *Iskusstvo kino*, no. 1, 1938, p. 14. For an engaging account of this use of photography in history, see Edith Wyschogrod, *An Ethics of Remembering: History, Heterology and the Nameless Others*, Chicago and London, 1998, p. 77.
90 Tsimbal, 'Obraz Lenina v kino', p. 14.

91 Vaisfel´d, 'Zamechatel´nyi fil´m', pp. vi, viii. However, in the post-Stalin era Stalin was edited out of the film. Alexander Sesonke, 'Re-Editing History: *Lenin in October:* 1937 Then and Now 1983', *Sight and Sound*, vol. 53 no. 1, 1983–1984, pp. 56–58.

92 Quoted in *Obraz V. I. Lenina v sovetskom kinoiskusstve*, ed. M. Serbera, Moscow, 1969, p. 31. Rostislav Yurenev, like all Soviet criticism on the subject, stresses the importance of a thorough study of the documents prior to the actor's performance of the Lenin role; Yurenev, 'Art and Ideology', p.71.

93 John Izod, *Myth, Mind and Screen: Understanding the Hoeroes of Our Times*, Cambridge, 2001, pp. 36–37.

94 André Bazin, 'The Myth of Stalin in the Soviet Cinema', in *Bazin at Work: Major Essays and Reviews from the Forties and Fifties*, ed. Bert Cardullo, trans. Alain Piette, New York and London, 1997, p. 30.

95 Tsimbal, 'Obraz Lenina v kino', p. 13.

96 Vaisfel´d does much the same without actually referring to Vertov's terminology: Vaisfel´d, 'Zamechatel´nyi fil´m'.

97 Tsimbal, 'Obraz Lenina v kino', pp. 13–14.

98 Tsimbal, 'Obraz Lenina v kino', p. 13.

99 *Lenin in October* was supposedly completed a mere three months after shooting began; Leyda, *Kino*, p. 339.

100 Katerina Clark, *The Soviet Novel: History as Ritual*, 3rd edn, Bloomington and Indianapolis, IN, 2000, pp. 146–147; Vaisfeld, 'Zamechatel´nyi fil´m', p. 5.

101 Selunskaya and Zezina, 'Documentary Films', in Taylor and Spring, *Stalinism and Soviet Cinema*, p. 179.

102 Lars T. Lih, 'Melodrama and the Myth of the Soviet Union', in Louise McReynolds and Joan Neuberger (eds), *Imitations of Life: Two Centuries of Melodrama in Russia*, Durham, NC, and London, 2002, p. 202.

Chapter 7

1 See, for example, Petrić: '[A]fter *Three Songs about Lenin*, Vertov was not able to make another major film.' Petrić, *Constructivism in Film*, p. 24. The notable exceptions are Deriabin, '"Kolybel´naia" Dzigi Vertova'; and Natascha Drubek-Meyer, 'Kolybel´ Griffith'a i Vertova. O "Kolybel´noi" Dzigi Vertova (1937),' *Kinovedcheskie zapiski*, no. 30, 1996, pp. 198–212.

2 Youngblood, *Soviet Cinema in the Silent Era*, p. 232; Taylor, *Film Factory*, pp. 345–355.

3 Vertov, Notebooks, Diaries 'On My Illness' (1934), *Kino-Eye*, p. 188; *Stat´i*, pp. 188–189.

4 Dziga Vertov, 'In Defence of Newsreel' (1939), *Kino-Eye*, pp. 146–147; *Stat´i*, pp. 152–153.

5 Deriabin, '"Kolybel´naia" Dzigi Vertova', pp. 37–38.

6 See, for example, Stalin's praise for the documentary film *Cheliuskin* and for its makers Shafran and Troianovskii as not 'posers' or 'loud-mouthed

boasters' in implicit contrast to Vertov. "'A driani podobno 'Garmon'' bol'she ne stavite?"', pp. 299–300.

7 Deriabin, "'Kolybel'naia" Dzigi Vertova', p. 36
8 Deriabin, "'Kolybel'naia" Dzigi Vertova', p. 37
9 Vertov, Notebooks, Diaries (1934), *Kino-Eye*, pp. 174–175; *Stat'i*, pp. 177–178.
10 Dziga Vertov, 'She' (1933), *Kino-Eye*, p. 296; *Stat'i*, pp. 285–286. For the unedited text see: Dziga Vertov, *Iz naslediia*, ed. with a foreword by Aleksander Deriabin, Moscow, 2004, p. 177.
11 Dziga Vertov, 'Songs of a Girl' (c. 1936), *Iz naslediia*, p. 191.
12 Deriabin, "'Kolybel'naia" Dzigi Vertova', p. 31.
13 Deriabin, "'Kolybel'naia" Dzigi Vertova', p. 31.
14 Vertov, 'Songs of a Girl' (c. 1936), *Iz naslediia*, pp. 494, 209–215.
15 One draft scenario is composed of heterogeneous elements including both songs and newspaper cuttings; Deriabin, "'Kolybel'naia" Dzigi Vertova', p. 33.
16 Vertov, 'Songs of a Girl' (c. 1936), *Iz naslediia*, p. 495.
17 Vertov, Notebooks, Diaries (1936), *Kino-Eye*, p. 200; *Stat'i*, p. 201.
18 Daniel and Dmitrii Pokrass were popular songwriters who wrote for theatrical productions, revues and latterly film music, before writing widely performed patriotic songs during World War II. See http://savethemusic .com/yiddish/bin/music.cgi?Page=zognitkeynmol&Composer=dpokras (last visited 09/09/05).
19 Deriabin notes that the high point of this genre was from 1937 to 1940; Deriabin, "'Kolybel'naia" Dzigi Vertova', p. 44.
20 Drubek-Meyer argues that this is informed by a general polemicising with D. W. Griffiths' *Intolerance*, which contains a repeated image of a mother (Lillian Gish) rocking a cradle in a highly staged studio shot. Drubek-Meyer, 'Kolybel' Griffith'a i Vertova', p. 202.
21 Feldman, "'Peace Between Man and Machine"', p. 51. Also see Drobashenko, *Istoriia sovetskogo dokumental'nogo kino*, p. 43.
22 I. Gunger, 'Zvukovoi obraz v dokumental'nom fil'me', in N. N. Sokolova (ed.), *Dokumental'noe kino segodnia*, Moscow, 1963, p. 189.
23 Gunger, 'Zvukovoi obraz v dokumental'nom fil'me', in Sokolova, *Dokumental 'noe kino segodnia*, p. 192.
24 Hans Günther, 'Mudryi otets Stalin i ego sem'ia (na materiale kartin D. Vertova i M. Chaureli)', *Russian Literature*, no. 43, 1998, p. 210.
25 Drobashenko, *Istoriia sovetskogo dokumental'nogo kino*, p. 43.
26 Drubek-Meyer, 'Kolybel' Griffith'a i Vertova', p. 208. Petrić argues something similar: Petrić, 'Vertov, Lenin, and Perestroika', pp. 3–4.
27 Drubek-Meyer, 'Kolybel' Griffith'a i Vertova', p. 209.
28 Drubek-Meyer, 'Kolybel' Griffith'a i Vertova', p. 202. Günther too sees the film as out of step with the times, but does not explain how; Günther, 'Mudryi otets Stalin i ego sem'ia', p. 212.
29 Deriabin, "'Kolybel'naia" Dzigi Vertova', p. 40.
30 Throughout this section I elaborate on Aleksandr Deriabin's excellent article: Deriabin, "'Kolybel'naia" Dzigi Vertova'.

31 Deriabin, '"Kolybel'naia" Dzigi Vertova', p. 59.
32 Deriabin, '"Kolybel'naia" Dzigi Vertova', p. 42.
33 Dziga Vertov, 'Excerpt from Speech of Comrade B. Z. Shumiatksii at the First All-Union Congress of Cinema Workers' (1937), RGALI 2091/2/497.
34 Deriabin, '"Kolybel'naia" Dzigi Vertova', p. 41.
35 Deriabin claims that there were no feature-length documentaries made of Stalin until after World War II; conversation with Aleksandr Deriabin, Moscow, 24 February 2005.
36 Deriabin, '"Kolybel'naia" Dzigi Vertova,' pp. 41–42. Deriabin comments that this was nothing by comparison with the mutilation of *Three Songs of Lenin.*
37 Deriabin, '"Kolybel'naia" Dzigi Vertova', p. 40.
38 '"A driani podobno 'Garmon'' bol'she ne stavite?"', p. 300.
39 Sartorti, *Pressefotographie und Industrialierung*, pp. 258–260.
40 However, this is not to say that there were no photographs of Stalin in this period. See A. Garanin's discussions of photographing Stalin: A. Garanin, 'Nezabyvaemye vstrechi', in Iu. Prigozhin (ed.), *Zapiski fotoreporterov*, Moscow, 1939, pp. 31–33.
41 Drubek-Meyer, 'Kolybel' Griffith'a i Vertova', p. 207.
42 Roshal', 'Vertov i Stalin', p. 111.
43 Listov, 'Vertov: Odnazhdy i vsegda', p. 138.
44 Dziga Vertov, 'A Day of the World' (1936), *Iz naslediia*, p. 238.
45 Drobashenko, *Istoriia sovetskogo dokumental'nogo kino*, p. 43.
46 Vertov, *Iz naslediia*, p. 497.
47 Leyda, *Kino*, pp. 359, 366.
48 Petrić, *Constructivism in Film*, p. 220.
49 Lev Roshal', 'Kommentarii k muzykal'nomu konspektu', *Kinovedcheskie zapiski*, no. 21, 1994, p. 192.
50 Vertov also made a newsreel, *Sovetskii Kazakhstan,* which was apparently not distributed; Semiramida Pumpianskaia, 'Ia mechtala rabotat' na kinostudii', *Kinovedcheskie zapiski*, no. 62, 2003, pp. 66–67.
51 Pumpianskaia, 'Ia mechtala rabotat' na kinostudii', p. 70.
52 Pumpianskaia, 'Ia mechtala rabotat' na kinostudii', p. 68.
53 Pumpianskaia, 'Ia mechtala rabotat' na kinostudii', p. 70.
54 Drobashenko, *Istoriia sovetskogo dokumental'nogo kino*, p. 60.
55 Kenez, 'Black and White: The War on Film', p. 163.
56 Listov, 'Vertov: odnazhdy i vsegda', p. 141.
57 Lev Roshal' (ed.), 'Protokol odnogo zasedaniia', *Iskusstvo kino*, no. 12, 1997, p. 132.
58 Dziga Vertov, 'Autobiography', in *Iz istorii kino. Materialy i dokumenty*, 2, Moscow, 1959, pp. 29–31.

Chapter 8

1   Thomas Tode, 'Un Soviétique escalade la Tour Eiffel: Dziga Vertov à Paris', *Cinémathèque*, no. 5, 1994, p. 69.

2   Tode refutes the claim that it was 'widely acclaimed' abroad; Roberts, *The Man with the Movie Camera*, p. 23. The one film-maker clearly influenced was Vertov's youngest brother, Boris Kaufman. Tode, 'Vertov à Paris', p. 72.

3   Moussinac published some articles on Vertov in the 1920s; he wrote reviews for the French Communist daily *L'Humanité*. See Tode, 'Vertov à Paris', p. 77.

4   Tode, 'Vertov à Paris', p. 70.

5   J. D., '"Living Russia" – Film Guild Cinema', *New York Herald Tribune*, 17 September 1929, p. 25.

6   Raymond Ganly, '*Man with the Camera*: No Appeal for American Fans' (1929), in Tsivian, *Lines of Resistance*, p. 363.

7   When Vertov showed *The Eleventh Year* in Germany in 1929 audiences recognised sections that had been used, unbeknown to Vertov, in Viktor Albrecht Blum's *In the Shadow of the Machines*. Blum had thought he could get away with using the footage. Dziga Vertov, and Siegfried Kracauer and Viktor Albrecht Blum, 'Vertov versus Blum' (1929), in Tsivian, *Lines of Resistance*, pp. 377–382; Vertov, Notebooks, Diaries (1934), *Kino-Eye*, p. 173; *Stat'i*, p. 175.

8   Certainly, Kracauer refers to the German premiere of *Man with a Movie Camera* at the Stuttgart 'Film and Photo' Exhibition of June 1929, and had seen a preview at the Soviet Trade Delegation earlier that year. Siegfried Kracauer, '*Man with a Movie Camera*' (1929), in Tsivian, *Lines of Resistance*, p. 356. Also see Sophie Kupers, *Kinovedcheskie zapiski*, no. 58, 2002, pp. 209–211.

9   Leyda, *Kino*, p. 251.

10 Montagu wrote to the Soviet trade delegation in Berlin twice in 1929; Dziga Vertov, RGALI 2091/2/542. Given the obstruction of the Soviet trade delegation towards the distribution of Vertov's films, it seems unlikely that he was ever made aware of this request; Dziga Vertov, 'Materials about Trip Abroad' (1931), RGALI 2091/2/419. Antonov even refused to give Vertov the film at one point.

11 'Impression of City Life in Modern Russia', *Morning Post*, 12 January, 1931, p. 6.

12 Ivor Montagu, 'Romance and Reality', *New Statesman and Nation*, 28 April 1934, p. 638.

13 John Grierson, '*Man with a Movie Camera*' (1931), in Tsivian, *Lines of Resistance*, p. 374.

14 Grierson, *Grierson on Documentary*, p. 39.

15 Grierson, '*Man with a Movie Camera*' (1931), in Tsivian, *Lines of Resistance*, p. 375.

16 Leyda, *Kino*, p. 195; *Grierson on Documentary*, pp. 25–28, 35.

17 Vertov, 'First Steps' (1931), *Kino-Eye*, p. 112; *Stat'i*, p. 128. Also see McKay, 'Disorganized Noise: *Enthusiasm* and the Ear of the Collective. Part 4: No

Noise', pp. 5–6. Shub perceives the possibilities of sound for documentary film-makers similarly: Shub, 'K prikhodu zvuka v kinematograf' (1929), *Zhizn' moia – kinematograf*, pp. 269–270.

18 Roshal', *Dziga Vertov*, p. 218.

19 Roshal', *Dziga Vertov*, p. 219; Dziga Vertov, 'Charlie Chaplin, The Workers of Hamburg and the Decrees of Dr Wirth', *Proletarskoe kino*, no. 3, 1932, pp. 40–41.

20 Dziga Vertov, 'Materials about Trip Abroad' (1931), RGALI 2091/2/419. Vertov considered that it was only the obstructive attitude of the Soviet trade delegation in Berlin that prevented him from travelling to Denmark, Belgium, Austria and Czechoslovakia, where leftist film organisations had all invited him.

21 'Propaganda by Film. "Enthusiasm" Shown in London', *Morning Post*, 16 November 1931, p. 13.

22 'A Soviet Film for Miners', *Daily Mail*, 16 November 1931, p. 17.

23 R. H. 'Contrasts in Two New Films. Russian Sound Film of Five-Year Plan', *Manchester Guardian*, 16 November 1931, p 11.

24 Robert Herring, 'Enthusiasm?', *Close-Up*, vol. 9 no. 1, 1932, p. 21.

25 Roshal', *Dziga Vertov*, p. 220.

26 Reprinted in *Stat'i*, p. 173.

27 Vertov, 'Charlie Chaplin, The Workers of Hamburg and the Decrees of Dr Wirth'.

28 Editorial, 'O "stat'e" t. Vertova', *Proletarskoe kino*, no. 3, 1932, pp. 44–45.

29 See Russell Campbell, *Cinema Strikes Back: Radical Filmmaking in the United States, 1930–1942*, Ann Arbor, MI, 1982, p. 31.

30 Roshal', *Dziga Vertov*, p. 235. It did not win any of the prizes at the festival, where Flaherty's *Man of Aran* (1934) was judged the best foreign film. See http://www.imdb.com/Sections/Awards/Venice_Film_Festival/1934 (last visited 27/07/05).

31 Ad in *New York Herald Tribune*, 5 November 1934, p. 14; '"Three Songs About Lenin" Premiere to Celebrate Revolution Anniversary', *Daily Worker* (US), 5 November 1934, p. 4. The film had opened in Moscow on 1 November 1934. See *Tri Pesni o Lenine*, p. 122.

32 *Daily Worker* (US), 5 November 1934, p. 4.

33 See Waugh, 'Joris Ivens' *The Spanish Earth*', pp. 108–109.

34 Samuel Brody, 'A Soviet Film Masterpiece. Three Songs About Lenin', *Daily Worker* (US), 6 November 1934, p. 7.

35 Otis Ferguson, 'Artists Among the Flickers', *New Republic*, 5 December, 1934, p. 103.

36 Richard Watts Jr, Review of 'Three Songs About Lenin', *New York Herald Tribune*, 7 November 1934, p. 24.

37 This is also the view taken by London's *News Chronicle*. A. T. B[orthwick], 'Lenin Glorified in Film', *News Chronicle*, 28 October 1935, p. 3.

38 H. G. Wells, *Experiment in Autobiography: Discoveries and Conclusions of a Very Ordinary Brain (Since 1866)*, 2 vols, London and Boston, 1969 [1934], vol. 1, p. 780.

Three Heroines (Tri geroinia,
1938), 108, 118–119, 185
Blood for Blood (Smert' za smert',
1941), 120
For You at the Front (Tebe front,
1942), 119–120, 185
The Oath of Youth (Kliatva
molodykh, 1944), 120
News of the Day no. 2 (1946), 122;
no. 6 (1947), 122; no. 43
(1947), 122

Volga-Volga (Grigori Alexandrov,
1938), 109
Vladimir Ilich Lenin (Mikhail
Romm, 1949), 101

Wells, H[erbert] G., 100, 127,
160n
West, Mae, 107
White Sea-Baltic Canal, The
(Belomor-baltiiskii vodnyi
put', Alexander Lemberg,
1933), 87
Whitman, Walt, 46–48, 146n
Winston, Brian, 24–25, 27, 30,
32, 160n
Worker Correspondent (*rabkor*),
16–18, 21, 37, 141n
World without Play (Mir bez igry,
L. Makhnach, 1968), 132

Yezhov, Nikolai, 115

Zhemchuzhny, Vitali, 53, 57, 59,
68, 149n

39 Walter Benjamin, 'The Work of Art in the Age of Mechanical Reproduction', in *Illuminations*, ed. with an intro. by Hannah Arendt, trans. Harry Zohn, New York, 1969, p. 231.

40 It was shown at Cercle du cinéma, on the Champs Elysées, from 26 February to 23 March 1935. BFI Special Collection, Cinema Ephemera Overseas, Programme (no item number).

41 R. H., 'Film Society. A Brilliant Programme', *Manchester Guardian*, 28 October 1935, p. 10.

42 Review by A Vesselo, *Sight and Sound*, vol. 4 no. 16, 1935–1936, p. 175.

43 A. V[esselo], *Monthly Film Bulletin*, vol. 2 no. 13, February 1935, p. 165.

44 'Plays and Pictures', *New Statesman and Nation*, 2 November 1935, p. 638.

45 'Plays and Pictures', *New Statesman and Nation*, 2 November 1935, p. 638.

46 BFI Film Society Special Collection, Item 21, BBFC Correspondence 1927–1934, letter dated 26 November 1935.

47 Typical of this tendency is the screening on 25 January 1936 (the twelfth anniversary of Lenin's death), when 'Dziga Vertov's famous documentary film' was screened at a Lenin memorial meeting at the Cambridge Theatre, in London's West End; *New Statesman and Nation*, 25 January 1936, p. 131. The screening was organised by the leftist film organisation Kino films.

48 See above, Chapter 6. Vertov Notebooks, Diaries (1934), *Kino-Eye*, p. 178; *Stat'i*, p. 181.

49 Roman Karmen, 'Soviet Documentary', in Roger Manvell (ed.), *Experiment in the Film*, London, 1949, p. 172.

50 Roberts, *Forward Soviet!*, p. 75.

51 Jean Vigo, 'Vers un cinéma social' [1930], quoted in Boris Kaufman, 'Jean Vigo's *À Propos de Nice*', in Lewis Jacobs, *The Documentary Tradition from Nanook to Woodstock*, New York, 1971, p. 77.

52 Bert Hogenkamp, 'Workers' Newsreels in Germany, the Netherlands and Japan During the Twenties and Thirties', in Waugh, *Show us Life*, p. 63.

53 Lord Rothermere, owner of *The Daily Mail*, also owned *British Movietone News*. *The March of Time* was linked to *Time* magazine. Glyn Roberts, 'News-Reels', *New Statesman and Nation*, 7 September 1935, pp. 304–305.

54 'The March of Time', 8 November 1935, in Graham Greene, *The Pleasure Dome: The Collected Film Criticism 1935–1940*, ed. John Russell Taylor, London, 1972, p. 34.

55 Greene, *The Pleasure Dome*, p. 34. Also see C. A. Lejeune, 'A New Screen Journalism', *Observer*, 3 November 1935, p. 18.

56 Waugh, 'Joris Ivens' *The Spanish Earth*', p. 111. Frequently the reference was to his writings and reputation rather than to his actual films.

57 Waugh, 'Joris Ivens' *The Spanish Earth*', p. 111.

58 Waugh, 'Joris Ivens' *The Spanish Earth*', p. 128.

59 Gunger, 'Zvukovoi obraz v dokumental'nom fil'me', in Sokolova, *Dokumental'noe kino segodnia*, pp. 189, 191; L. Derbysheva, 'Geroi prosit slova!', in Sokolova, *Dokumental'noe kino segodnia*, pp. 158–159. Derbysheva directed a film *The Voice of Virgin Soil* [Golos tseliny, 1961] which used

synchronous sound exclusively. Also see V. Mikosha, 'S tochki zreniia kinooperatora', in Sokolova, *Dokumental'noe kino segodnia*, pp. 168–169.

60   O. Podgoretskaia, 'Poiski kinoocherkistov', in Sokolova, *Dokumental'noe kino segodnia*, p. 88. Kopalin continued to pay respect to Vertov even in the late 1940s; see I. P. Kopalin, *Sovetskaia dokumental'naia kinematografiia*, Moscow, 1950, p. 5.

61   Podgoretskaia, 'Poiski kinoocherkistov', in Sokolova, *Dokumental'noe kino segodnia*, p. 84.

62   Drobashenko, *Istoriia sovetskogo dokumental'nogo kino*, pp. 67, 72.

63   Derbysheva, 'Geroi prosit slova!', in Sokolova, *Dokumental'noe kino segodnia*, p. 152. Roshal' mentions their collaboration: Roshal', *Dziga Vertov*, p. 255.

64   Roshal', *Dziga Vertov*, p. 252.

65   Pumpianskaia, 'Ia mechtala rabotat' na kinostudii', pp. 70, 73.

66   Abramov and Roshal' see it as Vertov's best work: Abramov, *Dziga Vertov*, p. 142; Roshal', *Dziga Vertov*, p. 199. Similarly, Drobashenko sees it as the high point of Soviet film until that point: Drobashenko, *Istoriia sovetskogo dokumental'nogo kino*, p. 40. This stands in contrast to the West, where from 1960 Vertov was associated primarily with *Man with a Movie Camera*; Roberts, *The Man with the Movie Camera*, p. 92.

67   Roshal', *Dziga Vertov*, p. 226. Michelson, 'The Kinetic Icon in the Work of Mourning', p. 18. See above, Chapter 6.

68   Georges Sadoul, 'Actualité de Dziga Vertov', *Cahiers du cinéma*, vol. 24 no. 144, June 1963, p. 23.

69   Thomas Waugh, 'The Films they Never Showed: The Flaherty Seminar and the Cold War', *Wide Angle*, vol. 17 nos 1–4, 1995, p. 219.

70   Jean Rouch, 'Cinq regards sur Vertov', in Georges Sadoul, *Dziga Vertov*, Paris, 1971, p. 13

71   Jean Rouch, in G. Roy Levin, *Documentary Explorations: 15 Interviews with Film-makers*, Garden City, NY, 1971, p. 135.

72   Rouch, in Levin, *Documentary Explorations*, pp. 135, 137.

73   Rouch, in Levin, *Documentary Explorations*, p. 135.

74   Roshal' refers to a 1955 evening of Soviet cinema in Paris at which Vertov's name figured centrally; Roshal', *Dziga Vertov*, p. 259.

75   Georges Sadoul, 'Dziga Vertov: Poète du ciné-oeil et prophète de la radio-oreille', *Image et son*, no. 183, 1965, pp. 10–11. Also see Sadoul's discussion of this translation in Sadoul, *Dziga Vertov*, pp. 139–140. However, Sadoul claims to have found late texts that treat the term 'Cine-Pravda' as programmatic.

76   James Roy McBean, 'Godard and the Dziga Vertov Group: Film and Dialectics', *Wide Angle*, vol. 26 no. 1, 1972, p. 33. Jean-Pierre Gorin, one of the Groupe Dziga Vertov, explicitly stated that there is no difference between fiction and non-fiction films. Jean-Pierre Gorin, in David Sterritt (ed.), *Jean-Luc Godard Interviews*, Jackson, MI, 1998, p. 60.

77   Steve Cannon, 'Godard, The *Groupe Dziga Vertov* and the Myth of "Counter-Cinema"', *Nottingham French Studies*, vol. 32 no. 1, 1993, p. 77.

78   Roberts, *The Man with the Movie Camera*, p. 100.

79 Sterritt, *Jean-Luc Godard Interviews*, p. 67.
80 Colin McCabe, *Godard: A Portrait of the Artist at 70*, London, 2003, p. 227.
81 Anon, '"Ne copiez pas sur les yeux" disait Vertov', *Cinéthique*, no. 15, 1972, p. 56.
82 *Afterimage*, no. 1, 1970. The first issue of the journal dispenses with the bourgeois tradition of page numbers.
83 Feldman, '"Peace Between Man and Machine"', p. 52.
84 I am referring to Petrić, *Constructivism in Film*, and Roberts, *The Man with the Movie Camera*.
85 Georges Sadoul, *Pravda*, 11 August 1959, p. 4.
86 Erik Barnouw, 'The Kaufman Saga: A Cold War Idyll', *Dox: Documentary Film Quarterly*, no. 3, 1994, p. 11.
87 Monovich, 'Database as Symbolic Form', p. 41.

Select Bibliography

i) Selected Writings of Vertov, Kaufman and Svilova

Kaufman, Mikhail. 'Poslednee interv'iu Mikhaila Kaufmana', *Kinovedcheskie zapiski* 18, 1993, 143–150.

Svilova[-Vertova], Elizaveta. 'U kinokov', *LEF* 4, 1924, 220.

_____ and V. I. Furtichev (eds). *Tri pesni o Lenine*, Moscow, 1972.

Vertov, Dziga. 'Kinoglaz, radioglaz i tak nazyvaemyi "dokumentalizm". Istoricheskaia spravka', *Proletarskoe kino* 4, 1931, 12–16.

_____. 'Charli Chaplin, gamburgskie rabochie i prikazy doktora Wirta', *Proletarskoe kino* 3, 1932, 40–43.

_____. 'Eshche raz o tak nazyvaemom dokumentalizme', *Proletarskoe kino* 4, 1932, 46.

_____. 'Rabotniki kino, vse sily, ves' tvorcheskii opyt – na realizatsiiu reshenii XVII partkonferentsii! Na podstupkakh k vtoroi piatiletke', *Proletarskoe kino* 4, 1932, 5–6.

_____. 'Polnaia kapituliatsiia Nikolaia Lebedeva. Istoricheskaia spravka', *Proletarskoe kino* 5, 1932, 12–18.

_____. 'Avtobiografiia', in *Iz istorii kino. Materialy i dokumenty* 2, Moscow, 1959, 29–31.

_____. 'Vospominaniia o s''emkakh V. I. Lenina', in *Iz istorii kino. Materialy i dokumenty* 2, Moscow, 1959, 32–35.

_____. 'Montazhnye listy fil'mov o Lenine', with a preface by S. Ginzburg, in *Iz istorii kino. Materialy i dokumenty* 2, Moscow, 1959, 35–62.

_____. 'Tvorcheskaia deiatel'nost' G.M. Boltianskogo', in *Iz istorii kino. Materialy i dokumenty* 2, Moscow, 1959, 63–67.

_____. *Stat'i, dnevniki, zamysly*, ed. Sergei Drobashenko, Moscow, 1966.

_____. 'Doklad na pervoi vsesoiuznoi konferentsii po zvukovomu kino', in *Iz istorii kino. Materialy i dokumenty* 8, Moscow, 1971, 178–188.

_____. *Kino-Eye: The Writings of Dziga Vertov*, ed. Annette Michelson trans. Kevin O'Brien, Berkeley: University of California Press, 1984.

_____. 'Intertitles to *Three Songs of Lenin*', *October* 52, Spring 1990, 40–51.

_____. 'Chelovek s kinoapparatom: muzykal'nyi konspekt', ed. Lev Roshal', *Kinovedcheskie zapiski* 21, 1994, 188–189.

_____. 'Tvorcheskaia kartochka 1917–1947', ed. Aleksandr Deriabin, *Kinovedcheskie zapiski* 30, 1996, 161–192.

_____. '"Kogda snimat' drug druga budete, ne snimaetes' bez kinoapparatov..." Pis'mo Dzigi Vertova iz Moskvy na Novuiu zemliu Samuilu Aleksandovichu

Benderskomu i Nikolaiu Konstantinovichu Iudinu', ed. B. D Pavlov, commentary Aleksandr Deriabin, *Kinovedcheskie zapiski* 30, 1996, 193–196.

_____. 'Kinomatografii ne sushchestvuet', ed. N. I. Nusinova, *Kinovedcheskie zapiski* 30, 1996, 197–198.

_____. 'Iz istorii rozhdeniia "Cheloveka s kinoapparatom"', ed. Aleksandr Deriabin, *Kinovedcheskie zapiski* 49, 2000, 199–204.

_____. *Iz naslediia*. vol 1: *Dramaticheskie opyty*, ed. with a foreword by Aleksandr Deriabin, Moscow, 2004.

Tsivian, Yuri (ed. and introduction) *Lines of Resistance: Dziga Vertov and the Twenties*, trans. Julian Graffy, Gemona: Le Giornate del Cinema Muto, 2004.

ii) Vertov Criticism

Abramov, N. P. *Dziga Vertov*, Moscow, 1962.

Anon. '"Ne copiez pas sur les yeux" disait Vertov', *Cinéthique* 15, 1972, 55–57.

Barnouw, Erik. 'The Kaufman Saga: A Cold War Idyll', *Dox: Documentary Film Quarterly* 3, Autumn 1994, 10–13.

Benjamin, Walter. 'The Work of Art in the Age of Mechanical Reproduction', in *Illuminations*, ed. with an introduction by Hannah Arendt, trans. Harry Zohn, New York: Schocken Books, 1969.

Bordwell, David. 'Dziga Vertov: An Introduction', *Film Comment* 8, 1972, 38–45.

Bulgakova, Oksana. 'LEF i kino', *Kinovedcheskie zapiski* 18, 1993, 165–197.

_____. 'Prostranstvennye figury sovetskogo kino 30-kh godov', *Kinovedcheskie zapiski* 29, 1996, 49–62.

Deleuze, Gilles. *The Movement Image*, trans. Hugh Tomlinson and Barbara Habberjam, Minneapolis: University of Minnesota Press, 1986.

Deriabin, Aleksandr. '"Plod sozrel i ego nado sniat'." K istokam vertovskogo shedevra', *Kinovedcheskie zapiski* 49, 2000, 192–198.

_____. '"Kolybel'naia" Dzigi Vertova: zamysel-voploshchenie-ekrannaia sud'ba', *Kinovedcheskie zapiski* 51, 2001, 30–65.

_____. 'Vertov i animatsiia: roman, kotorogo ne bylo', *Kinovedcheskie zapiski* 52, 2001, 132–144.

Drobashenko, Sergei. 'Teoreticheskoe nasledie Dzigi Vertova', *Iskusstvo kino* 12, 1965, 74–83.

_____. *Istoriia sovetskogo dokumental'nogo kino. Uchebno-metodicheskoe posobie*, Moscow, 1980.

Drubek-Meyer, Natascha. 'Kolybel' Griffith'a i Vertova', *Kinovedcheskie zapiski* 30, 1996, 198–212.

_____ and Jurij Murasov (eds). *Apparatur und Rhapsodie: Zu den Filmen des Dziga Vertov*, Frankfurt: Peter Lang, 2000.

Eisenstein, Sergei. *Selected Works*. vol. 1: *Writings, 1922–1934*, ed. and trans. Richard Taylor, London, Bloomington and Indianapolis, IN: BFI, 1988.

Esquenazi, Jean-Pierre (ed.), *Vertov: L'Invention du réel, Actes du colloque de Metz*, Paris: L'Harmattan, 1997.

Feldman, Seth, *Evolution of Style in the Early Work of Dziga Vertov*, New York: Arno Press, 1975 [as PhD thesis, University of New York, Buffalo, 1975].

_____. *Dziga Vertov: A Guide to References and Resources*, Boston, MA: G. K. Hall, 1979.

_____. '"Peace Between Man and Machine": Dziga Vertov's *The Man with a Movie Camera*', in Barry Keith Grant and Jeanette Sloniowski (eds), *Documenting the Documentary: Close Readings of Documentary Film and Video*, Detroit, MI: Wayne State University Press, 1998, 40–54.

Fevral'skii, A. 'Dziga Vertov i pravdisty', *Iskusstvo kino* 12, 1965, 68–74.

Fischer, Lucy. '*Enthusiasm*: From Kino-Eye to Radio-Eye', *Film Quarterly* 31:2, Winter 1977–1978, 25–34.

Fofanova, M. V. 'Tri pesni o Lenine', *Iskusstvo kino* 8, 1970, 45–48.

Grierson, John. *Grierson on Documentary*, ed. with an introduction by Forsyth Hardy, London and Boston: Faber and Faber, 1979.

Günther, Hans. 'Mudryi otets Stalin i ego sem'ia (na materiale kartin D. Vertova i M. Chaureli)', *Russian Literature* 43, 1998, 205–220.

Guneratne, Anthony R. 'The Birth of a New Realism: Photography, Painting and the Advent of Documentary Cinema', *Film History* 10, 1998, 165–187.

Iampol'skii, Mikhail. 'Chuzhaia real'nost'', *Kinovedcheskie zapiski* 10, 1991, 137–149.

Kirby, Lynne. 'From Marinetti to Vertov: Woman on the Track of Avant-Garde Representation', *Quarterly Review of Film Studies* 10:4, 1989, 309–323.

Kleiman, Naum. '"National'noe", "Internationalal'noe" i sovetskii kinoavangard', *Kinovedcheskie zapiski*, 24, 1994–1995, 69–82.

Kletskin, A. Ia. 'Dziga Vertov i Robert Flaerti', *Kinovedcheskie zapiski* 16, 1992, 94–99.

Latteier, Pearl. 'Gender and the Modern Body: Men, Women, and Machines in Vertov's *Man with a Movie Camera*', *Post Script* 22:1, 2002, 23–34.

Lawton, Anna. 'The Futurist Roots of Russian Avant-Garde Cinema', in *Kul'tura russkogo modernizma, stat'i, esse i publikatsii*, ed. Ronald Vroon and John E. Malmsted, Moscow, 1993, 188–205.

Lemberg, Aleksandr. 'Dziga Vertov prikhodit v kino', *Iz istorii kino* 7, Moscow, 1968, 45–48.

Leyda, Jay. *Films Beget Films*, London: Allen and Unwin, 1964.

Listov, Viktor. 'Pervyi fil'm Dzigi Vertova', *Prometii*, Moscow, 1966, 127–135.

_____. 'Kak chitalas' "Kinopravda"', *Iskusstvo kino* 7, 1972, 96–106.

_____. 'Mikhail Kol'tsov i "Desiataia muza"', *Kinovedcheskie zapiski* 5, 1990, 41–52.

_____. 'Vertov: odnazhdy i vsegda', *Kinovedcheskie zapiski* 18, 1993, 121–143.

McKay, John. 'Disorganized Noise: *Enthusiasm* and the Ear of the Collective', http://www.kinokultura.com/articles/jan05-mackay.html (last visited 27/07/05).

Magidov, V. M. 'Iz arkhiva Vertova', *Kinovedcheskie zapiski* 18, 1993, 161–164.

Manvell, Roger (ed.). *Experiment in the Film*, London: Grey Walls Press, 1949.

Marshall, Herbert. *Masters of the Soviet Cinema: Crippled Creative Biographies*, London: Routledge and Kegan Paul, 1983.

Mayne, Judith. 'Ideologies of Metacinema', unpublished PhD thesis, State University of New York, Buffalo, 1975.

_____. *Kino and the Woman Question: Feminism and Silent Film*, Columbus: Ohio State University Press, 1989.

Michelson, Annette. 'From Magician to Epistemologist: Vertov's *The Man with a Movie Camera*', in P. Adams Sitney (ed.). *The Essential Cinema: Essays on Films in The Collection of Anthology Film Archives*, vol. 1, New York: Anthology Film Archives and New York University Press, 1975, 95–111.

_____. 'The Kinetic Icon in the Work of Mourning: Prolegomena to the Analysis of a Textual System', *October* 52, 1990, 16–39.

_____. 'Dr Craze and Mr Clair', *Kinovedcheskie zapiski* 8, 1990, 151–167.

Mil'don, Valerii. 'Monolog dlia khora: dvoinik-prizrak. Obrazy Lenina i Stalina v sovetskom kino 30-kh–40-kh godov', *Kinovedcheskie zapiski* 43, 1999, 338–349.

Monovich, Lev. 'Database as Symbolic Form', *Millennium Film Journal* 34, Fall 1999, 24–43.

Murray-Brown, Jeremy. 'False Cinema: Dziga Vertov and Early Soviet Film', *The New Criterion* 8:3, 1989, 21–33.

Petrić, Vlada. 'Dziga Vertov as Theorist', *Cinema Journal* 18:1, 1978, 29–44.

_____. *Constructivism in Film: The Man with the Movie Camera: A Cinematic Analysis*, Cambridge: Cambridge University Press, 1987.

_____. 'Vertov, Lenin, and Perestroika', *Historical Journal of Film, Radio and Television* 15:1, 1995, 3–17.

Pirog, Gerald. 'Iconicity and Narrative: The Vertov–Eisenstein Controversy', *Semiotica* 39:3–4, 1982, 297–313.

Richter, Hans. '"Protivopolozhnost' revoliutsionnomu." Pis'mo Gansa Richtera Dzige Vertovu o Mezhdunarodnom kongresse nazavismogo kino v La Sarraze, 1929', ed. Thomas Tode, *Kinovedcheskie zapiski* 49, 2000, 208–211.

Roberts, Graham. *Forward Soviet! History and Non-fiction Film in the USSR*, London, New York: I. B. Tauris, 1999.

_____. *The Man with the Movie Camera*, London and New York: I. B. Tauris, 2000.

Roshal', Lev. *Dziga Vertov*, Moscow, 1982.

_____. 'Kommentarii k muzykal'nomu konspektu', *Kinovedcheskie zapiski* 21, 1994, 190–199.

_____. 'Stikhi kinopoeta', *Kinovedcheskie zapiski* 21, 1994, 80–96.

_____. 'Vertov i Stalin', *Iskusstvo kino* 1, 1994, 104–113.

_____. (ed.) 'Protokol odnogo zasedaniia', *Iskusstvo kino* 12, 1997, 124–133.

Ruby, Jay. 'Speaking for, Speaking about, Speaking with, or Speaking alongside: An Anthropological and Documentary Dilemma', *Journal of Film and Video* 44:1–2, 1992, 42–66.

Sadoul, Georges. 'Zhivaia istoriia kino', *Pravda*, 11 August 1959, 4.

_____. 'Actualité de Dziga Vertov', *Cahiers du cinéma* 24:144, 1963, 23–31.

_____. 'Dziga Vertov: Poète du ciné-oeil et prophète de la radio-oreille', *Image et son* 183, 1965, 9–18.

_____. *Dziga Vertov*, Paris: Champ libre, 1971.

Sarkisova, Oksana. 'Envisioned Communities: Representations of Nationalities in Non-Fiction Cinema in Soviet Russia, 1923–1935', Unpublished PhD Dissertation, Central European University, Budapest, 2004.

Schaub, Joseph. 'Presenting the Cyborg's Futurist Past: An Analysis of Dziga Vertov's Kino-Eye', *Postmodern Culture* 8:2, 1998, 27 paras, http://project. cyberpunk.ru/ibd/cyborg_futurist_past.html (last visited 02/06/05).

Selezneva, T. *Kinomysl' 1920-kh godov*, Leningrad, 1972.

Singer, Ben. 'Connoisseurs of Chaos: Whitman, Vertov and the "Poetic Survey"', *Literature/Film Quarterly* 15:4, 1987, 247–258.

Stollery, Martin. *Alternative Empires: European Modernist Cinemas and Cultures of Imperialism*, Exeter: Exeter University Press, 2000.

Strathausen, Carsten. 'Uncanny Spaces: The City in Ruttmann and Vertov', in Mark Shiel and Tony Fitzmaurice (eds), *Screening the City*, London and New York: Verso, 2003, 15–40.

Taylor, Richard. *Film Propaganda: Soviet Russia and Nazi Germany*, 2nd edn revised, London and New York: I. B. Tauris, 1998.

Thompson, Kristin. 'Early Sound Counterpoint', *Yale French Studies* 60, 1980, 115–140.

Tode, Thomas. 'Un Soviétique escalade la Tour Eiffel: Dziga Vertov à Paris', *Cinémathèque* 5, Spring 1994, 68–85.

Tolchan, Ia. M. 'Kollektivnyi portret dlia ekster'era (v knigu Guinnessa)', *Kinovedcheskie zapiski* 18, 1993, 160–161.

Tsivian, Yuri. 'Homeless Images: D. W. Griffith in the Eye of Soviet Filmmakers', *Griffithiana* 20:60–61, 1997, 51–75.

_____. 'Man with a Movie Camera, Reel One. A Selective Glossary', *Film Studies* 2, 2000, 51–76.

Tupitsyn, Margarita. *Malevich and Film*, Yale University Press, London and New Haven, CT, 2002.

Turvey, Malcom. 'Can the Camera See? Mimesis in *Man with a Movie Camera*', October 89, 1999, 25–50.

Vertova-Svilova, E. I., and A. L. Vinogradova (eds). *Dziga Vertov v vospomiinaniakh sovremennikov*, Moscow, 1976.

Wells, H. G. *Experiment in Autobiography: Discoveries and Conclusions of a Very Ordinary Brain (Since 1866)*, London and Boston, MA: Faber and Faber, 1969.

Widdis, Emma. *Visions of a New Land: Soviet Film from the Revolution to the Second World War*, New Haven, CT, and London: Yale University Press, 2003.

Zimmermann, Patricia R. 'Reconstructing Vertov: Soviet Film Theory and American Radical Documentary', *Journal of Film and Video* 44:1–2, 1992, 80–90.

iii) Other Works

Barnouw, Erik. *Documentary: A History of the Non-Fiction Film*, 2nd revised edn, Oxford: Oxford University Press, 1993.

Barsam, Richard Maran. *Nonfiction Film: A Critical History*, foreword by Richard Dyer McCann, London: George Allen and Unwin, 1974.

Bazin, André. 'The Myth of Stalin in the Soviet Cinema', in *Bazin at Work: Major Essays and Reviews from the Forties and Fifties*, ed. Bert Cardullo, trans. Alain Piette, New York and London: Routledge, 1997, 23–40.

Bogorov, Ansel'm. 'Leningradskie kinokhronikery', in *Iz istorii kino. Materialy i dokumenty* 9, Moscow, 1974, 155–174.

Bruzzi, Stella. *New Documentary: A Critical Introduction*, London and New York: Routledge, 2000.

Corner, John. *The Art of Record: A Critical Introduction to Documentary*, Manchester: Manchester University Press, 1996.

Denkin, Harvey. 'Linguistic Models in Early Soviet Cinema', *Cinema Journal* 17:1, Fall 1977, 1–13.

Deriabin, Aleksandr. '"Nasha psikhologiia i ikh psikhologiia – sovershenno raznye veshchi". "Afganistan" Vladimira Erofeeva i sovetskii kul'turfil'm dvadtsatykh godov', *Kinovedcheskie zapiski* 54, 2001, 53–71.

———. (ed.) '"Tam ia uvidel neobychainye veshchi," Sovetskie kinematografisty o svoikh poezdkakh v Germanii. (ARK, 1928–1929)', *Kinovedcheskie zapiski* 58, 2002, 239–285.

———. (ed.) '"A driani podobno 'Garmon'' bol'she ne stavite?" Zapiski besed B. Z. Shumiatskogo s I.V. Stalinym posle kinoprosmotrov, 1934g.', *Kinovedcheskie zapiski* 61, 2002, 281–346.

Dzhulai, Liudmila. *Dokumental'nyi illiuzion. Otechestvennyi kinodokumentalizm – opyty sotsial'nogo tvorchestva*, Moscow, 2001.

Gan, Aleksei. '"Bolezn' moia inogo poriadka" Pis'ma Alekseia Gana Esfiri Shub', *Kinovedcheskie zapiski* 49, 2000, 222–230.

Le Giornate del cinema muto 2004. 23rd Pordenone Silent Film Festival Catalogue, Pordenone: Giornate del cinema muto, 2004.

Jacobs, Lewis. *The Documentary Tradition from Nanook to Woodstock*, New York: Hopkinson and Blake, 1971.

Karmen, Roman. *No Pasaran!*, Moscow, 1972.

Kenez, Peter. *The Birth of the Propaganda State: Soviet Methods of Mass Mobilisation, 1917–1929*, Cambridge: Cambridge University Press, 1985.

———. 'Black and White: The War on Film', in Richard Stites (ed.), *Culture and Entertainment in Wartime Russia*, Bloomington and Indianapolis: Indiana University Press, 1995, 157–175.

Levin, Roy. *Documentary Explorations: 15 Interviews with Film-makers*, Garden City, NY: Doubleday, 1971.

Leyda, Jay. *Kino: A History of the Russian and Soviet Film. A Study of the Development of Russian Cinema, from 1896 to the Present*, London: George Allen and Unwin, 1983.

Lih, Lars T. 'Melodrama and the Myth of the Soviet Union', in Louise McReynolds and Joan Neuberger (eds), *Imitations of Life: Two Centuries of Melodrama in Russia*, Durham, NC, and London: Duke University Press, 2002, 178–207.

Listov, Viktor. 'Mikhail Kol´tsov i "Desiataia muza"', *Kinovedcheskie zapiski* 5, 1990, 41–52.

Miller, Frank J. *Folklore for Stalin: Russian Folklore and Pseudofolklore of the Stalin Era*, Armonk, NY, and London: M. E. Sharpe, 1990.

Molchanov, L. A. *Gazetnaia pressa Rossii v gody revoliutsii i grazhdanskoi voiny (okt. 1917–1920 gg.)*, Moscow, 2002.

Nichols, Bill. *Representing Reality: Issues and Concepts in Documentary*, Bloomington and Indianapolis: Indiana University Press, 1991.

Plantinga, Carl R. *Rhetoric and Representation in Nonfiction Film*, Cambridge: Cambridge University Press, 1997.

Rhode, Eric. *A History of the Cinema from its Origins to 1970*, New York: Da Capo, 1976.

Sartorti, Rosalinde. *Pressfotographie und Industrialisierung in der Sowjetunion: die Pravda, 1925–1933*, Berlin and Wiesbaden: Osteuropa Institut, 1981.

Selunskaya, Valeriya, and Maria Zezina 'Documentary Films – A Soviet Source for Soviet Historians', in Richard Taylor and Derek Spring (eds), *Stalinism and Soviet Cinema*, London: Routledge, 1993, 171–185.

Sesonke, Alexander. 'Re-Editing History: *Lenin in October*: 1937 Then and Now 1983', *Sight and Sound* 53:1, 1983–1984, 56–58.

Shklovskii, Viktor. *Za 60 let. Raboty o kino*, Moscow, 1985.

Shub, Esfir´. *Zhizn´ moia – kinematograf. Krupnym planom. Stat´i, vystupleniia. Neosushchestvlennye zamysly. Perepiska*, ed. L. Poznanskaia, Moscow, 1972.

Soviet Writers' Congress 1934. The Debate on Socialist Realism and Modernism in the Soviet Union, London: Lawrence and Wishart, 1977.

Taylor, Richard (ed. and trans.). *The Film Factory: Russian and Soviet Cinema in Documents*, co-ed. with an introduction by Ian Christie, Cambridge, MA: Harvard University Press, 1988.

Tumarkin, Nina. *Lenin Lives! The Lenin Cult in Soviet Russia*, 2nd edn enlarged, Cambridge, MA, and London: Harvard University Press, 1997.

Waugh, Thomas. 'Joris Ivens' *The Spanish Earth*: Committed Documentary and the Popular Front', in Thomas Waugh (ed.), *'Show us Life': Towards a History and Aesthetics of the Committed Documentary*, Metuchen, NJ, and London: Scarecrow Press, 1984, 105–132.

_____. 'The Films they Never Showed: The Flaherty Seminar and the Cold War', *Wide Angle* 17:1–4, 1995, 217–226.

Winston, Brian. *Claiming the Real: The Documentary Film Revisited*, London: BFI, 1995.

_____. *Lies, Damned Lies and Documentaries*, London: BFI, 2000.

Wollen, Peter. *Signs and Meaning in the Cinema*, 3rd edn revised and enlarged, London: Secker and Warburg, 1979.

Youngblood, Denise J. *Soviet Cinema in the Silent Era, 1918–1935*, Ann Arbor, MI: UMI Research Press, 1985.

Filmography

This filmography is largely based on published sources, such as that in *Lines of Resistance*, and the author's research at RGAKFD (Krasnogorsk).

Cine Week nos 1–43 [Kinonedeliia May 1918–June 1919]
Moscow Cine Committee of the People's Commissariat of Education
Directors: Mikhail Kol′tsov, Nikolai Tikhonov, Evgenii Schneider, Dziga Vertov.

Anniversary of the Revolution [Godovshchina revoliutsii 1919]
12 reels. 2710 metres.
Moscow Cine Committee of the People's Commissariat of Education
Directors: Dziga Vertov, Aleksei Savelev.

The Brain of Soviet Russia [Mozg Sovetskoi Rossii 1919]
1 reel. 317 metres.
Moscow Cine Committee of the People's Commissariat of Education
Director: Dziga Vertov.

The Battle for Tsaritsyn [Boi pod Tsaritsynom 1919]
1 reel. 350 metres.
Moscow Cine Committee of the People's Commissariat of Education and the Revolutionary Military Soviet
Director: Dziga Vertov. Cameraman: Aleksandr Lemberg.

The Trial of Mironov [Protsess Mironova 1919]
1 reel. 300 metres.
Moscow Cine Committee of the People's Commissariat of Education
Director: Dziga Vertov. Cameraman: Petr Ermolov.

Exhumation of the Remains of Sergius of Radonezh [Vskrytie moshchei Sergeia Radonezhskogo 1919]
2 reels. 166 metres [incomplete].
Moscow Cine Committee of the People's Commissariat of Education
Directors: Lev Kuleshov, Dziga Vertov.

'Red Star' Instructional Steamer of the All-Russia Central Executive Committee [Literaturno-Instruktorskii agit-parokhod VTSIK 'Krasnaia zvezda' 1919]
2 reels. 335 metres.
Moscow Cine Committee of the People's Commissariat of Education
Director: Dziga Vertov. Cameramen: Aleksandr Lemberg, Petr Ermolov.

Agit-train of the Central Committee [Agitpoezd VTsIK 1921]
1 reel.
Moscow Cine Committee of the People's Commissariat of Education and the All-Russia Central Executive Committee
Author and Director: Dziga Vertov.

The History of the Civil War [Istoriia grazhdanskoi voiny 1921]
13 reels. 3643 metres.
All-Russian Photo-Cine Department (VFKO) and the People's Commissariat of Education
Director: Dziga Vertov.

Trial of the Right Socialist Revolutionaries [Protsess pravykh eserov/Protsess eserov 1922]
3 reels. 671 metres.
All-Russian Photo-Cine Department (VFKO) and the People's Commissariat of Education
Author and Director: Dziga Vertov.
Cameramen: Aleksandr Levitskii, Mikhail Kaufman.
Assistant Director: Elizaveta Svilova.

Cine-Pravda nos 1–23 [Kinopravda 1922–1925]
Goskino
Director: Dziga Vertov.

Named issues of Cine-Pravda:
Cine-Pravda no. 13. Yesterday, Today, Tomorrow. A Film Poem Dedicated to the October Revolution/October Cine-Pravda [Vchera, Segodnia, Zavtra. Oktiabr'skaia Kinopravda 1922]
3 reels. 900 metres.
Author, Director and Editor: Dziga Vertov. Intertitles: Aleksandr Rodchenko.

Cine-Pravda no. 16. Spring Cine-Pravda. A Picturesque, Lyrical Newsreel [Vesennaia Kinopravda. Vidovaia liricheskaia khronika 1923]
3 reels. 1110 metres.
Director: Dziga Vertov.

Cine-Pravda no. 17. *For the First Agricultural and Cottage Industries Exhibition in the USSR* [Pervoi sel´skokhoziastvennoi i kustarnoprmyshlennoi vystavke SSSR 1923]
1 reel. 332 metres.
Director: Dziga Vertov. Editor: Elizaveta Svilova.

Cine-Pravda no. 18. *A Movie Camera Race over 299 metres and 14 Minutes and 50 Seconds in the Direction of Soviet Reality* [Probeg kinoapparata v napravlenii sovetskoi deistvitel´nosti 299 metrov 14 min. 50 sek 1924]
1 reel. 299 metres.
Director: Dziga Vertov.

Cine-Pravda no. 19. *Black Sea – Arctic Ocean – Moscow. A Movie Camera Race from Moscow to the Arctic Ocean* [Chernoe more– Ledovityi okean – Moskva. Probeg kinoapparata Moskva – Ledovityi okean 1924]
1 reel. 358 metres.
Director: Dziga Vertov.

Cine-Pravda no. 20. *Pioneer Pravda* [Pionerskaia pravda 1924]
1 reel. 352 metres.
Director: Dziga Vertov. Cameraman: Mikhail Kaufman.

Cine-Pravda no. 21. *Leninist Cine-Pravda* [Leninskaia kinopravda. Kinopoema o Lenine 1925]
3 reels. 800 metres.
Cameramen: Grigorii Giber, Aleksandr Levitskii, Aleksandr Lemberg, Petr Novitskii, Mikhail Kaufman, Eduard Tisse and others. Director: Dziga Vertov.

Cine-Pravda no. 22. *Peasant Cine-Pravda. In the Heart of a Peasant Lenin Lives on* [Krest´ianskaia kinopravda. V serdtse krest´ianina Lenin zhiv 1925]
2 reels. 606 metres.
Cameramen: Mikhail Kaufman, Aleksandr Lemberg, Ivan Beliakov. Director: Dziga Vertov.

Cine-Pravda no. 23. *Radio-Pravda* [Radiopravda 1925]
4 reels. 1400 metres.
Director: Dziga Vertov. Cameramen: Mikhail Kaufman, Ivan Beliakov. Animation Design: Aleksandr Bushkin.

State-Cine-Calendar 1–53 [Goskinokalendar´ May 1923–April 1925]
Goskino
Director: Dziga Vertov.

Give Us Air! [Daesh′ vozdukh! 1923]
Issue 1: 1 reel. 652 metres. Issue 2: 1 reel. 280 metres. Issue 3: 1 reel. 280 metres.
Goskino
Director-Author: Dziga Vertov. Cameramen: Mikhail Kaufman, Ivan Beliakov.
Intertitles and diagrams: Ivan Beliakov.

Today [Segodnia 1923]
1 reel. 195 metres.
Goskino
Director: Dziga Vertov.
Cameraman: Mikhail Kaufman.
Animators: Ivan Beliakov, Boris Volkov.

Automobile (GUM) [Avtomobil′ (GUM) 1923]
2 reel. 600 metres.
Goskino
Directors: Dziga Vertov, Mikhail Doronin.

Soviet Toys [Sovetskie igrushki 1924]
1 reel. 350 metres.
Goskino (Kul′tkino)
Author and Director: Dziga Vertov.
Cameraman: Aleksandr Dorn.
Animators: Ivan Beliakov, A. Ivanov.

Humoresques [Iumoreski 1924]
1 reel. 60 metres.
Goskino (Kul′tkino)
Author and Director: Dziga Vertov. Art Director: Aleksandr Bushkin.
Cameraman: Ivan Beliakov. Animators: Boris Volkov, Boris Egerev.

1 May in Moscow/1 May Celebration in Moscow [Pervoe maia v Moskve/Prazdnik
pervogo maia v Moskve 1923]
1 reel. 403 metres.
Proletkino
Director: Dziga Vertov. Cameraman: Petr Novitskii.

*Cine-Eye/Kino-Eye on its First Reconnaissance. First Episode of the Cycle 'Life Off-
Guard'* [Kinoglaz/ Kinoglaz na pervoi razvedke: pervaia seriia tsikla 'Zhizn′
vrasplokh' 1924]
6 reels. 1627 metres.
Goskino

Director: Dziga Vertov. Cameraman: Mikhail Kaufman.
Editor: Elizaveta Svilova.

The First October without Il'ich [Pervyi Oktiabr' bez Il'icha 1925]
3 reels. 895 metres.
Goskino (Kul'tkino)
Director: Dziga Vertov.
Assistant Director: Elizaveta Svilova. Cameraman: Mikhail Kaufman.

*Forward, Soviet/The Moscow Soviet in the Present, Past and Future/The Moscow
Soviet* [Shagai, Sovet!/Mossovet v nastoiashchem, proshlom i budushchem/
Mossovet 1926]
7 reels. 1650 metres.
Goskino (Kul'tkino)
Author and Director: Dziga Vertov. Assistant Director: Elizaveta
Svilova.
Cameraman: Ivan Beliakov. Cine-Scout: Il'ia Kopalin.

*A Sixth Part of the World/A Cine-Eye Race Around the USSR: Export and Import by the
State Trading Organisation of the USSR* [Shestaia chast' mira. Probeg kinoglaza
po SSSR: Eksport i import Gostorga SSSR 1926]
6 reels. 1718 metres.
Goskino (Kul'tkino)
Author-Director: Dziga Vertov. Assistant Director: Elizaveta Svilova.
Head Cameraman: Mikhail Kaufman.
Cameramen: Ivan Beliakov, Samuel Benderskii, Petr Zotov, Nikolai Konstantinov,
Aleksandr Lemberg, Nikolai Strukov, Iakov Tolchan.
Cine-Scouts: Aleksandr Kagarlitskii, Il'ia Kopalin, Boris Kudinov.

The Eleventh Year [Odinnadtsatyi 1928]
6 reels. 1600 metres.
The All-Ukrainian Photo-Cine Directorate (VUFKU)
Director: Dziga Vertov. Assistant Director: Elizaveta Svilova.
Head Cameraman: Mikhail Kaufman. Assistant Cameraman: Konstantin Kuliaev.
Laboratory Technician: I. Kotel'nikov.

Man with a Movie Camera [Chelovek s kinoapparatom 1929]
6 reels. 1839 metres.
The All-Ukrainian Photo-Cine Directorate (VUFKU)
Director: Dziga Vertov. Assistant Director: Elizaveta Svilova.
Head Cameraman: Mikhail Kaufman.

Enthusiasm: Symphony of the Donbas [Entuziazm: Simfoniia Donbassa 1931]
6 reels. 1854 metres.
Ukrainfilm
Director: Dziga Vertov. Assistant Director: Elizaveta Svilova.
Cameraman: Boris Tseitlin. Sound: Petr Shtro. Composer: N. Timareev.

Three Songs of Lenin [Tri pesni o Lenine 1934]
Sound version: 6 reels. 1794 metres. / 7 reels. 1848 metres. / 6 reels. 1607 metres.
(1934/1938/1970)
Silent version: 2100 metres. / 6 reels. 1474 metres. (1935/1938)
Mezhrabpomfilm
Director: Dziga Vertov. Assistant Director: Elizaveta Svilova.
Cameramen: Dmitrii Surenskii, Mark Magidson, Bentsion Monastyrskii.
Sound: Petr Shtro. Composer: Iurii Shaporin.

Lullaby [Kolybel'naia 1937]
7 reels. 1606 metres.
Union Newsreel [Soiuzkinokhronika]
Author and Director: Dziga Vertov. Assistant Director: Elizaveta Svilova.
Cameramen: Dmitrii Surenskii and the Cameramen of Union Newsreel.
Sound: I. Renkov. Composers; Dmitrii and Danil Pokrass.
Text: Vasilii Lebedev-Kumach (songs), Dziga Vertov (narration).

In Memory of Sergo Ordzhonikidze [Pamiati Sergo Ordzhonikidze 1937]
2 reels. 439 metres.
Union Newsreel [Soiuzkinokhronika]
Director: Dziga Vertov. Assistant Director: Elizaveta Svilova.
Voice-over: V. Kachalov, A. Shvarts.

*In Memory of Sergo Ordzhonikidze/In Memory of Sergo Ordzhonikidzhe, Ardent Fighter
for the Cause of the Working Class, for the Cause of Communism, Fearless Leninist-
Bolshevik, Friend and Comrade-in-Arms of Stalin the Great* [Pamiati plamennogo
bortsa za delo rabochego klassa, za delo kommunizma, besstrashnogo bol'shevika-
Lenintsa, druga i soratnika velikogo Stalina, Sergo Ordzhonikidze 1938]
5 reels. 1247 metres.
Moscow Studio of Union Newsreel [Soiuzkinokhronika]
Authors and Directors: Dziga Vertov, Iahkov Bliokh.
Assistants: Elizaveta Svilova, Kulagina
Cameramen: M. Oshurkov, Ivan Beliakov, V. Dobronitskii, A. Solovev, N.
Adzhibegishvili.
Composer: Isaak Dunaevskii.
Text: Vasilii Lebedev-Kumach (songs), Pyklin, Katsman (narration).

Conductor: David Blok.
Voice-over: V. Kachalov, M. Lebedev.

Glory to the Soviet Heroines [Slava sovetskim geroiniam 1938]
2 reels. 280 metres.
Moscow Studio of Union Newsreel [Soiuzkinokhronika]
Author and Director: Dziga Vertov. Director: Elizaveta Svilova.

Three Heroines [Tri geroinia 1938]
5 reels. 1466 metres.
Moscow Studio of Union Newsreel [Soiuzkinokhronika]
Authors and Directors: Dziga Vertov and Elizaveta Svilova.
Train sequence: Mark Troianovskii.
Text of songs: Vasilii Lebedev-Kumach. Composers: Dmitrii and Daniil Pokrass.

Blood for Blood, Death for Death; We Will Not Forget the Crimes of the German-Fascist Invaders in the Territory of the USSR [Krov´ za krov´, smert´ za smert´; zlodeianiia nemetsko-fashistkikh zakhvatchikov na territorii SSSR my ne zabudem, 1941]
1 reel. 236 metres.
Central Newsreel Studio
Director: Dziga Vertov.

Soiuzkino Journal no. 77 [Soiuzkinozhurnal 1941]
1 reel. 282 metres.
Central Newsreel Studio
Directors: Dziga Vertov Elizaveta Svilova. Cameraman: V. Vikhirev.

Soiuzkino Journal no. 87 ('In the Region of the "A" Heights') [Soiuzkinozhurnal. V raione vysoty 'A' 1941]
1 reel. 223 metres.
Central Newsreel Studio.
Director: Dziga Vertov. Cameramen: T. Bunimovich, P. Kasatkin.

For You at the Front! [Tebe, front! 1942]
5 reels. 1285 metres.
Alma-Ata Newsreel Studio.
Author and Director: Dziga Vertov. Director: Elizaveta Svilova. Assistant Director: S. Pumpianskaia.
Chief Cameraman: Boris Pumpianskii.
Composers: Gavriil Popov, V. Velikanov. Consultant: D. Kurmanov.

The Oath of Youth [Kliatva molodykh 1944]
3 reels. 853 metres.
Central Studio of Documentary Films (TsSDF)
Author and Director: Dziga Vertov.
Cameramen: Ivan Beliakov, G. Amirov, B. Borkovskii, B. Dementev, S. Semenov, B. Kositsin, E Stankevich.
Voice-over: L. Khmara.
Musical arrangements: D. Astradantsev. Director: Elizaveta Svilova. Sound: V. Kotov.

News of the Day [Novosti dnia]
All 1 reel. All Central Studio of Documentary Films (TsSDF)
1944, no. 18
1945, nos 4, 8, 12, 15, 20
1946 nos 2, 8, 18, 24, 34, 42, 67, 71
1947 nos 6, 13, 21, 30, 37, 43, 51, 65, 71
1948 nos 8, 19, 23, 29, 34, 39, 44, 50
1949 nos 19, 27, 43, 45, 51, 55
1950 nos 7, 58
1951 nos 15, 33, 43, 56
1952 nos 9, 15, 31, 43, 54
1953 nos 18, 27, 35, 55
1954 nos 31, 46, 60

Particular issues referred to:
News of the Day no. 2, January 1946
1 reel. 248 metres.
Central Studio of Documentary Films (TsSDF)
Director: Dziga Vertov.

News of the Day no. 6, January 1947
1 reel. 258 metres.
Central Studio of Documentary Films (TsSDF)
Director: Dziga Vertov.

News of the Day no. 43, June 1947
1 reel. 278 metres.
Central Studio of Documentary Films (TsSDF)
Director: Dziga Vertov.

Availability

DVD

Man with a Movie Camera, BFI, 2000
Kino-Eye / Three Songs About Lenin, Kino-International/Image Entertainment, 1999
Enthusiasm: Symphony of the Don Basin [Entuziazm (Simfonija Donbassa)], Austrian Film Museum, 2005

Video

Kino-Pravda [Compilation of nos 1–9] Available from www.nyfavideo.com ISBN 1-55881-057-9
Enthusiasm: Symphony of the Don Basin Available from www.nyfavideo.com ISBN 1-55881-056-0

Film Archives

The most comprehensive collections are to be found in Russia at RGAKFD (Krasnogorsk) and Gosfil'mofond (Belye Stolby). Many archives outside Russia have copies of Vertov's films, but the Austrian Film Museum in Vienna has the most extensive collection.

Index

A Propos de Nice (France, Jean Vigo, 1930), 129
Abramov, Nikolai, 132, 168n
Alexandrov, Grigori, 72, 109
Anger, Kenneth, 135
Auden, W(ystan) H., 128
Awakening of a Woman, The (Das Erwachen des Weibes, Fred Sauer, 1927), 65

Baiganin, Nurpeis, 119
Battle for our Soviet Ukraine, The (Bitva za nashu sovetskuiu Ukrainu, Alexander Dovzhenko, 1943), 120
Battleship 'Potemkin', The (Sergei Eisenstein, 1926), 41, 71, 124, 127
Bazin, André, 104
Bedny, Demian, 95, 160n
Beliakov, Ivan, 29, 149n, 181–184, 186
Benjamin, Walter, 128
Bentham, Jeremy, 34
Beria, Lavrenti, 115
Berlin (Yuli Raizman, 1945), 112, 120
Bezymensky, Alexander, 126
Bialystok (Belostok), 4
Bliokh, Iakov, 117, 184
Boltiansky, Grigori, 32–33
Brakhage, Stan, 135
Brik, Osip, 59, 63, 68, 102

Brody, Samuel, 127, 134n
Bruzzi, Stella, 23
Bukharin, Nikolai, 17

Chapaev (Vasilev Brothers, 1934), 91–92, 95–96, 103
Chaplin, Charlie, 126
Cheliuskin (Arkady Shafran and Mark Troianovsky, 1934), 89, 95, 98, 162n
Chopin, 97
Chronicle of a Summer (Chronique d'un été, Edgar Morin and Jean Rouch, 1961), 133
Churchill, Winston, 121
Cine-Eye. See Vertov
Cinéma vérité. See Vertov
Circus (Tsirk, Grigori Alexandrov, 1936), 109, 115, 117
Clark, Katerina, 105
Constructivism, 3, 14, 64

Day of the New World, A (Den' novogo mira, Roman Karmen and Mikhail Slutsky, 1940), 116
Deleuze, Gilles, 63
Derbysheva, L., 132
Deren, Maya, 135
Deriabin, Alexander, 136, 164n
Documentary. See Vertov and performance
Drobashenko, Sergei, 92, 132, 135

Dunaevsky, Isaak, 117
Dzerzhinsky, Felix, 37
Dziga and his Brothers (Dziga i ego brat´ia, Evgeny Tsymbal, 2002), 135

Earth (Zemlia, Alexander Dovzhenko, 1930), 124
Eisenstein, Sergei, 41, 52, 55, 62, 71–72, 80, 84–85, 102–103, 107, 123–124, 129–130, 134
Eisler, Hans, 125
Erofeev, Vladimir, 27, 49, 55, 77–78, 85–88, 150n, 156n

Fall of the Romanov Dynasty (Padenie dinastii Romanovykh, Esfir Shub, 1927), 53
Fahrenheit 9/11 (Michael Moore, USA, 2004), 2
Fefer, V., 52–53
Film Society, 99, 124–126
Fitzpatrick, Sheila, 37
Flaherty, Robert, 3, 28, 49, 133, 146n, 161n, 166n, 168n
Formalism, 42, 46, 64, 70, 80, 84, 90, 91, 114, 151n
Foucault, Michel, 34
Futurism, 1, 3, 64, 90, 95

Gan, Aleksei, 14, 56
Glass Eye (Stekliannyi glaz, Lili Brik and Vitali Zhemchuzhny, 1928), 68
Godard, Jean-Luc, 134–135
Gorin, Jean-Pierre, 168n
Gorky, Maxim, 95
GPU (Gosudarstvennoe politicheskoe upravlenie), Soviet secret police 1922–1934, 36–37

Graffy, Julian, xi, 143n
Great Patriotic War, The (Velikaia otechestvennaia, Roman Karmen, 1965), 131–132
Greene, Graham, 130
Grierson, John, 3, 28, 32, 124, 126, 130, 133, 136, 141n, 165n

Higher and Higher (Vse vyshe, 1940), 109
Housing Problems (Arthur Elton, 1935), 99

Ibarrurí, Dolores [La Pasionaria], 102
In Spring (Vesnoi, Mikhail Kaufman, 1929), 59, 68
Ivens, Joris, 130

Jazz Singer (Alan Crossland, USA, 1927), 71

Kaplan, Fanny, 13, 30, 101
Karmazinsky, Nikolai, 86, 88
Karmen, Roman, 86, 89, 112, 116, 122, 129, 131, 160
Kaufman, Boris, 82, 129, 165
Kaufman, Mikhail, 6, 8, 27, 29–30, 35, 56, 59, 68–69, 74, 80, 138n, 143n, 152–153n, 180–183
Kenez, Peter, 102
Koltsov, Mikhail, 11–15, 116
Komsomol: Patron of Electrification (Komsomol-shef elektrifikatsii, Esfir Shub, 1932), 79
Kopalin, Ilya, 20, 55, 82, 83, 100, 102, 120, 132, 147n, 149n, 168n, 183
Kracauer, Siegfried, 123, 165n

Kuleshov, Lev, 67, 180
Kulturfilm, 62–63, 150n

Lebedev, Nikolai, 84, 87, 150n
Lebedev-Kumach, Vasilii, 109,
    117, 118, 184–185
LEF, 3, 14, 53, 56, 144n
Lenin (Ilya Kopalin, 1938), 100
Lenin, Vladimir Ilich, 8, 10–15,
    17, 28, 37, 44, 49, 59, 84,
    90–104, 110, 113, 122,
    127–128, 132, 139n, 141n,
    154n, 182n, 167n
Lenin in October (Lenin v oktiabre,
    Mikail Romm, 1937),
    102–104, 115–116, 162n
Leyda, Jay, 91, 123, 129, 160n,
    161n
Listov, Viktor, 136
Lloyd, Harold, 70

McCabe, Colin, 134
Malevich, Kazimir, 60
Man of Aran (Robert Flaherty,
    UK, 1934), 28
Mao, Zedong, 134
March of Time, 130, 167n
Mayakovsky, Vladimir, 43, 46,
    56, 150n
Medvedkin, Aleksandr, 87, 120
Michelson, Annette, 135, 142n,
    151n, 158n
Modern Times (Charlie Chaplin,
    USA, 1936), 126
Moholy-Nagy, László, 125
Montagu, Ivor, 123–124, 165n
Moore, Michael, 2, 147n
Morin, Edgar, 133
Moscow–Kara–Kum–Moscow
    (Moskva-Kara-Kum-
    Moskva, Roman Karmen,
    1933), 86, 89, 112, 116

Moscow Strikes Back [Razgrom
    nemetskikh voisk pod
    Moskvoi, Ilya Kopalin and
    Leonid Varlamov, 1942), 55
Moussinac, Léon, 123

Nanook of the North (Robert
    Flaherty, USA, 1922), 27, 49
Nebylitsky, Boris, 94

O'Brien, Kevin, xi, 135, 142n,
    159n
October (Oktiabr´, Sergei
    Eisenstein, 1927), 102–103
Olympiad of the Arts (Olimpiada
    iskusstv, Vladimir Erofeev,
    1930), 78, 85
One of Many (Odin iz mnogikh,
    Ilya Kopalin, 1930), 82–83
Ordinary Fascism (Obyknovennyi
    fashizm, Mikhail Romm,
    1965), 101, 132
Osipov, G., 53

People (Liudi, Mikhail Slutsky,
    1934), 87
Peoples' Court, The (Sud narodov,
    Roman Karmen, 1946), 122
Podgoretskaia, O., 131
Pokrass, Daniel and Dmitrii,
    109, 118, 163n, 184–185
Productivism, 3, 64
Propaganda. See Vertov and
    journalism
Pudovkin, Vsevolod, 72,
    123–124, 148n

Reconstruction. See Vertov and
    performance
Rodchenko, Alexander, 14
Roger and Me (Michael Moore,
    USA, 1989), 147n

Romm, Mikhail, 101–103, 132
Room, Abram, 72
Roshal, Lev, 136
Rouch, Jean, 133–134
Russian Military Newsreel
    (Russkaia voennaia
    khronika), 5
Ruttmann, Walter, 124

Sadoul, Georges, 132–135, 168n
Safronov, Nikolai, 87
Shaporin, Iurii, 97, 184
Shchukin, Boris, 103
Shklovsky, Victor, 42, 45–46,
    51–52, 132, 137n
Shub, Esfir', 53–55, 62, 69, 72,
    77, 79, 89, 100, 102, 148n,
    153–154n, 161n, 166n
Shumiatsky, Boris, 91, 106–107,
    115
Slutsky, Mikhail, 87, 116, 131
Soiuzkinozhurnal, 86–87, 185
Sokolov, Ippolit, 72, 148n
Song of Heroes (Pesnia o
    geroiakh, Joris Ivens, 1932),
    131
Song of Stalin (Pesnia o Staline,
    Iosif Poselsky, 1938), 116
Sovkino-journal, 39, 53
Stalin [Dzhugashvili], Iosif, 46,
    48, 77, 86, 91–93, 100–106,
    110, 112, 114–117, 131–132,
    135, 159n, 161–162n, 164n
Svilova, Elizaveta, 6, 56, 65, 68,
    69, 80, 99, 101, 108, 114,
    117–118, 120–122, 138n,
    161n, 180–181, 183–186
Swan Lake, Petr Tchaikovsky,
    97–98

Tarzan, 104
Tretiakov, Sergei, 32, 103

Trotsky, Lev, 3, 26–27, 44, 84,
    103, 135, 145n
Tsivian, Yuri, 65, 136

Ulianova, Maria,17
Urazov, Izmail, 53
Utesov, Leonid, 86

Vertov:
Cine-Eye
the film. See Vertov, films by
the method [kinoglaz],18, 22,
    23, 31–33, 35–36, 55, 65,
    70, 72, 80, 84, 133–134,
    157n, 183
the movement and its members
    [kinoki], 14–21, 31, 36–37,
    40, 49, 52–53, 55, 57, 65, 82,
    140–142n, 149n
Cine-Pravda, the concept
    (cinéma vérité), 22, 33,
    133–134, 168n
Cine-Pravda, the film. See Vertov,
    films by
and folklore, 2, 94–98, 119
and hidden camera, 1, 23–25, 28,
    30, 33–34, 54, 69, 81, 110,
    132, 142–143
and journalism, 1–3, 5, 8–21, 37,
    45, 50, 60, 82, 130
and life caught unawares; life
    caught off-guard [zhizn'
    vrasplokh]. See Vertov and
    performance
and newsreel, 1–3, 5–11, 14–16,
    18, 23, 26, 32–33, 39–40, 42,
    45, 50–57, 60, 62, 71, 82–89,
    94, 103–104, 107, 114–115,
    117–118, 120–123, 127,
    129–130, 132, 138–139n,
    148–149n, 154n, 156n, 160n,
    164n

and performance, 1, 10, 22–35, 38, 52, 68–69, 72–73, 81–89, 98, 109–111, 129, 132, 136, 142–143n

and poetry, 1, 3, 14–15, 17–18, 27, 43, 45–48, 50, 60, 79, 80, 94–95, 109, 126–127, 136, 145n

and surveillance, 1, 33–38, 70

films by,

Cine Week (Kinonedelia, 1918–1919), 6, 11, 15, 26, 44, 138–139n, 145n, 179

Battle for Tsaritsyn, The (Boi pod Tsaritsynom, 1919), 6, 179

Trial of Mironov (Protsess Mironova, 1919), 26, 179

History of the Civil War, The (Istoriia grazhdanskoi voiny, 1921), 6, 40, 44, 180

Cine-Pravda (Kinopravda, 1922–1925), 6, 11, 16, 27, 29–30, 39–40, 44–45, 52, 58, 84, 135, 180

individual issues

Cine-Pravda no. 1, 7–8; no. 2, 27; no. 5, 10, 29; no. 6, 46; no. 7, 10; no 8, 10, 29; no. 9, 46; no. 13, 45, 145n, 180; no. 14, 145n; no. 15, 29; no. 17, 147n, 181; no. 18, 29, 45, 147n, 181; no. 19, 45, 181; no. 20, 31, 36, 147n 181; no. 21 (Leninist Cine-Pravda), 11–15, 28, 30, 37, 43, 45, 90, 93, 130, 181; no. 22, 10, 181

State Cine Calendar (Goskinokalendar' 1923–1925), 11, 181

Cine Eye (Kinoglaz, 1924), 10, 15–16, 18–20, 23, 27–28, 30–32, 34–36, 40, 46, 50, 59, 65–66, 81–82, 84–85, 94, 123, 140n, 142–143n, 147n, 182, 187

Forward, Soviet! (Shagai, sovet!, 1926), 39–47, 50–53, 58, 71, 129, 135, 145n, 147–148n, 183

A Sixth Part of the World (Shestaia chast' mira, 1926), 28, 39, 45–54, 56–58, 71, 89, 93, 107, 129, 145–149n, 183

The Eleventh Year (Odinnadtsatyi, 1928), 37, 50, 55–63, 66, 68, 71, 74, 79, 82, 122–123, 129, 135, 144n, 147n, 149–153n, 153n, 165n, 183

Man with a Movie Camera (Chelovek s kinoapparatom, 1929), 1, 3, 18, 26, 28, 35, 43, 46, 50, 54–59, 62–71, 73–75, 79–81, 90, 96, 100, 108, 120, 122–123, 129–130, 134–135, 147n, 149n, 152–153n, 165n, 168n, 183, 187

Enthusiasm (Entuziazm, 1931), 71–83, 90, 95, 97–98, 100, 124–126, 129, 134, 147n, 154–156n, 165–166n, 184, 187

Three Songs of Lenin (Tri pesni o Lenine, 1934), 2, 28, 37, 44, 65, 90–102, 104, 106–112, 116, 119, 126–129, 131–132, 134–135, 140n, 147n, 155n, 158–161n, 164n, 184, 187

Lullaby (Kolybel'naia, 1937), 65, 106–119, 129, 184

In Memory of Sergo Ordzhonikidze (Pamiati Sergo Ordzhonikidze, 1937), 108, 116–118, 184